Maria Sibylla Merian

Illuminating Women Artists: Renaissance and Baroque

The series *Illuminating Women Artists* launches at a critical moment in contemporary culture. It marks a significant intervention within the broader movement underway among scholars, museums, collectors and the wider world of cultural heritage to make evident and contextualise historically the contributions of women artists. As such, the books, each written by a leading specialist in the field of art history, will appeal to audiences from the academic sphere to the general public. Beautifully illustrated, the volumes collectively offer an unprecedented visual contextualisation of the lives and works of their subjects, to whom in some cases a monograph has yet to be dedicated.

Books in the sub-series *Illuminating Women Artists: Renaissance and Baroque* critically reappraise the lives and works of female artists in Europe from the fifteenth to the early eighteenth centuries. Many of the women represented by the volumes were celebrated professional artists in their own eras, yet their names and works have not been passed down continually in the history of art. As the first series dedicated to correcting this omission, the books interweave established conclusions with new discoveries to reframe how women's artistic production is approached and understood.

Maria Sibylla Merian

CATHERINE POWELL-WARREN

GETTY PUBLICATIONS
LOS ANGELES

This book is dedicated to two spirited, independent women:
my sister Dominique and my stepdaughter Hadley.

In memory of my grandmother, Olive Allard (1925–2024), who taught me to paint and,
through her example, encouraged me to challenge expectations.

Published in the United States of America by Getty Publications, Los Angeles
1200 Getty Center Drive, Suite 500
Los Angeles, California 90049-1682
getty.edu/publications

Distributed in the United States and Canada by the University of Chicago Press

Printed in China

ISBN 978-1-60606-992-9
Library of Congress Control Number: 2025933137

Published simultaneously in the United Kingdom by Lund Humphries
Originated by Lund Humphries
Second Home Spitalfields
60-80 Hanbury Street
London E1 5JH
UK
lundhumphries.com

Copy edited by Julie Gunz
Project managed and designed by Crow Books
Set in Adobe Caslon Pro

Front cover: Maria Sibylla Merian, *Metamorphosis of a Small Emperor Moth on a Damson Plum* (detail), 1679, watercolour on parchment, 18.7 × 14.9 cm (7⅜ × 5⅞ in), J. Paul Getty Museum, Los Angeles, CA

Back cover: Maria Sibylla Merian, *The Rocu Tree with Caterpillars, Moths, and Butterflies* (detail), 1730/71, watercolour, 52.7 × 34.8 cm (20¾ × 13¾ in), J. Paul Getty Museum, Los Angeles, CA

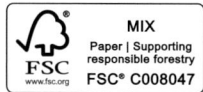

Contents

Series Foreword

The series *Illuminating Women Artists: Renaissance and Baroque* was conceptualised at a pivotal moment in contemporary life, when the call to dismantle structural bias was taking on a new urgency. As social justice movements, such as #MeToo, #BlackLivesMatter, and #TransLivesMatter, exposed assumptions about gender, race, and sexual identity, academic research has been infused with a new energy around these topics. Although approaches to, and even the very applicability of, identity categories as they are defined today vary in regard to the past, early modernity and the contemporary moment share a desire to contend with the power structures that have repressed individuals and groups, albeit in historically distinct ways. Books in *Illuminating Women Artists* advance a specific aspect of this study – the feminist academic enterprise – by making evident various ways that early modern women of the fifteenth through eighteenth centuries negotiated, and sometimes resisted, structural constraints in the sphere of the visual arts.

The series is indebted to feminist art-historical studies produced from the beginning of the 1970s that aimed to disrupt the traditional academic focus on early modern male artists by writing their female counterparts into the discipline of art history. These and other scholarship also began to investigate gender norms in the Renaissance and Baroque, which created different conditions for women and men who sought to practice art as professionals or amateurs. Societal limitations disadvantaged most women (and some men) who aspired to a life in the visual arts. For example, girls were excluded from the formal apprenticeship system through which most male artists were trained, and therefore they sought informal instruction, often from male relatives. Women practitioners who married and became mothers generally experienced a lapse in artistic production while they attended to the responsibilities that came with these roles. On the other hand, fathers sometimes supportively promoted their daughters as artists, which also aggrandised the family and improved its financial standing through patronage and sales.

This series considers early modern women artists within their social, cultural, temporal, and geographic contexts. These female artmakers worked in a period when a literary defence of women's merits began to challenge the patriarchal misogynist ideas that sought to suppress women and their potential. Some women artists may have been aware of this incipient feminism or have visually voiced related issues in their art. But the female artists represented by the series also identified with the social structures of their place and time. These structures, prominent among them gender and class, contributed to shaping their identities and to forming their conceptions about others. While women challenged normative structures in important ways (some more overtly than others), they also were acculturated into dominant cultural attitudes and thus complicit in supporting social hierarchies of class and race. Renaissance and Baroque women artists themselves derived from a spectrum of social classes – artisan, merchant, professional, or patrician. Membership in these classes made it possible for some women artists to have servants or even to enslave persons who contributed to their households. This practice reduced their own domestic obligations and freed time for artmaking, but in turn contributed to reinforcing existing systems of social stratification regarded as the norm.

Some gendered conditions with which female artists contended did not necessarily impede their success, but, even when women's artistic production was critically acclaimed, it was often evaluated according to gender stereotypes. Yet, certain women independently challenged, and circumvented or broke, restrictive gender protocols to enable prolific art production. In the process, they revised those protocols and influenced the history of art. Some established their own professional studios and trained pupils, both female and male, who in turn established themselves as professionals in workshops of their own. Others produced large bodies of work as amateurs, and some rendered porous the boundaries between these two statuses by bridging them. Still others produced works for members of communities to which they belonged, such as professed nuns in enclosed convents, or for personal reasons, such as to have in their possession a portrait of a family member. Some worked under contract for patrons, producing images for prestigious European courts and churches, where their art came under the eyes of the public. These women in the aggregate produced works that varied widely in subject, including both sacred and secular themes, and in artistic media. Represented in the latter category were the familiar forms of sculpture, painting, and printmaking, and also other ways of artmaking that were valued more highly in the past than they are in the present, including papercutting, embroidery, and weaving.

Five decades of sustained research have transformed our understanding of early modern women artists. *Illuminating Women Artists: Renaissance and Baroque* takes stock of this work through books that offer state-of-the-question analyses of their subjects. These peer-reviewed volumes variously interweave established conclusions with new discoveries investigated through emerging modes of analysis to reframe our understanding of the lives, artistic production, and works of art by European women. Together the books reveal the varied ways in which women of the fifteenth through the seventeenth centuries skilfully and often successfully navigated restricting gender norms to stake out productive lives as artmakers and develop innovative approaches to the works they produced. The volumes offer an unprecedented contextualisation of the lives and works of their subjects, to whom in some cases a monograph has not previously been dedicated.

Marilyn Dunn, Loyola University Chicago
Andrea Pearson, American University, Washington, DC
April 2021

Acknowledgements

Learning and writing about Maria Sibylla Merian and her superlative art has been a fascinating endeavour, filled with marvellous artworks, intriguing stories and puzzles. A number of individuals provided me with invaluable assistance and made my efforts so much more productive, and enjoyable.

At Lund Humphries, I am deeply grateful to Erika Gaffney, commissioning editor, and to the series editors Andrea Pearson and Marilyn Dunn for the opportunity to contribute to the series *Illuminating Women Artists*. It is an honour to be part of this important undertaking. I also wish to thank them for their forbearance, as well as their close reading of the manuscript and their feedback, which was enormously helpful. I would also like to thank Rebeccah Williams, a model of patience, who shepherded the book through the publishing process.

Over the many years during which I have been focused on (not to say obsessed with) Maria Sibylla Merian, I have benefited from enriching discussions with many colleagues, mentors and friends. Among many others, I wish to acknowledge the stimulating conversations I have shared with Jeffrey Chipps Smith, Mirka Beneš, Claudia Swan, Babette Bohn, Judith Noorman, Lieke van Deinsen, Kay Etheridge, Henrietta Ward, Eric Jorink and Dániel Margócsy. I am particularly thankful to Hans Mulder, who has shown me endless patience and generosity, and to Jaya Remond for her insights, thoughtfulness and friendship. Inanna Martens's Master's thesis on Merian and watercolour, written under my supervision, has given me much to think about over the past two years, for which I am thankful. For their kindness, friendship and continued cheerleading, I wish to thank Maximiliaan Martens, Koenraad Jonckheere, Marjan Sterckx, Maude Bass-Krueger, Alexis Slater, Arianna Ray, Sarah Farkas, Clio Rom, Sheila Reda, Saskia Beranek, Lien Vandenberghe, Marlise Rijks, Henrietta Ward and V.E. Mandrij.

A number of individuals and institutions went well beyond the call of duty in assisting me with images and imaging rights and gaining access to primary sources. Thank you to Sophie Suykens, Lien Vandenberghe, Hans Mulder, Florence Pieters, Michelle Moseley, Lizzie Marx and the National Gallery of Ireland, Sarah Mallory and the Morgan Library and Museum, Leora Siegel and the Chicago Botanic Garden, Kate Heard and Lauren Stark and the Royal Collection Trust, Joost Depuyt and Denis van Velthoven and the Museum Plantin-Moretus, Alison Petretti and Arader Galleries, New York, Henrietta Ward and the Fitzwilliam Museum, Juliette Parmentier and the Fondation Custodia, the Rijksmuseum, and the Amsterdam Museum.

The research included in this book was carried out over several years and made possible in part by

funding from the Samuel H. Kress Foundation, The
Renaissance Society of America, the Rolf und Ursula
Schneider-Stiftung, and The University of Texas
at Austin. The book also draws from my research
for the project *Hive Mind: Networks, Collectivity,
and Mentorship amongst Women Artists, Patrons, and
Collectors in the Low Countries in Early Modernity*
(2021–4), funded by the Fonds Wetenschappelijk
Onderzoek – Vlaanderen (FWO).

As always, my family has been supportive,
encouraging and good humoured about my
distractedness and absences. All of my love to my
father, Paul, my sister, Dominique, and Michelle.

This book would not have been possible without
the unconditional love, encouragement, devotion and
unfailing support of my beloved husband, Robert. I
am heartbroken that he did not live to see the result.
His memory lives in every page and in me, always.
With all of my soul, I miss you.

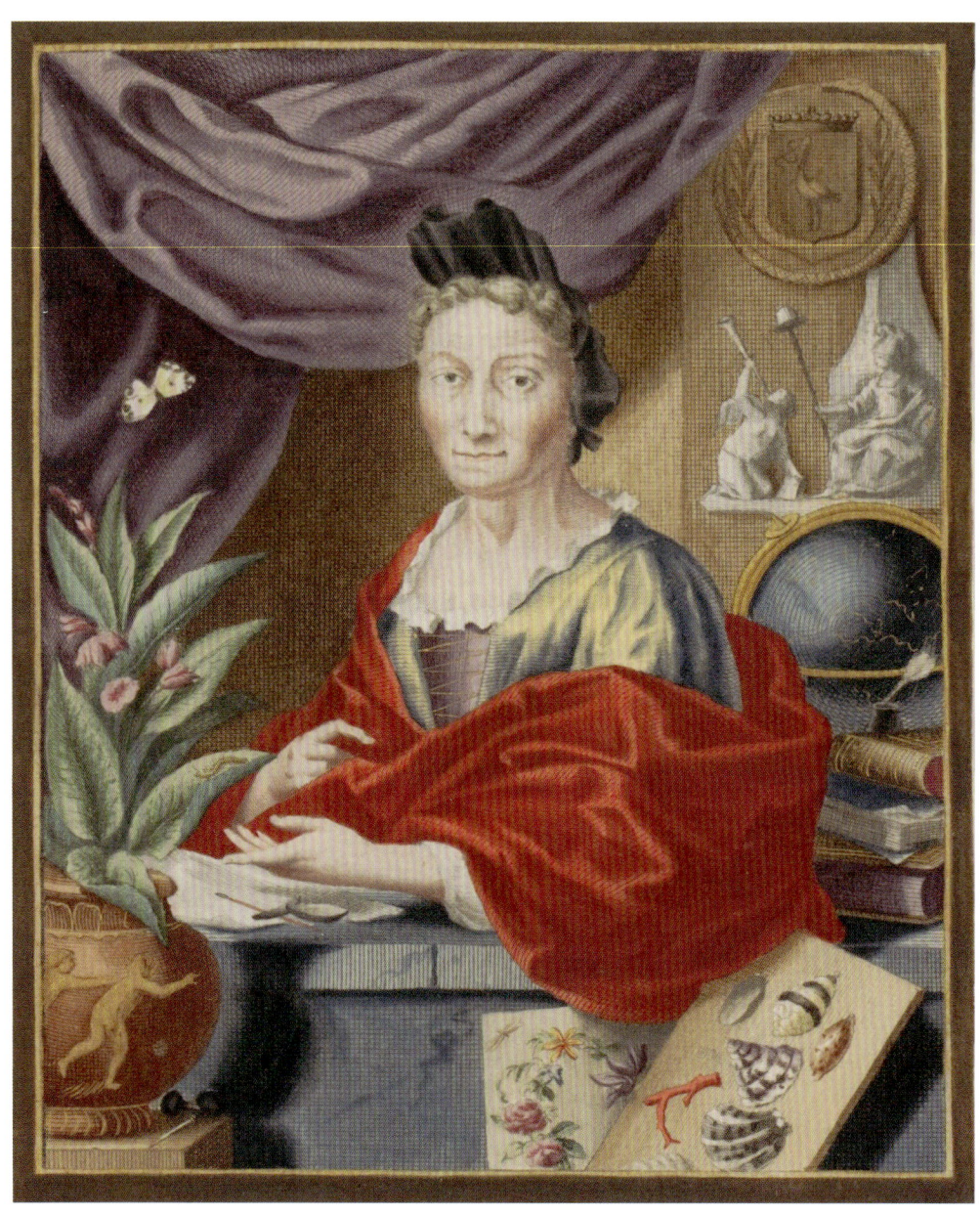

1   Jacob Houbraken (after Georg Gsell), 'Portrait of Maria Sibylla Merian', *c.*1715, in Maria Sibylla
    Merian, *Erucarum ortus, alimentum et paradoxa metamorphosis*, Joannes Oosterwyk, Amsterdam, 1718,
    printed book, hand-coloured, Allard Pierson, Amsterdam

Introduction

Only one portrait survives for which we can be certain that the sitter is Maria Sibylla Merian (1647–1717).[1] It is an engraving made by Jacob Houbraken after a drawing of Merian made by her son-in-law Georg Gsell in or about 1715, two years before her death (fig.1). The engraving allowed the portrait to be printed multiple times and to be disseminated widely. This is the portrait that would be included in the posthumous edition of the last part of Merian's book on caterpillars, *Der rupsen begin*, in 1717, and reproduced in part in Arnold Houbraken's *De Groote schouburgh der Nederlantsche konstschilders en schilderessen* (The Great Theatre of Dutch Painters) in 1721. Seated in three-quarters pose, Merian seems tired; she is near the end of her life and had not been feeling well. Wearing her best dress, however, she is proud of what she has achieved, and so will sit for this portrait. Seated at a table, the space around her is crowded with illustrations that she has made, thick volumes and a celestial sphere. The tools of her work are at hand: two burins, a paintbrush with a mussel shell to hold paint, and a quill in an inkwell. Merian, with an open hand, points to the subject matter that has fascinated her since she was a young girl: a plant on which crawl caterpillars and to which are attached a pupa and a chrysalis; a butterfly flutters above the plant. This is metamorphosis, emphasised by the depiction of the myth of Apollo and Daphne on the vase that holds the plant. Viewers of the portrait would have known that in Ovid's *Metamorphoses*, Daphne is transformed into a tree to avoid capture by Apollo.

In Merian's life, metamorphosis was not about the inexorable transformation from one form of self to another, like Daphne or the caterpillars she raised, but rather about the coexistence of multiple selves that evolved over time. She was a painter and a printmaker, a teacher, a workshop master and manager, a collector, a trader in artistic supplies and curiosities, and a naturalist. She was also a daughter and stepdaughter, mother and mother-in-law, a wife and an ex-wife. The insistence on classifying Merian has produced a number of narratives, some unfortunately reductive: she has joined the ranks of 'radical women' and 'exceptional women artists', of 'first ecologists' and 'first women in science'. The scholarly works that fall into these categories, although helpful (and, indeed, relied upon in writing this book), cannot help but result in a narrowing of Merian, of her world, and of her legacy.

The objective of this book is to provide a more nuanced and encompassing narrative for this undeniably extraordinary woman, told through her art and artistic practices and in context. In telling

Merian's story, I am mindful of the 'undivided territory' between the history of science and the history of art, which Janice Neri cautioned against specifically in the case of Merian, arguing (correctly) that those who sought to parse the 'scientific' aspects of her illustrations from the 'artistic' ones created an opposition of 'forces engaged in a perpetual battle for dominance' that did not exist in reality, and certainly not in Merian's time or in her case.[2] This book does not engage with the nature, extent or validity of Merian's activities as a naturalist, which is to say that it does not examine nor does it offer an opinion on whether her empirical methods were novel or appropriate, or whether every element in her artworks is a true and exact representation of a given specimen (scholars have identified a relatively small number of errors). It does, however, frequently engage with the concept of 'scientific accuracy', which I consider to be a feature of artistic practice governed by its own set of pictorial guidelines, as discussed in Chapter 2. Throughout, illustrations are assessed and discussed on the basis of their artistic sophistication – meaning composition, line, form, colour, proportionality – as well as their level of scientific accuracy. These ideals are inseparable and they are discussed this way throughout the book.

There exist a number of excellent biographies of Maria Sibylla Merian, including (in English) an early one by Natalie Zemon Davis and a more recent one by Kim Todd. With enthusiasm about the artist-naturalist having grown, especially over the past two decades, newly discovered archival documents and references are constantly being added to the scholarship. I could not begin to improve on the biographical work that has been done to date and this book does not purport to be a comprehensive biography. Readers are encouraged to consult two recent collections of essays about Merian, namely *Maria Sibylla Merian. Metamorphosis 1705*, a facsimile of *Metamorphosis* edited by Marieke van Delft and Hans Mulder that includes new translations by

Patrick Lennon and essays (2016); as well as *Maria Sibylla Merian: Changing the Nature of Art and Science*, edited by Bert van de Roemer, Florence Pieters, Hans Mulder, Kay Etheridge and Marieke van Delft (2022). The latter includes a helpful timeline setting out the major events in the lives of Merian and her daughters, Johanna Helena Herolt and Dorothea Maria Graff; I have referred to it often. Also helpful is Kay Etheridge's *The Flowering of Ecology*, which casts a new eye on Merian's Caterpillar Book and includes a translation of the text of part 1 (published in 1679). This work contains the most up-to-date information about the historical scientific consideration of Merian's work on metamorphosis and insect generation, as well as regarding the history of the book's production and publication in Nuremberg, Frankfurt and, after Merian's death, Amsterdam.

Scholarship on Merian has benefited greatly from the digital turn. Many of the scholars who have contributed to the volumes mentioned above are members of the Maria Sibylla Merian Society, which maintains a website in collaboration with the University of Amsterdam.[3] On the site, one can find links to digital versions of Merian's publications, transcriptions of letters by Merian in their original language accompanied by English translations, and links to a number of other primary sources. I bookmarked the website at the time of the 2017 symposium on Merian organised by the Society; it has been indispensable to my work since then. Margot Lölhöffel, also a contributor to the above volumes, has since launched a website with Dieter Lölhöffel devoted to Merian, with a particular focus on her Nuremberg and Wieuwerd periods.[4] The website includes images of many archival sources that the authors have uncovered, unavailable elsewhere.

In light of the foregoing, one would be forgiven for asking 'Why another book on Merian – let alone a book on Merian as a *woman artist*, and why *now*?' Surprisingly enough, there is relatively little scholarship on Merian as a subject of feminist art-historical analysis, or as an artist. The first modern treatment of Merian by an art historian came thanks to an exhibition curated by Elisabeth Rücker in Nuremberg in 1967, for which there was a catalogue.[5] But the artist was not included in the landmark exhibition *Women Artists 1550–1950*, curated by Ann Sutherland Harris and Linda Nochlin in 1976, although she was part of the related exhibition catalogue.[6] Two of her works, both bouquets of flowers in blue and white porcelain vases, were included in the exhibition *A chacun sa grâce: Femmes artistes en Belgique et aux Pays-Bas, 1500–1950*, co-curated by Katlijne van der Stighelen and Mirjam Westen in 1999, and she has been a regular feature of group exhibitions about women since.[7]

Yet, Merian remains understudied as an artist – as opposed to as a naturalist. Writing in 1998, Sam Segal pointed to the number of re-editions and facsimiles of Merian's books in support of his assertion that not only had Merian been 'widely admired during her lifetime', but she remained a popular figure. Still, he concluded that 'A critical study of her oeuvre remains to be undertaken.'[8] Notwithstanding Segal's dedication to the investigation of flower and botanical artists, it was not until 2017 that Carin Grabowski published a comprehensive monograph on Merian, in which she categorised her works based on their subject matter and the periods in Merian's life during which they were produced.[9] Grabowski's tome, although the closest thing to a catalogue raisonné of Merian, is a dense scholarly work not yet translated from the German, which makes it accessible to a limited audience. Furthermore, that work only gives limited contextual information and does not examine how the socio-economic, political and early scientific historical contexts may have influenced Merian, her work, her reception and her legacy.

Recent research on early modern women artists has revealed the critical role of informal social networks to their artistic practices.[10] In the Northern Europe of Merian's time, women could not belong to art academies, universities or scientific societies, which were essential especially if one intended to pursue the art of science. When it came to obtaining unusual specimens, information about certain insects or plants, or even access to rare pigments, Merian could not simply turn to her colleagues or fellow members of the Royal Society in the manner that so many of her male contemporaries did. Rather, she was able to achieve the same results as her male peers because she developed lasting relationships with the men who were members of these formal institutions. Relationships played an essential role in Merian's artistic career: this is how she gained pupils, specimens, other connections, commissions and even assistance in marketing her work. Any examination of her artistic practice, consequently, should take into consideration her relationships, which I have aimed to do.

Merian was as talented an artist as any painter of landscape or flowers or scientific illustrator of her time, male or female. She had an eye for interesting and dynamic compositions; she was able to manipulate colour to create volume, texture and depth; she was an exquisite draughtsperson; and, above all, she was enormously creative and innovative in all aspects of her artistic production. The genre to which she devoted her career was not inherently gendered. Nevertheless, navigating gender expectations and barriers to entry – in art and in science – was a constant concern. Gender was a feature of Merian's career from the outset: it determined her training, limited the genres and media in which she could work, set social expectations with respect to her marriage and role as a mother, and even informed her reception and legacy.

Merian possessed what Andrea Pearson has termed 'situational agency', meaning 'a situational form of power claimed by or for the socially restricted or disadvantaged, even if visible change was not, or is not, apparent'.[11] Thus, she managed to publish, end a marriage, work and travel, not by forcing a change of the legal or social order or by demanding recognition equal to the work and worth of men for herself, but by building and maintaining relationships and using her creativity, innovativeness, curiosity and remarkable mind to create a universe in which she could have decision-making power on important matters in her life, and in her art. This book, therefore, refers to gender and to the concept of agency throughout, both explicitly and implicitly.

EDITORIAL CHOICES AND ORGANISATION OF THIS BOOK

I have chosen to refer to Maria Sibylla Merian simply as Merian throughout. Feminist scholars have argued, correctly in my view, that referring to a woman artist only by her first name unnecessarily diminishes her stature. Nevertheless, for the sake of clarity and consistency, I have allowed some exceptions to the rule in this book. Merian's daughters, Johanna Helena and Dorothea Maria, adopted several surnames during their lives: Graff, Herolt and Merian for Johanna Helena; and Graff, Hendrik, Gsell and Merian for Dorothea Maria. For the sake of concordance with earlier scholarship and simplicity, I refer to Merian's daughters by their first names while they are children, and as Herolt or Graff after they marry, unless there is a risk of confusion, in which case I use their first names. Readers will notice that the titles of Merian's books appear to be inconsistently italicised; *Metamorphosis*, which is the short form of the original Dutch title, is in italics, while the translated titles of Merian's Flower Books, New Flower Books, and Caterpillar Book are not – but their original German titles are. Finally, plant names in Latin are italicised but plant names in English are not. Capitalisation follows the conventions of the original languages.

Given the limitations inherent in writing a concise book, I have elected to focus only on a relatively small body of works in order to better demonstrate Merian's outstanding talents and impressive range as an artist. The long arc of her career, which is examined in context in Chapter 1, serves as a scaffold for the chapters that follow. I have chosen her early books of flower and caterpillar illustrations to demonstrate her grasp of engraving and her familiarity with the state-of-the-art in the illustration of natural history (Chapter 2). *Metamorphosis*, the book for which she is best known, provides a case study in creativity and innovation (Chapter 3), while her individual works on parchment provide the opportunity to admire her ability to manipulate line and colour, and to appeal to elite collectors (Chapter 5). Merian's enterprising nature and her role as the head of a women-only, high-production-volume workshop that included her daughters and most likely other pupils, establishes her sophistication as a working artist (Chapter 4). The book concludes with an examination of Merian's early reception and legacy (Chapter 6), which is as interesting for the reactions she generated as for the varied kinds of individuals who had an opinion to share.

Maria Sibylla Merian deserves extended consideration as an artist, driven by the most recent developments in feminist art history. This is a beginning which, I hope, will serve as a starting point for new research, new perspectives and new approaches.

I

The Arc of a Peripatetic Career

Maria Sibylla Merian was a multi-talented artist: she embroidered, painted on silk and linen (a new method that she devised, which allowed the textile to be washed and the design to remain), engraved images onto copper plates for printing, and painted. She was born into an artistic milieu, which, as a woman in seventeenth-century Northern Europe, placed her at a distinct advantage in becoming an artist. The successful pursuit of artmaking as a for-profit activity, however, demanded far more than simply being born in the right family: Merian needed to navigate the boundaries imposed upon her, and the hindrances she experienced, as a result of her gender. To do so required a propitious social and economic environment and the development of relationships inside and outside of her family network. As will become clear throughout this chapter, the relationships that Merian forged at the outset of her career, in Frankfurt am Main and Nuremberg, would endure for the remainder of her career. Without access to formal institutions, such as guilds or academies, these informal networks were critical in the development of nature as Merian's chosen subject matter and in the distribution and recognition of her work.

GROWING UP IN AN ARTISTIC MILIEU

Maria Sibylla Merian was born in Frankfurt am Main during the first few days of April, 1647 (she was baptised on the 4th).[1] She was the daughter of the Basel-born printmaker and publisher Matthäus Merian (1593–1650) and his second wife, Johanna Sibylla Heim (c.1620–90), a Walloon from the Southern Netherlands.[2] Theirs was a large family: Matthäus had seven children from his first marriage. There were two children of the second marriage; first-born Maria Sibylla, and a son who died at age three. Maria Sibylla was only three years old when Matthäus passed away. In 1651, Johanna Sibylla married the successful still-life painter Jacob Marrel (1613/14–81), who ran a painting workshop and was an art dealer. Matthäus's sons Matthäus the Younger (1621–87) and Caspar (1627–86) took over the printing and publishing shop that their maternal great-grandfather, Theodor de Bry, had established in the sixteenth century.[3] There are no suggestions that Maria Sibylla had anything to do with the operation thereafter, although she appears to have remained in touch with her half-brother Caspar, since she would later reunite with him in the religious Labadist community of Wieuwerd, Friesland.

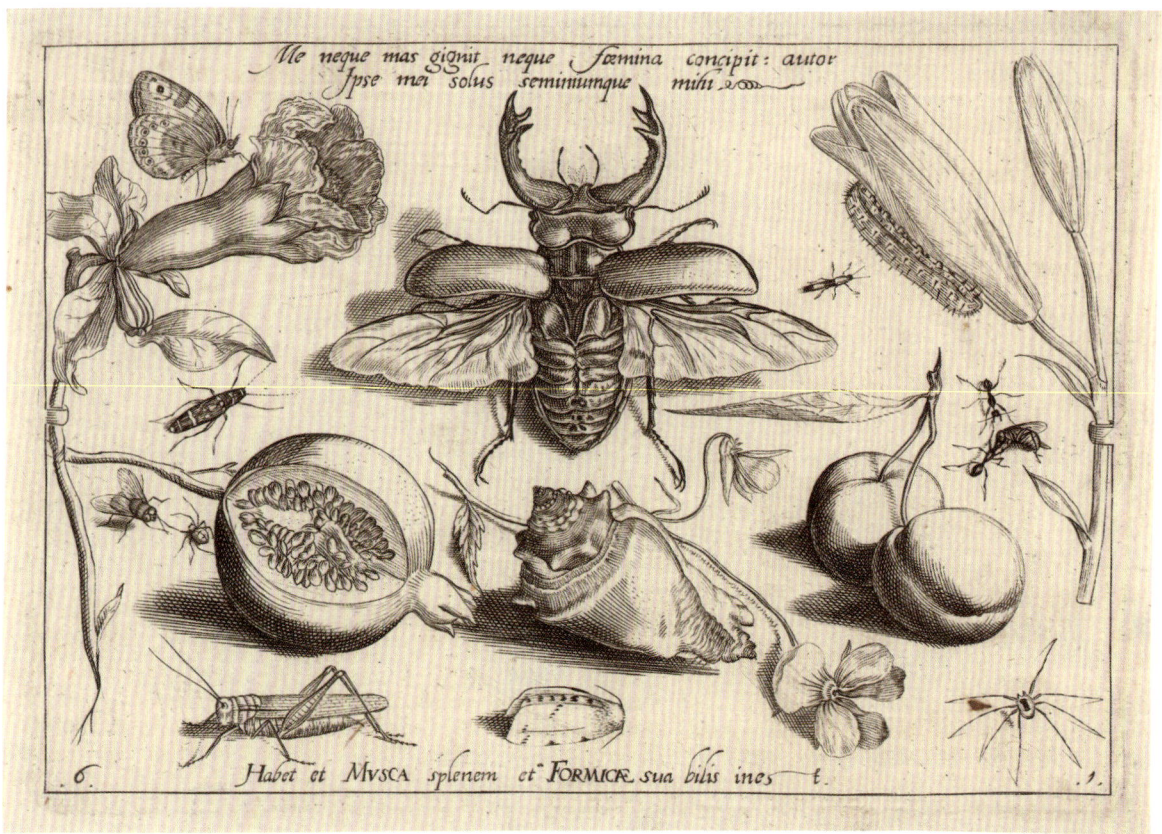

Me neque mas gignit neque fœmina concipit: autor
Ipse mei solus seminiumque mihi

Habet et MVSCA splenem et FORMICÆ sua bilis ines t

2　Jacob Hoefnagel (after Joris Hoefnagel), *Insects, Flowers and Fruits Surrounding a Stag Beetle*, 1592 and/or 1693–1726, engraving, 15.3 × 21.5 cm (6 × 8 ½ in), Rijksmuseum, Amsterdam

Born just one year before the official end of the Thirty Years War, Merian and her family were fortunate to find themselves in Frankfurt, a free imperial city. This meant that it benefited from considerable autonomy from the Holy Roman Emperor and was not subject to the rule of a territorial prince, but rather reported directly to the Emperor. An important locus of commerce in the Holy Roman Empire, Frankfurt had remained neutral during the war; therefore, unlike other areas of Germany, it did not experience the devastation of repeated attacks nor the destabilisation of military occupation, with the attendant pilfering, destruction and infliction of violence upon civilians. The city's comparatively stable political and economic environment allowed Matthäus (who had obtained citizenship) to continue running the family printing and publishing business and to pass it on to his sons upon his death as a successful, going concern.

Jacob Marrel, Merian's stepfather, spent the second half of the Thirty Years War in Utrecht, in the Northern Netherlands. He returned to his native Germany in 1650 and established himself in Frankfurt, where he gained citizenship. There, he would have found socio-economic circumstances propitious for the establishment of his business as a master with apprentices and as an art dealer. (Here, the term 'master' is used in a strictly historical sense to describe a hierarchical position in a workshop, and not as an indication of the significance of an artist or of the quality of that artist's work.)

These socio-economic conditions likely played an important part in setting Merian on her path. In the first place, she was able to receive an education typical for German girls of her economic and social background. This would have included reading and writing, with a particular focus on religious texts, and basic mathematics, as well as skills such as embroidery and household management. Her peers in wealthier or patrician families would also likely have been taught poetry and learned to read and play music and draw – activities that formed part of a traditional humanist education in early modernity.[4]

In the second place, Merian was able to remain within the ambit of the family workshop. There, she was in contact with the art that circulated through Marrel's art-dealing business, his books and his own works, which she could use as models. She learned to draw and paint, initially from Marrel and later from his apprentices, Abraham Mignon (1640–79) and Johann Andreas Graff (1636–1701), Merian's future husband. Marrel and Mignon specialised in flower painting, while Graff became known primarily as a draughtsman and printmaker. Part of Merian's training would have entailed reproducing the work of other artists, including that of Marrel, Mignon and Graff, but also older examples found in the workshop, such as Joris Hoefnagel's *Archetypa*, a collection of miniature models of insects and animals with emblems published in Frankfurt in 1592 (fig.2).[5] In the workshop, she learned how to use paints, as well as to engrave on copper, as explored more fully in Chapter 2.

Anecdotal evidence suggests that Merian was far more interested in spending time in the workshop than in the house, assisting her mother with chores.[6] There, she could refine her drawing and painting skills, as well as tend to silkworms,

which she carefully observed and depicted. An often told story is that when she was 13, she received a gift of silkworms, a present that opened a world previously unknown to her, which would fill her with curiosity and passion throughout her life. In a study journal that she kept (now in St Petersburg, Russia), she recorded and drew her observations of the metamorphosis of silkworms. In the very first entry, she wrote: 'I began this study, God be praised, in Franckfurt in 1660.'[7]

A drawing by Graff from that period conveys the close relationship that existed between apprentices and masters and their family (fig.3). The rectangular drawing in red pencil and with grey ink wash shows a young girl absorbed in her embroidery. Wearing a handkerchief on her head and her dress protected by an apron, she is seated at a table with her pattern, linen and thread. Graff has inscribed the drawing as being of 'Jacob Marrel's daughter'. Since it is dated 1658, the young woman is probably Sara Marrel, Merian's half-sister, who would have been around ten years old at the time. The drawing is an intimate one likely done in the studio, as evidenced by the empty easel that stands behind Sara.

Merian was not officially an apprentice in Marrel's workshop and she was not registered with the guild. Many painters' guilds in early modern Europe did not admit women, although some of them did. The primary functions of a guild were to assess the qualification of members, thereby performing a form of quality control, as well as to protect the economic interests of their members. Limiting the admission of women to a guild, therefore, was an effective way to limit competition.[8] Nevertheless, it was not uncommon for daughters in artistic families to be trained and contribute to the activities of the family workshop. Some of the daughters received the same training as their male siblings. One significant difference, however, is that young women could not travel and complete additional apprenticeships in other cities or countries after their main apprenticeship, as young men

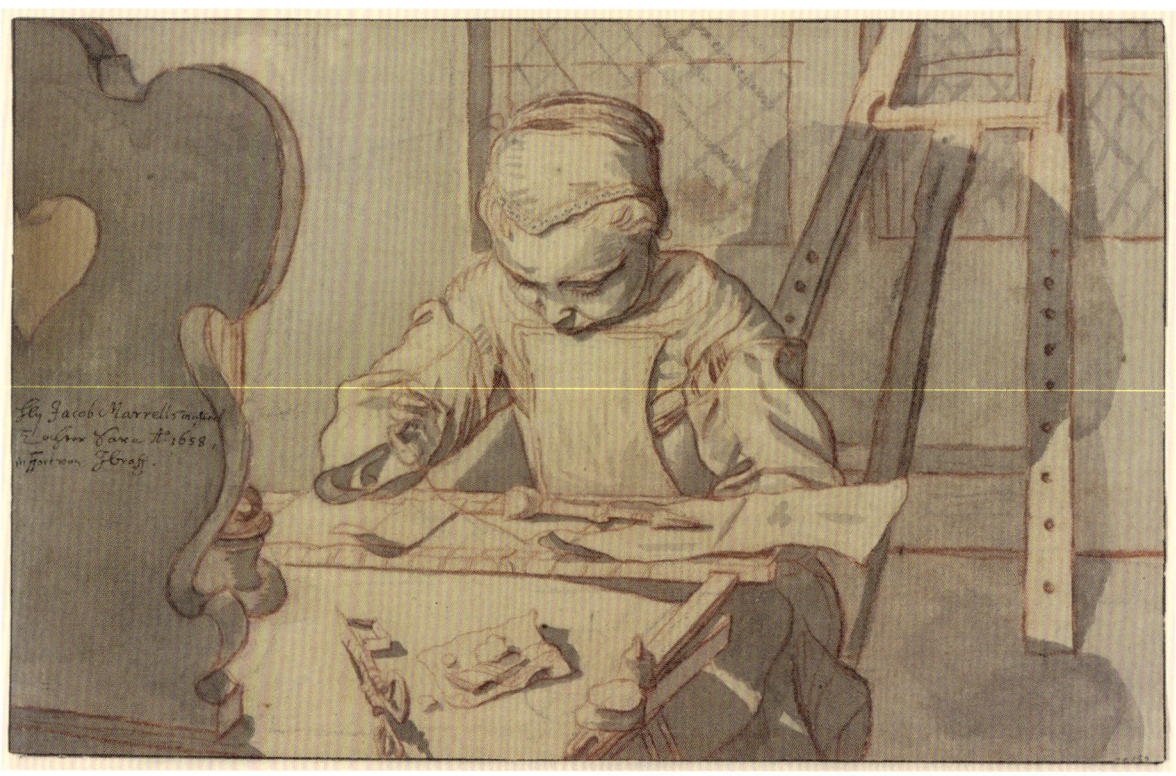

3   Johann Andreas Graff, *Girl Embroidering by Candlelight in an Interior (possibly Sara Marrel)*, 1658, drawing, 18.7 × 29 cm (7⅜ × 11⅜ in), Staedelmuseum, Frankfurt am Main

frequently did. Thus, whereas Merian's half-brother Matthäus the Younger spent time in Amsterdam, London, Paris, Nuremberg and Italy after being apprenticed in his father's workshop, she was to remain in place in Frankfurt until she married, at which point she would follow her husband.

It is important to note that even when not trained as artists, women frequently provided 'assisting labour' in family workshops, meaning that it would not have seemed exceptional or inappropriate to see Merian coming and going in the workshop.[9] Indeed, as hinted in Graff's drawing of Sara Marrel (fig.3), the workshop seems to have functioned as part of the household. The names of the women who provided this labour are mostly forgotten, however, as their

functions did not require guild or official registration. The operation of an artistic workshop was a complex and demanding business, requiring the involvement of many hands. Women performed bookkeeping, engaged in sales and marketing, and performed a range of unskilled and skilled tasks – from sweeping to preparing canvasses, and even acting as figure models. This type of training, in turn, made early modern women particularly attractive brides. Being trained and experienced in the family workshop provided women with a particular kind of social capital that could be appealing to potential grooms looking to set up their own workshop. The archives confirm that, not surprisingly, families of painters, or sculptors, frequently intermarried.

Few works survive from Merian's period in Marrel's workshop, except for a series of 17 drawings in pen and ink attributed to her.[10] Representing flowers and insects, they were likely exercises in copying and drawing from models. These earliest known of Merian's works attest to her fascination with these subjects from the outset of her artistic career, an interest she continued to pursue and develop in the decades that followed.

THE NUREMBERG YEARS: WIFE, MOTHER, ARTIST

In 1665, Maria Sibylla Merian married Johann Andreas Graff, her stepfather's apprentice. The young couple continued to live in Frankfurt for at least three years. It was there that their first daughter, Johanna Helena, was born in 1668. Little is known about Merian's artistic activities during this period. Although she likely did not stop drawing and painting altogether, one can assume that as a recently married woman in charge of setting up a household and looking after an infant, she had limited time to devote to these pursuits. An illustration of a shoot of a pomegranate tree, undated but signed 'Maria Sibylla Gräffin, born Merian', which is believed to be the earliest signed work by the artist, is likely from these early years after her marriage (hence the use of the name 'Gräffin', which is the feminine form of Graff) (fig.4). The composition is simple, with the pomegranate shoot bisecting the image plane into two vertical halves. Three flowers, in various stages of bloom, are attached to the uppermost branches, while two heavy fruits, one ripe and the other overripe, hang lower. In the left-hand bottom corner, behind the shoot, a fruit has fallen to the ground, bursting open to reveal its juicy seeds and attracting a butterfly. This early work lacks the dynamism that exemplifies Merian's later production. Nevertheless, her focus on representing different stages of the flowering of the fruit and the inclusion of the insect would become hallmarks of Merian's illustrations. The pomegranate

flowers and bursting fruit are motifs that would recur multiple times in her oeuvre.

The small family relocated to Nuremberg in 1668, shortly after Johanna Helena's birth, and Merian would remain there until 1681. Before the Thirty Years War, Nuremberg (like Frankfurt, also a free imperial city) had been one of the most influential artistic centres in Germany. In the sixteenth century, it was the home of Albrecht Dürer, Hans von Kulmbach, Georg Pencz, and Hans and Sebald Beham, as well as of the sculptors Veit Stoß and Adam Kraft. When Merian, Graff and Johanna Helena arrived in 1668, the city was still reeling economically from the devastation of the war, although it continued to be the home of an important patrician class.

At the outset of the sixteenth century, the practice of several trades in Nuremberg, including that of painting, was 'free', meaning that it was not subject to guild membership and regulations. Lifting these requirements created favourable conditions for newcomers who wished to establish themselves as masters and resulted in Nuremberg becoming one of the foremost centres of artistic production and innovation in early modern Germany. Eventually, however, local painters sought protection from foreign arrivals and the city council, composed of the leaders of Nuremberg's patrician families, enacted a Painters' Ordinance in 1596, which remained in effect when Merian lived in the city.[11] In addition to referring to masters and apprentices in the masculine form only, the ordinance specifically forbade women to paint (for profit) live models or biblical and mythological scenes (also referred to as history painting) in oils. Engraving and painting on glass, textile or furniture, however, were not subject to these restrictions.[12]

The period that she spent in Nuremberg was a critical part of Merian's development as an artist, both in terms of the maturation of her skills and with respect to the relationships that she would forge there. In addition to building and carrying out her own artistic practice, it is likely that Merian also assisted her

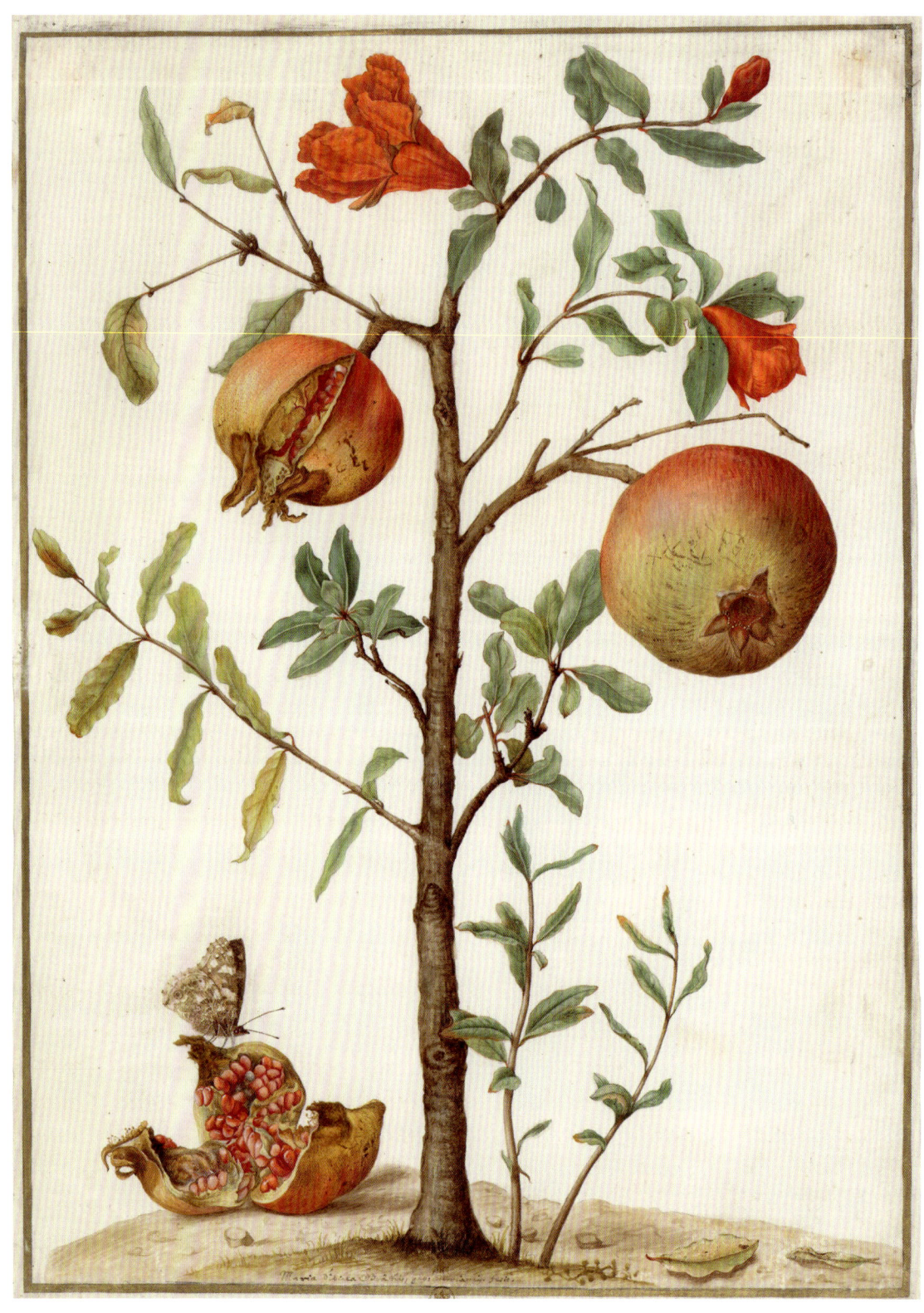

4   Maria Sibylla Merian, *Pomegranate Shoot and Fruit*, *c.*1665, gouache on vellum, 46 × 30.8 cm (18 ⅛ × 12 ⅛ in),
Bibliothèque Nationale de France, Paris

husband in the workshop. After all, she was a trained artist and, having spent her early and teenage years in Marrel's workshop, she would have been intimately familiar with the needs of the business and with the complexity of running a commercial artistic practice.

Auspicious Surroundings and Relationships

In Nuremberg, Graff and his family belonged to a relatively prosperous class, although not part of the patriciate. His father had been a poet laureate and the rector of the Egidiengymnasium (today known as the Melanchthon Gymnasium or High School), a school of higher learning founded by the Reformer Philip Melanchthon and at the time one of the most prestigious educational institutions in Germany.[13] Merian and Graff moved into the house he had inherited from his family, known as 'The Golden Sun' (*zur goldenen Sonne*), located in the Old Milk Market district (*Alte Milchmarkt*).[14] This was an affluent district near the Imperial Castle (*Keizerburg*), St Sebald's Church (*Sebalduskirche*) and the imposing City Hall (*Rathaus*) (fig.5). It was home to many craftsmen and patricians.[15] The family owned a small garden adjacent to the castle, something that Merian noted in her Study Book (*Studienbuch*), in which she would record her observations with text and sketches for much of her life.[16]

Merian could hardly have wished for more auspicious surroundings in which to pursue her artistic career, which she did with great momentum. As the couple's second daughter, Dorothea Maria, was not born until 1678, Merian benefited from a number of years without the burdens associated with pregnancy – from the swollen abdomen that makes working at an easel difficult, to the physical and emotional demands of a newborn, to say nothing of the health risks associated with pregnancy in early modernity.[17] Johanna Helena, a newborn when she arrived in Nuremberg, would grow more independent and eventually attend school. This was a rare period

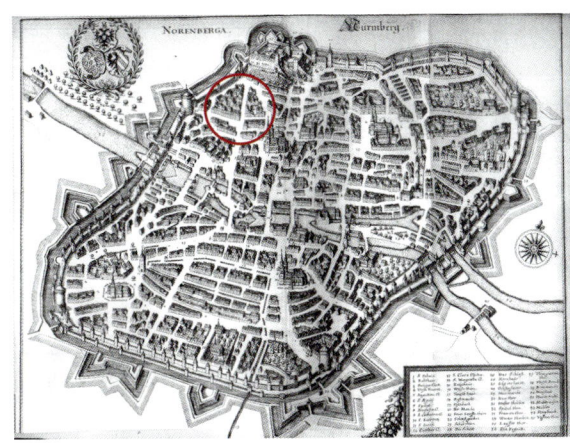

5   Matthäus Merian, 'Norenberga', in *Topographia Franconiae*, Merian, Frankfurt am Main, 1648, p.90. The circle marks the general area of the *Alte Milchmarkt* district

during which it would have been easier for Merian to leave the house and focus on artmaking.

In short succession, self-styled as Maria Sibylla Gräffin, daughter of Matthäus Merian the Elder, she designed and engraved 36 plates depicting flowers and insects for her Flower Book (*Blumenbuch*), which was released in three parts of 12 illustrations in 1675, 1677 and 1680. The three parts were reissued, together with a new frontispiece, as the New Flower Book (*Neues Blumenbuch*) in 1680. In 1679, the first part of her book on caterpillars (*Der Raupen wunderbare*), which contained 50 original illustrations, appeared. The books were published by Merian's husband, Johann Andreas Graff, and represented the state-of-the-art in the illustration of nature (Chapter 2).

It was also during her Nuremberg period that Merian began taking on pupils to teach them embroidery and painting, an activity that she would carry on for much of her career. Her students, whom she referred to as her 'Maiden's Company', were the daughters of Nuremberg's wealthier families. They included Dorothea Auer (dates unknown) and

Magdalena Fürst (1652–1717), both the daughters of artists, and Clara Regina Imhoff (dates unknown), who belonged to two of the oldest patrician families in Nuremberg, the Imhoff and Volkamer clans. Merian's relationship with Imhoff endured for much of her life and provided her with a number of opportunities, in addition to income from tuition. With the exception of her period in Wieuwerd, in the Labadist community, it seems that Merian remained in contact with her pupil from 1682 until at least 1697. The tone of Merian's letters conveys a genuine fondness for Imhoff, who, notably, continued to paint and to share her artworks with her teacher. Imhoff relied on Merian to provide her with supplies such as pigment and, on one occasion, an illustration for her to colour. Imhoff's brother, through the intercession of his sister, asked Merian to contribute to his *album amicorum*; he eventually visited her in Amsterdam.[18]

In the early Nuremberg years, Merian's relationship with Imhoff enabled her to widen her network. Clara Regina's maternal grandfather, Friedrich Volkamer, was an important official in Nuremberg whose duties included the stewardship of the Imperial Castle. He also owned his own garden. In her Study Book, Merian wrote that not only was it thanks to Clara that she gained access to the gardens at the castle and to Friedrich Volkamer's personal garden, but that Clara accompanied her on her visits.[19] During one of those visits, Merian found a 'unique caterpillar', which she would go on to draw.[20]

Merian's pupil Dorothea Auer came from a well-to-do but non-patrician family. This relationship between pupil and tutor was just as important to Merian as her connection to Imhoff, and perhaps even more so. Indeed, Merian and Graff's youngest daughter, Dorothea Maria, was named after her.[21] One of Auer's brothers-in-law was the merchant and *liefhebber* (meaning a devoted enthusiast of a subject matter, a *virtuoso*) Johann Christoph Volkamer, who was in turn the brother of Johann Georg Volkamer, a well-known physician and botanist.[22]

Merian maintained a lengthy correspondence with Johann Georg. In 1702, upon her return from Suriname (a trip detailed below), Merian reached out to him to share her plans for *Metamorphosis*, which she hoped would be completed shortly (it would take three more years). Merian described for him how she saw wondrous creatures, and how unique the book she envisioned would be. She looked to him to gauge interest for a sale by subscription of the book in Germany, and attempted to induce him to buy from her dried and preserved specimens from Suriname, including 'snakes, a crocodile in liquor, twenty boxes with butterflies, hummingbirds and lanternflies'.[23] Merian corresponded with Volkamer until at least 1705. Although there would be insufficient interest to produce a German-language version of *Metamorphosis*, Merian had in Volkamer an emissary who was learned, wealthy and, above all, connected. On 16 April 1705, Merian sent Johann Georg two copies of *Metamorphosis*; one for him, and one for his brother, Johann Christoph.[24] A few years later, Johann Christoph would go on to write a book entitled the *Nürnbergische Hesperides* (1708–14), an important botanical treatise on lemons, limes and oranges. In it, he refers to Merian's *Metamorphosis*.

These relationships were rich and imbued with trust. Through them, Merian maintained links with Nuremberg decades after she left the city. As her life changed dramatically, these connections provided Merian with a conduit through which she could engage in trade, distribute her art, and maintain and enhance her goodwill and reputation.

A KIND OF EMANCIPATION

Life changed abruptly for Merian when her stepfather, Jacob Marrel, passed away in 1681. Together with her daughters, she returned to Frankfurt to assist her mother, who had fallen into financial difficulties. It appears that Graff joined them there for extended periods of time, although he evidently returned to

Nuremberg on occasion.[25] During this time, Merian continued her teaching and took on young women as pupils. In 1683, the second instalment of her Caterpillar Book was published. As in the first part, it contained 50 original illustrations depicting the life cycle of caterpillars and their ecology. Like the other books, the author is Maria Sibylla Gräffin, daughter of Matthäus Merian the Elder. Unlike the other books, however, part II of the Caterpillar Book was not published by Graff, but rather by David Funken, in Frankfurt. Three years later, in 1686, Merian, her mother and her daughters left Germany and travelled to the province of Friesland, in the Northern Netherlands, where they joined the Labadist community at Waltha Castle, Wieuwerd.[26] Merian would not live with her husband again, nor return to Germany.

The Labadists were a community of strict Protestants led by Jean de Labadie (1610–74). Anna Maria van Schurman (1607–78) – a (German-born) Dutch linguist, philosopher, poet and artist who remained unmarried and famously withdrew from public life – was also a member of the community from 1669 until her death. Although she and Merian never met, one could expect that they would have been *ad idem* on a number of matters, including the importance of female intellectual independence. Caspar Merian, Maria Sibylla's half-brother, had joined the community when he was widowed, in 1677.[27] He would die shortly after his relatives joined him. An account attributed to Johann Gabriel Doppelmayr and dated 1730 tells that Graff travelled to Friesland in an attempt to convince Merian and his daughters to return to Nuremberg, to no avail.[28] This account is supported by a drawing that Graff made of Waltha Castle, *c.*1686.[29]

Based on the Study Book, it appears that Merian kept up her drawing and painting practice while with the Labadists. Her focus on and fascination with nature would have been consistent with a strict Protestant ethos that encouraged meditation upon nature, thought to be a divine creation. Johanna Helena spent her teenage years in Wieuwerd, and that is where Dorothea Maria came of age. Although Johanna Helena's artistic training would have likely begun earlier, it would have continued during this period. It was also with the Labadists that Dorothea Maria would have been initiated into artistic practice, and that Merian, as it were, established the foundations of the workshop that she would later operate with her daughters. In addition to providing the women with time to draw and practice, the Wieuwerd stay also furnished them with specimens as subjects. Waltha Castle, which was owned by the family of Cornelis van Aerssen van Sommelsdijck, the Governor of Dutch Suriname (whose sisters belonged to the Labadists), held a collection of insects from the West Indies.

TAKING IN THE BUSY EMPORIUM OF AMSTERDAM

With the death of her brother in 1686 and that of her mother in 1690, it seems that there was little to keep Merian with the Labadists. In 1691, she and her daughters resettled in Amsterdam. In 1692, Johanna Helena, by then 24, married Jacob Hendrik Herolt (b.*c.*1660), who had been a member of the Labadist colony at Wieuwerd and was a trader with Suriname. Johann Andreas Graff obtained a divorce in 1694, so that he could remarry.[30] Her status as a divorced woman, however, does not appear to have affected Merian's prospects in Amsterdam.

The city was a bustling metropolis, a place where the entire world – or so it must have seemed – came to meet. The canal-lined streets would have resonated with Dutch, French, German, Italian and Portuguese, among other languages. Officially, the Dutch Republic subscribed to the Reformed church, which was Protestant. In practice, however, Amsterdam was home to sizeable Mennonite, Catholic and Jewish communities and the adherents of these religions worshipped in 'secret churches', which were frequently hidden in plain sight.

Amsterdam was a pragmatic city: tolerance attracted trade and merchants from the four continents; wealth flowed in. This was a city with an affluent merchant class and a seemingly inexhaustible supply of food, spices, goods and art.

In Amsterdam, Merian came into contact with botanical enthusiasts and experts, as well as collectors, including importantly Jan Commelin (1629–92), Caspar Commelin (1668–1731) and Frederik Ruysch (1638–1731), the father of the still-life painters Rachel (1664–1750) and Anna Ruysch (1666–c.1754) and professor at the Amsterdam medical garden (or *hortus medicus*), as well as Simon Schijnvoet (1653–1727), a polymath with a particular devotion to botany and landscape architecture, and Nicolaas Witsen (1641–1717), a merchant, director of the Dutch East India Company (VOC) and Burgomaster of Amsterdam. These were the best-known, and best-connected, individuals whom an artist with a passion for flowers and insects could possibly hope to meet.

In addition to being conduits of botanical knowledge, these individuals provided Merian with access to Amsterdam's intertwined pastimes: collecting and the pursuit of nature. In the second half of the seventeenth century, the Northern Netherlands was in the throes of a passion for collecting, which included objects of natural history – or '*naturalia*', for example shells and corals, dried butterflies and insects mounted in boxes. These collections were assembled in rooms filled with books, art, and cabinets to hold them all, usually simply referred to as cabinets of curiosity. These cabinets of curiosity and the private and public gardens of the seventeenth century revealed a particular fondness for all things strange and foreign (sometimes referred to as '*exotica*' – simply meaning from outside the Dutch Republic, as well as exceptional, unusual or otherwise curious things), which created an 'atmosphere of wonderstruck novelty that suffused natural philosophy and natural history throughout the seventeenth century'.[31]

The Dutch presented themselves as having primacy in the trade of exotic and rare goods.[32] An advertisement in the local newspaper *Amsterdamsche Courant* of 21 November 1684, for example, promised the delivery of gold, elephant tusks and civet cats from a ship returning from the West Indies.[33] Collections of *exotica* and *naturalia* were a mark of curiosity about the world, as well as status symbols. 'Luxury', as a category, was no longer restricted to precious metals or gemstones, but now also included 'rare books and manuscripts, exotic plants, animals and seashells or minerals from foreign parts'.[34]

Amsterdam, for Merian, would have been a radical departure from the life of quiet contemplation, physical labour and asceticism that she had experienced in Wieuwerd. Surrounded by collectors and their vast cabinets, which she visited, she could give free reign to the curiosity that she had first observed in herself at the age of 13.

Important Friends and a Community

Merian and Herolt came under the patronage of Agnes Block, an amateur botanist and collector whose collection of works by Merian is addressed in Chapter 5. At this juncture, it suffices to say that the relationship that Merian and Herolt formed with Block seems to have lasted approximately from the time they arrived in Amsterdam until Block's death in 1704. Theirs was a lengthy and productive association, from which trust and friendship can be inferred. Block assembled one of the largest private collections of botanical watercolours, which she commissioned from the best specialised artists of the time. Receiving commissions from Agnes Block, for the women, meant income, but also access to an artistic network in their new home.

Merian became friends with the painter Michiel van Musscher (1645–1705), a successful portraitist, whose sitters included Rachel Ruysch, Nicolaas Witsen, the patrician Van Loon and Trip families, and relatives of Agnes Block.[35] Although there exists no supporting textual evidence, it is almost certain that, when in Amsterdam, Merian became acquainted with specialists of natural illustration, such as Pieter Withoos (1654/5–92) and, through her connection with Frederik Ruysch, his daughters Rachel and Anna Ruysch. Among other circumstantial evidence, we know that Alida Withoos (c.1662–1730) and her brother Pieter also worked for Block, and that Rachel Ruysch was familiar with the work of the artists Block commissioned, which included her and Anna's brother-in-law, Jan Moninckx (c.1656–1714). One of the members of the loose artistic community that Merian and her daughters joined in Amsterdam was Joanna Koerten (1650–1715), whose intricate papercuttings fetched enormous sums and attracted collectors at the highest echelon of society.[36] We know that Merian wrote at least two poems for Koerten, each accompanied by an illustration of flowers, one of which survives (fig.6). Both poems praise Koerten's skills, but one is particularly touching in the manner in which it expresses both community with Koerten and empathy regarding attitudes towards women artists. On behalf of their mother, Merian's daughters wrote:

> Dear Friend, with thy
> Silhouette Paper-cutting
> So innovatively employed
> And never enough praised
> Thou hast connected thy skilled
> Art with ours.[37]

These Amsterdam connections were critical in the development of the workshop that Merian and her daughters would operate from their rented house in the centre of the city, which is the subject of Chapter 4.

LOOKING AND DRAWING IN SURINAME

In June of 1699, Merian, aged 52, and Dorothea Maria, aged 21, boarded a ship bound for Suriname.

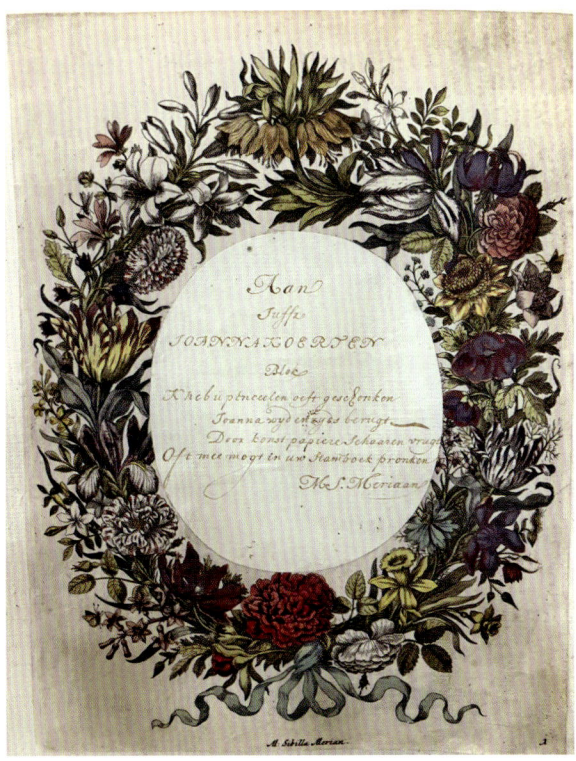

6   Maria Sibylla Merian, Poem to Joanna Koerten Blok, undated, engraving, hand-coloured, Allard Pierson, Amsterdam

This voyage would have been planned well in advance: the trip was expensive and the women were self-funded, meaning that they had had to sell artworks and other belongings in order to finance their journey. Furthermore, this was a three-month, highly risky affair – one that could only be undertaken with significant preparation, from booking passage to ensuring the supply of provisions and materials that would be required upon arrival. Merian was aware of the risk she was taking; she prepared a will in case she should not survive. She entrusted the management and disposition of her affairs to her son-in-law, Jacob

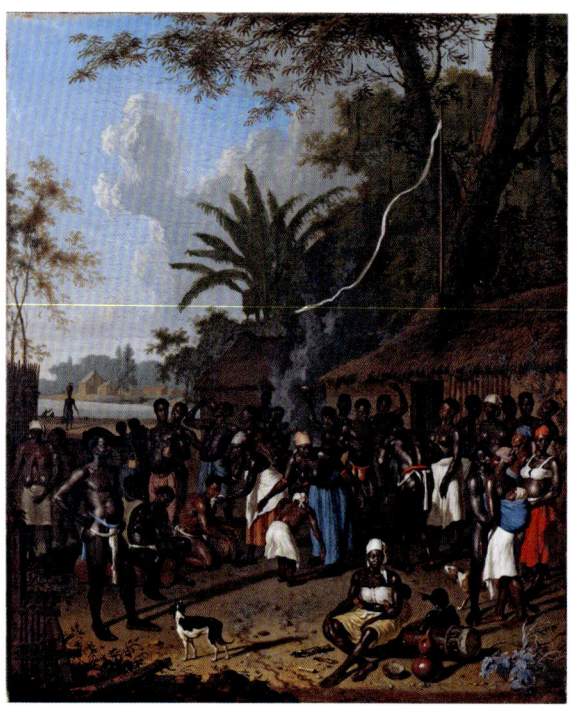

7   Dirk Valkenburg, *Gathering of Enslaved People on one of the Plantations of Jonas Witsen in Surinam*, 1706–8, oil on canvas, 58 × 46.5 cm (22 ⅞ × 18 ¼ in), Statens Museum for Kunst (SMK), Copenhagen

Governor, Cornelis van Aerssen van Sommelsdijck, also owned Waltha Castle, where Merian and her daughters had spent several years with the Labadists. Nicolaas Witsen, whom Merian knew well in Amsterdam, had a nephew named Jonas who owned a plantation called Palmeneribo in Suriname. Merian knew Jonas Witsen and acknowledged him in the preface of her book *Metamorphosis* (introduced below). Although he did not run the plantation himself and remained in Amsterdam while others ran it for him, he owned 156 enslaved people.[39] Jonas Witsen commissioned the artist Dirk Valkenburg to draw and paint his plantation, so he could visualise what he owned.[40] One of the resulting paintings, of a ritual enacted by enslaved people, while purporting to depict a placid countryside and its 'exotic' inhabitants, is a reminder of the profound othering and inhumane treatment of Black and Indigenous peoples by the colonisers (fig.7).

Merian's writings evidence some ambivalence about the living conditions and deprivation of liberty experienced by the enslaved population, as discussed in Chapter 3.[41] It is unquestionable, however, that she and Dorothea Maria benefited from the labour of enslaved persons and Indigenous servants, who hacked a path through the dense jungle so the women could make observations and capture specimens: caterpillars and insects with their food, and even birds and reptiles. Back at their shelter, Merian nurtured the caterpillars, patiently waiting for their transformation, and recording her observations with drawings in her Study Book. She complemented her empirical knowledge with information she gathered from the local population.

Merian's travels and field observations in the jungle of Suriname fed her creativity and allowed her to produce remarkable illustrations that featured an ecological approach to insects by including their sources of food and habitat, which would be published as *Metamorphosis*, the work for which she remains best known (Chapters 3 and 6).

Herolt, and to Van Musscher, who is referred to in the notarial instrument as 'well known to her'.[38]

Merian's and Dorothea Maria's daily lives in Suriname would have been unlike anything they had experienced in Europe. We know that the two women lived in a house with a garden, a residence that was undoubtedly very different from the types of lodging afforded to enslaved individuals and Indigenous people. The nature of the women's interactions with white Europeans, which included government officials, plantation owners, traders and sailors, is unknown. Merian, however, would have known a number of them. After all, the family of the

Merian and Dorothea Maria left Suriname in 1701, returning to Amsterdam. The women experienced heat and jungle conditions the likes of which they likely could not have imagined. When Merian wrote to Johann Georg Volkamer in 1702, upon her return, she mentioned how crippled she had been by the climate: 'there is such great heat in the country that no work could be done, except with great difficulty; I would have had to pay for it with death, which is why I could not stay there longer'.[42]

Merian and Dorothea Maria were accompanied by a native of Suriname about whom nothing is known. They were laden with crates filled with specimens, some dried and others preserved in alcohol solutions – and big plans. Merian resettled in the centre of the city and, together with Herolt, who had remained in Amsterdam, set to work, shoring up support for her exceptional *Metamorphosis*. Reaching out to her old friend Volkamer in Nuremberg, and to James Petiver, an English apothecary and contact likely acquired through her circle of Amsterdam botanists and collectors (and whose role is discussed further in Chapter 3), she expressed her vision: this book was to be unlike anything else that had been published before, both in form and content.[43]

In addition to carrying out work on *Metamorphosis*, the three women continued producing watercolours for sale to collectors (Chapter 5) and selling hand-coloured copies of the Caterpillar and Flower Books. Dorothea Maria married twice, first to a German-born surgeon, Philip Hendriks (1671–1711), in 1701, and again in 1715 to the Swiss-born painter Georg Gsell (1673–1740).[44] In between, Herolt and her husband relocated to Suriname, in 1711, where she died in 1730. During the last two years of her life, Merian, who is believed to have suffered a stroke, relied increasingly on the assistance of her younger daughter. She died on 13 January 1717, in Amsterdam.[45]

THE MAKING OF AN ARTIST: FAMILY, RELATIONSHIPS AND INGENUITY

An often repeated trope in writings about Maria Sibylla Merian is that her career path was ready-made, having been born a Merian and raised in the household of Marrel. It is undeniable that the botanical works printed by her father, and Marrel's flower paintings, were an important part of Merian's intellectual and creative environment. The foregoing demonstrates, however, that equally (if not more) important to the development of Merian as an artist were the relationships that she built in Nuremberg, Wieuwerd and Amsterdam, which allowed her to navigate the boundaries imposed upon her by her gender with relative fluidity, notwithstanding her lack of formal education or apprenticeship, and the fact that she was never a member of a guild, or an institution of higher learning.

Ultimately, it was Merian's ingenuity and creativity – in forging relationships, developing her own empiricism, in honing her artistic skills – that were responsible for her remarkable life and success.

The Art of Nature in Print: Merian's Early Books

COURTING DIFFERENT AUDIENCES

One of Merian's greatest strengths as an artist was her ability to adapt her art to the needs of different audiences without sacrificing technique or quality. An example of her artistic flexibility lies in her manipulation of compositions and the primacy she accords to the image in her earliest published works. The Book of Flowers, which, to recall, appeared in three parts in 1675, 1677 and 1680, represented the first public distribution of Merian's work. The book contains no text other than the information conveyed on the title page. Textual description is also absent from the New Book of Flowers (*Neues Blumenbuch*, 1680), which does however, contain a preface, in which Merian addresses her intended audience: 'the teachable youth', who might find the images suitable for 'milling and tearing'; the sewing rooms of women; and 'all art-loving enthusiasts'. Altogether, Merian offered 36 illustrated plates depicting flowers and insects in various compositions. Each image is given one entire page, underscoring their importance.

The Caterpillar Book, whose publication in two parts in 1679 and 1683 overlaps with the publication of the Book of Flowers and New Book of Flowers, reflects an entirely different paradigm. The relationship between images and text, quasi absent in the first publication, is inverted. Part 1 of the Caterpillar Book contains a preface, in which Merian addresses 'naturalists, artists, and garden lovers'.[1] It also contains a 'Song of Praise' addressed to Merian and a 'Caterpillar Hymn', both by Christoph Arnold.[2] Critically, the work contains on average one to two pages of text setting out Merian's observations for each illustrated plate. As with the Book of Flowers and New Book of Flowers, illustrations of insects with plants or flowers, totalling 50, are each given an entire page. Their importance, however, has shifted, as they both support and are supported by the text.

Evidently, Merian was aware of the needs of her intended audiences, and she set out to meet them. As we will see in this chapter, Merian did more than manipulate the balance between text and image: she also adapted her art to ensure that her books would find their public.

ILLUSTRATING NATURE THROUGH TIME

Merian's works were not the first ones in their respective genres. To appreciate the rich visual rhetoric of Merian's illustrations, it is helpful to situate her works within the lengthy tradition of the illustration of nature.

The dependence of humans on nature – for food, shelter and healing, among other uses – is inextricable from the human experience itself. From this perspective, it is unsurprising that some of the very first texts produced were herbals. Essential guides to the identification and uses of plants based on their characterisation and properties, these scrolls were copied and transmitted over time, oblivious to geographic, political and religious boundaries. The earliest known herbal illustrations on record were contained in Pliny the Elder's *Naturalis Historia*, which dates to 77–79 CE.[3] In that work, as well as in other herbals produced until the sixth century, the text was subordinated to the illustrations. This was true both as a method of production and from the perspective of knowledge creation: scribes would first illustrate the papyrus roll or codex, and then add the text in the remaining space. The text, in turn, would frequently be abridged, depending on the availability of space.[4]

Although the production process of herbals evolved and, in later centuries, the relationship between text and image was frequently inverted (meaning both that the text was inscribed first and that text sometimes dominated), it remains that illustrations have been of paramount importance in the history of natural knowledge. As noted by plant scientist and historian Stephen Harris: 'Publications, and hence reputations, are enhanced by the right illustrator, making the right illustrations of the right subjects.'[5] This was perhaps never truer than in the sixteenth and seventeenth centuries. Accompanying the growth of European expeditions to the Americas, Africa and Asia was a strong desire to record or document new 'discoveries' of nature.[6] Frequently, expeditions employed artists specifically to illustrate the flora, fauna and peoples of faraway lands. This served national-colonial and commercial interests, but also the creation of natural knowledge.

The German botanist Leonhard Fuchs (1501–66) was one of the first individuals of his time to address the significance of images as didactic tools and to make images an inextricable part of the knowledge he imparted.[7] In the preface of his *De historia stirpium* (On the History of Plants) of 1542, he stated that 'each picture was taken from a plant, and was rendered "absolutissima" by including its roots, stems, leaves, flowers, seeds, and fruits'.[8] Thus, the images included in Fuchs's treatise could be used as objects of study in the same manner as the plants themselves. Put another way, Fuchs recognised the epistemic value of images, meaning that they were 'made with the intent not only of depicting the object of scientific inquiry but also of replacing it'.[9] In a similar spirit, from the early years of its foundation, the Royal Society (an academic society created in London in 1660 to promote empirical knowledge and learning) encouraged its members to learn to draw and paint, based on the belief that the ability to accurately depict observations was a tool of significance equal to that of microscopes and other optical instruments.[10]

In addition to facilitating the identification of specimens and complementing the text, illustrations also served to make works such as *De historia stirpium* as accessible as possible. Indeed, Latin – the *lingua franca* of early modern science – was widely read and spoken in learned environments, but could often be a barrier to learning in other, less elite circles.

'After Life'

Key to the importance of images in early modern treatises on natural history was their description as having been made 'after life', 'ad vivum', 'd'après le naturel' or, in Dutch, 'naer het leven'.[11] Using this terminology was akin to using a special code known amongst admirers and observers of nature, an 'internationally valid password in a community spread across a continent and joined by correspondence and publication'.[12] It was a promise of accuracy and of faithful depiction of the specimen by the artist. At its best, it could '[deceive] the eye into thinking that

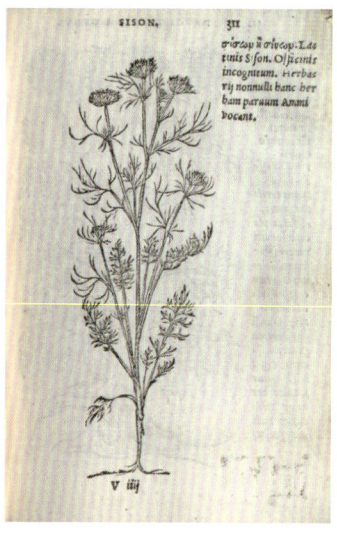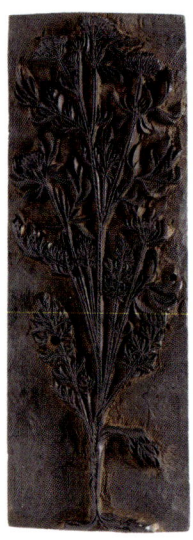

faithful lifelikeness'.[16] Notwithstanding the desire to represent nature as faithfully as possible, however, artists followed certain principles in the illustration of nature, rooted in *De historia stirpium*: things that should be avoided in order not to detract from the 'innate form' of the plant, according to Fuchs, were shadows, unnecessary elements or embellishments and artistic licence that would obscure the characteristics of the plant.[17]

These considerations and requirements inherent to the illustration of nature are of particular relevance with respect to the brief survey of the history of printed illustrations that follows, as well as in our understanding of Merian's contributions to the tradition of this genre of illustration.

8 Anonymous, '*Sison amomum*', in Rembert Dodoens, *Trium priorum de stirpium historia commentariorum imagines ad vivum expressae*, Ex officina Jan van der Loe, Antwerp, 1553, p.311, printed book, Collectie Stad Antwerpen, Museum Plantin-Moretus, Antwerp

9 Anonymous, *Sison amomum*, c.1553, woodblock, 11.5 × 4.1 cm (4½ × 1⅝ in), Collectie Stad Antwerpen, Museum Plantin-Moretus, Antwerp

it was real'.[13] In effect, the representation of natural history 'after life' was an exercise in translation: the recording of visual observations of live, three-dimensional objects onto a two-dimensional surface.[14]

The development of early modern science was an empirical world where first-hand observation superseded other modes of knowledge acquisition. Accordingly, to certify an illustration of a flower or plant as having been made 'from life' was to vouch for its truth.[15] This was the case even if the artist in fact relied on an illustration made by someone else who had directly observed the specimen, as long as 'the image realises (or aspires to) a condition of

Printed Nature

Quite apart from the production of manuscripts, illustrated herbals and *florilegia* intended for private use, the sixteenth century saw the publication of several seminal works of natural history in Europe.[18] These included illustrated histories of animal life (although treatises focusing on insects would come later), as well as human anatomy. In botany, in addition to Fuchs's *De historia stirpium*, these included Otto Brunfels's *Herbarum vivae eicones* (1530), Christian Egenolff's *Lustgärten und Pflantzungen* (1530) and Hieronymus Bock's *Kreüter Buch* (1539). Whereas these works originated in the German-speaking world, the locus of production of many of the most important natural history treatises of the period shifted to the Southern Netherlands during the second half of the century, specifically to Antwerp. There, the printing and publishing house of Christoffel Plantijn (also referred to as *Officina Plantiniana*) published Rembert Dodoens's still famous *Cruijdeboeck* of 1554, which is reported to have been the second most translated book in Europe, after the Bible.[19] Plantijn also published Mathias de Lobel's *Plantarum seu stirpium icones* of 1581 and, at the turn of the seventeenth century, Carolus Clusius's *Rariorum plantarum historia* of 1601.

In these illustrated texts, plants are usually shown flattened – as if a cut plant had been pressed between the pages and left to dry.[20] One can apprehend the general shape of blooms, leaves and roots, as well as their respective proportions (in line with Fuchs's stipulations) but there is no sense of volume and little to no impression of texture. The illustration of *sison amomum*, commonly known as *sison* or stone parsley, which first appeared in Dodoens's 1553 *Trium priorum de stirpium historia* and was reprinted in his *Cruijdeboeck*, is representative (fig.8). The central stem shoots straight up; on either side are thinner stems with small, pointed leaves. The leaves are attached in small clusters and each cluster is connected to the stem to form a triangular configuration, with the apex of the pyramid pointing outwards at the extremity of the stem. One can guess that the blooms, principally located on the taller stems, are circular and consist of clusters of very small flowers or petals. As depicted, they appear oval, where shown as if from the face, or pie-shaped, where shown as if from the side. The small flowers are joined together by thin, filament-like peduncles.

This illustration was made with a woodcut, a type of relief printing.[21] A wooden block (of pear wood, for example) would have been carved with a mirror of the image of the *sison*, as if it were a photographic negative. The surface of the block, with the exception of the stems, leaves and flowers, would have been cut away, revealing thin lines (fig.9). These lines would then be inked and pressed on the paper, yielding the illustration.[22] This method of image-making did not allow for many fine details, especially when the block was of a relatively small size. In these circumstances, the illustration was not always sufficient, on its own, to permit certain and unerring identification. The generous addition of text, however, supplements the image and provides the details that cannot otherwise be ascertained from the illustration, thereby giving the user a complete guide to the appearance, characteristics and properties of *sison*.

The illustration of works like Dodoens's *Cruijdeboeck* was a complex and expensive enterprise. The *Cruijdeboeck* itself required the use of hundreds of woodblocks, each carved carefully by an artist after a drawing made or approved by Dodoens. The value and quality of these woodblocks was such that they were reused for several other works; nearly all of them survive to this day.[23]

The popularity of natural history treatises only increased during the seventeenth century. In the Dutch Republic, enthusiasts of the natural sciences – whether focused on human, animal, plant or material life, from anatomy to the description and classification of minerals – developed well-stocked libraries, acquiring treatises published locally or abroad. Conrad Gessner's *Historia animalium*, published in 1551–8, was followed by Ulisse Aldrovandi's *Historiam naturalem* [. . .] *de animalibus insectis libri septem* (1618), among others. In 1685, Martin Lister published *Historiae conchyliorum*, which was illustrated by his daughters, Anna and Susanna, based on their own observations of the shells and molluscs.[24] In botany, this was the era of Emanuel Sweert's *Florilegium amplissimum et selectissimum* (1612), Crispijn van de Passe's *Hortus floridus* (1614–16), Caspar Bauhin's *Pinax theatri botanici* (1623), and John Parkinson's *Paradisi in Sole* (1629) and *Theatrum botanicum* (1640). This frenzy of publishing activity continued unabated until the end of the seventeenth century and for much of the eighteenth century. Most important, for Merian, was likely the publication by Theodor de Bry of the *Florilegium novum* (1612), which was revised by Johann Theodor de Bry and reprinted in 1641 by her father Matthäus Merian.

In addition to evidencing the continued expansion of natural knowledge, these works marked a turning point in the illustration of nature. Whereas Dodoens's *Cruijdeboeck* had been illustrated with the use of woodcuts, the later publications made

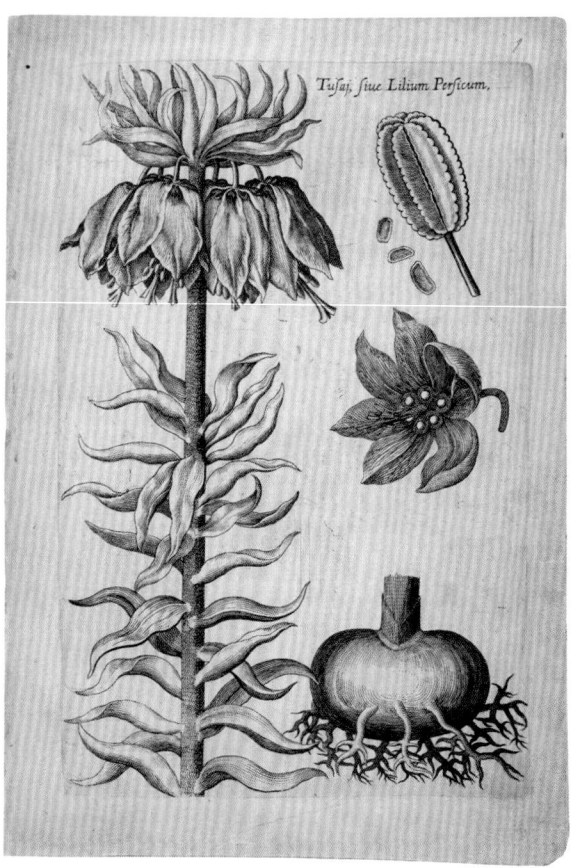

10 Johann Theodor de Bry, 'Imperial Crown Lily', in *Florilegium novum hoc est*, Merian, Frankfurt am Main, 1641, plate 1, printed book, Chicago Botanic Garden, Glencoe, IL

(mirrored) image was transferred onto a damp sheet of paper. Just as was the case with woodcuts, this process could be repeated hundreds of times.

An illustration of an imperial crown lily, included in the 1641 edition of the *Florilegium novum*, demonstrates how engraving could be used to great effect to transmit not only the three-dimensionality of the tall flower, but also the strength of its thick stem and the concave structure of its undulating leaves (fig.10). The addition of seeds and roots, as well as of a single, fully opened bloom, reinforce the scientific nature of the book. Like Dodoens's illustrations before it, the *Florilegium novum* does not include shadows or anything to distract from the characteristic traits of the plant.

Merian would have had no memories of her father's engraving and printing activities. Nevertheless, it is likely that De Bry's *Florilegium novum*, De Passe's *Hortus floridus* and other, similar books could have been found in Jacob Marrel's workshop, especially since he specialised in the depiction of flowers. These works, and others like them, were part of Merian's intellectual and creative environment.

MERIAN'S BOOK OF FLOWERS AND NEW BOOK OF FLOWERS

When the first 12 plates of the Book of Flowers were published, unbound, in 1675, they were informed by the traditions reviewed above; but, in small ways, they were different from anything that had been previously published, not only because they were entirely engraved by Merian herself.

This is not to say, of course, that Merian did not find inspiration elsewhere and, in particular, in the works of French artist Nicolas Robert (1614–85). His *Fiori diversi* (1640), a small book consisting of 25 illustrations of flowers, and his *Variae ac multiformes florum species expressae ad vivum* (1660), which contained 31 illustrations of plants and flowers, some

use of engraving (a print-making method known as *intaglio*), which permitted the creation of more detailed images.[25] Engravings were made by using a burin to score a metal plate (usually copper) with a design. Once the design was completed, the plate would be inked and then cleaned, so that ink remained only in the grooves created by the burin. This plate was then placed in a printing press, and the

of which were accompanied by insects, were not scientific treatises. Like the Book of Flowers, the only text in the two works was that found on the title pages. Nevertheless, as can be seen with this illustration of daffodils (or narcissi, fig.11), Robert's illustrations evidence a careful consideration of composition, volume and texture. Two *Narcissus maximus* occupy the centre of the composition. Their stems cross just beneath their large blooms, one of which faces the viewer while the other offers a profile view. The waxy texture of the petals is rendered through a manipulation of thin, etched lines that create deep shadows and highlights. On the left side of the composition there is a shorter stem of miniature daffodils with three blooms arranged as an inverted triangle. The balance of the composition is achieved through the addition of a large butterfly with serrated wings on the right-hand side. Robert's careful composition and his liberal use of shadows on the plants suggest that he privileged artistic considerations in his work.

Merian reproduced Robert's large daffodils almost exactly in the third part of the New Book of Flowers (fig.12). She did, however, make an important change by including only the two large daffodils in her composition and omitting the miniatures, thereby simplifying the design. Each leaf is clearly delineated, as are the petals. While the stems cross, the space between them is easy to outline. These features would have made the illustration easier to cut out or use as a pattern for embroidery or other needlework, as the book was intended to be used.[26]

Notwithstanding the simplification of the composition, Merian made other changes that provide clues to the significance she accorded to the observation of nature and to the accurate depiction of flowers which were, to her, specimens. Thus, Merian included additional leaves in her design of the daffodils and depicted them from various angles to show their concave structure and the difference in texture between the front and the back of the

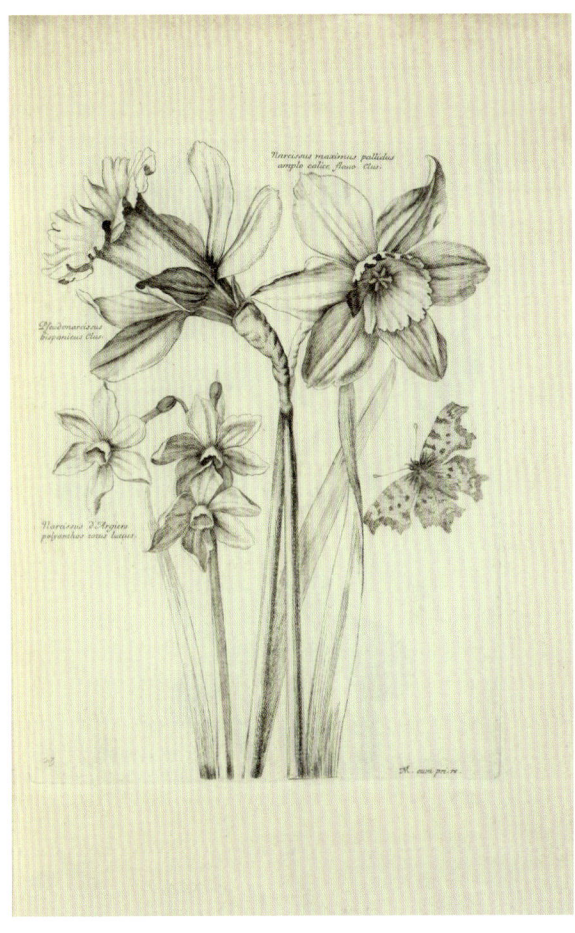

11   Nicolas Robert, 'Narcissus', in *Variae ac multiformes florum species expressae ad vivum*, F. Poilly, Paris, 1660, plate 23, printed book, Biblioteca Orto Botanico, University of Padua, Padua

leaf. Two further additions highlight Merian's equal commitment to artistic and scientific principles: she included an unopened bloom in order to illustrate the growth cycle of the narcissus and added a caterpillar to the right-hand side, which balances the composition but also draws the reader's attention to the life cycle of the butterfly. Remarkably, Merian

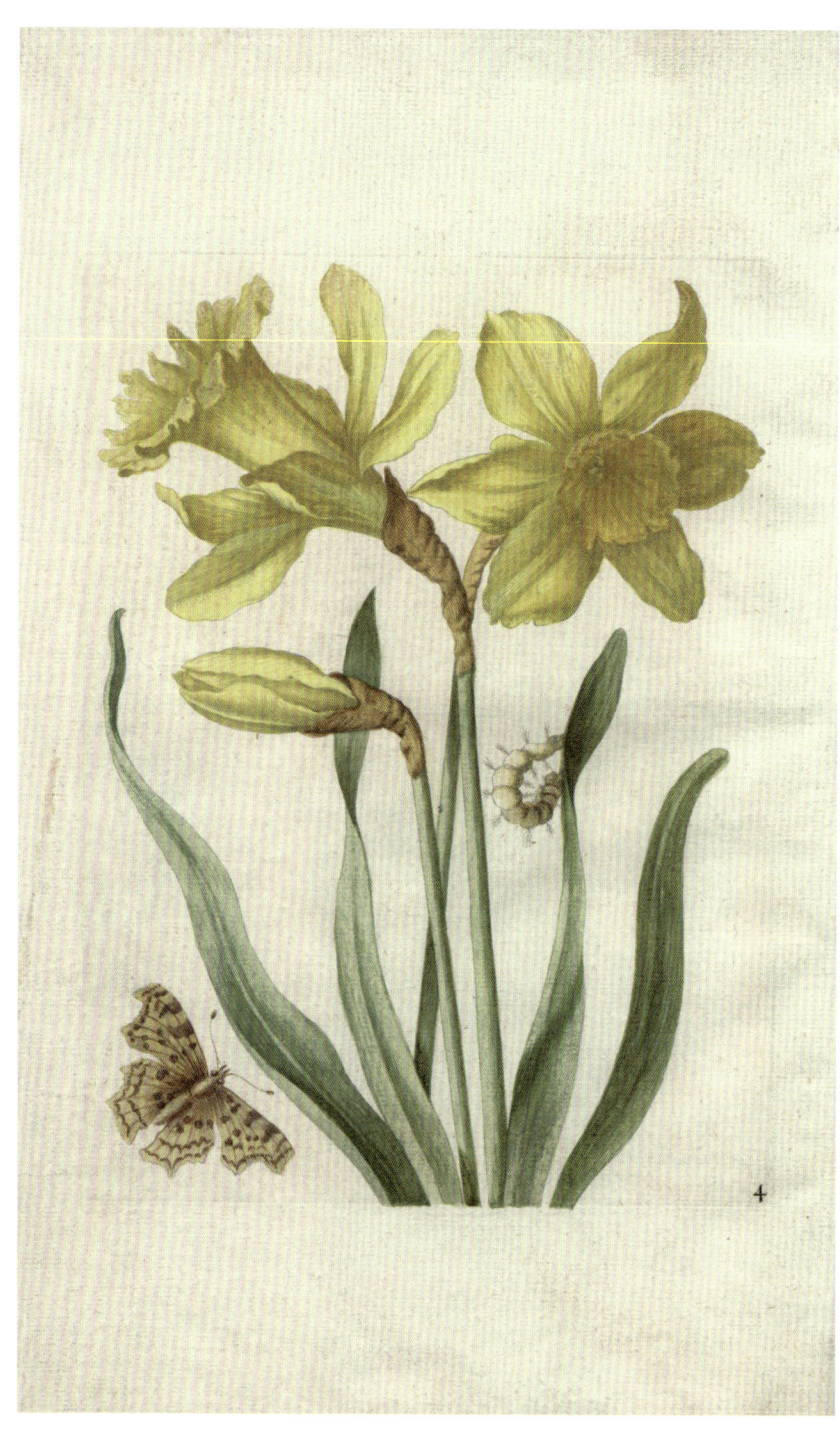

12 Maria Sibylla Merian, 'Narcissus with Butterfly', in *Neues Blumenbuch*, part III, Johannes Andreas Graff, Nuremberg, 1680, plate 4, printed book, hand-coloured, Sächsische Landesbibliothek – Staats- und Universitätsbibliothek (SLUB), Dresden

produced an image that observed Fuchs's stipulations regarding the illustration of nature, embraced aesthetic principles, and met the needs of artists and artisans relying upon the illustration for their work in other media.

To the extent that many of Merian's illustrations for the Book of Flowers and New Book of Flowers borrow motifs and compositions from the works of Nicolas Robert, they were not made 'after life' in the strictest sense. Merian, however, likely observed first-hand the insects that she added to the compositions, and she would have been able to observe the flowers to satisfy herself that her representation of them was accurate and, thus, after life.

The visual characteristics observed in relation to Merian's daffodils – the simplification of line, the use of negative space, the depiction of natural elements from different perspectives in the pursuit of illustrations that were at once aesthetically sophisticated and scientifically accurate – can also be seen in the other plates of the Book of Flowers and New Book of Flowers. The depiction of a primrose (fig.13), in part II, disregards several of Fuchs's dicta: the plant is represented growing from an undulating mound of soil, rather than showing its roots; an abundance of curling leaves gather at the base of the stem, overlapping with each other and casting shadows onto the soil beneath. Similarly, the top of the plant is crowned with numerous flowers and the composition is completed with the addition of a dragonfly on the left, and a moth on the right. The inclusion of these elements by Merian denotes an aesthetic sensibility. Yet, they do not detract from the plant's essential characteristics, which was Fuchs's principal concern. Indeed, the spoon-shape of the serrated leaves is easily recognised, as are the small, rounded, frilled, trumpet-like flowers. Moreover, Merian has included blooms in three different growth stages – closed, semi-open and open – and shows them from every angle: front, back, left and right, and even upside-down. The image would have been more difficult to embroider, but Merian kept the overall outline of the flower simple, and placed the insects so that they could easily be embroidered on their own, or else cut away.

A purple passion flower, from part III of the New Book of Flowers (figs 14 and 15), displays a similarly deft fusion of fitness for purpose, artistic considerations and scientific accuracy. The vine-like flower, which seems to hover above the branch to the left, is depicted in tantalising detail: a crown of pistils stands erect in the centre of the flower, which is denoted by a series of concentric circles in the manner of a target. Delicate, spindle-like wavy petals flutter above larger, downcast ones. The undulating stem of the vine bends slightly to the right, with fuller leaves at the bottom and new, not yet opened ones at the top. Merian has depicted a closed flower bud and suggested the delicateness and climbing possibilities of the vine by the addition of a number of curlicued tendrils. This is not the idealised specimen of earlier botanical treatises: various stages of development have been condensed into a single, still frame. Moreover, some of the leaves have holes in them, presumably created by the caterpillar of the moth that now glides above the flower. Notwithstanding the elaborate design, however, the viewer would have noticed that the various elements of the flower did not overlap with each other, and that Merian had used negative space to great effect, making it easier to cut out or reproduce the design with a needle, while highlighting the elaborate use of curves.

Some of the illustrations of the Book of Flowers and New Book of Flowers seem more obviously intended for decorative purposes, such as a bouquet of poppies, fritillaries and a lily (fig.16). The bouquet is arranged in an oval composition, with a large, variegated poppy at the top, and the smallest and unopened flowers in the lower half of the bouquet. The top-heavy composition is offset by a loose, ribbon bow with curls that echo those of the narrow leaves

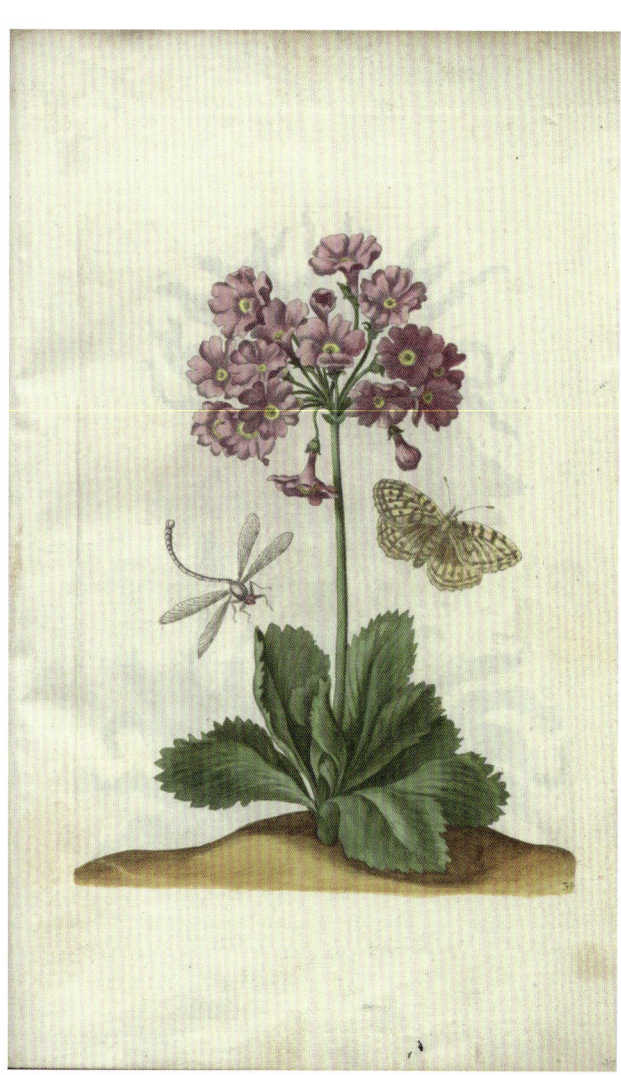

13 Maria Sibylla Merian, 'Primrose with Dragonfly and Moth', in *Neues Blumenbuch*, part II, Johannes Andreas Graff, Nuremberg, 1680 (originally published 1677), plate 4, printed book, hand-coloured, Sächsische Landesbibliothek – Staats- und Universitätsbibliothek (SLUB), Dresden

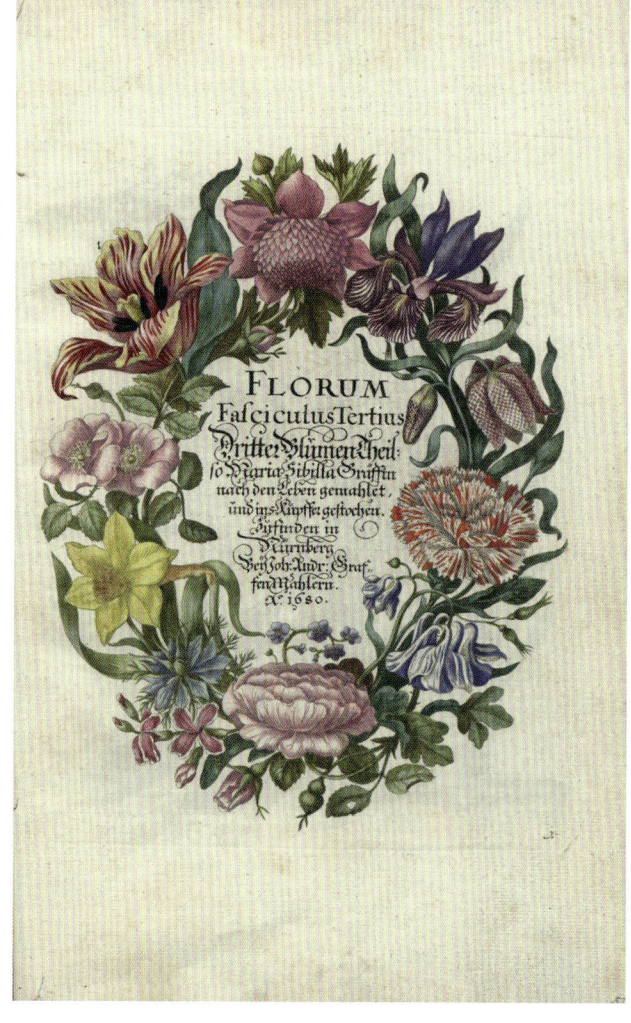

14 Maria Sibylla Merian, 'Frontispiece', in *Neues Blumenbuch*, part III, Johannes Andreas Graff, Nuremberg, 1680, printed book, hand-coloured, Sächsische Landesbibliothek – Staats- und Universitätsbibliothek (SLUB), Dresden

16 Maria Sibylla Merian, 'Bouquet with Poppies, Fritillary and Lily', in *Neues Blumenbuch*, part 1, Johannes Andreas Graff, Nuremberg, 1680 (originally published 1675), plate 7, printed book, hand-coloured, Sächsische Landesbibliothek – Staats- und Universitätsbibliothek (SLUB), Dresden

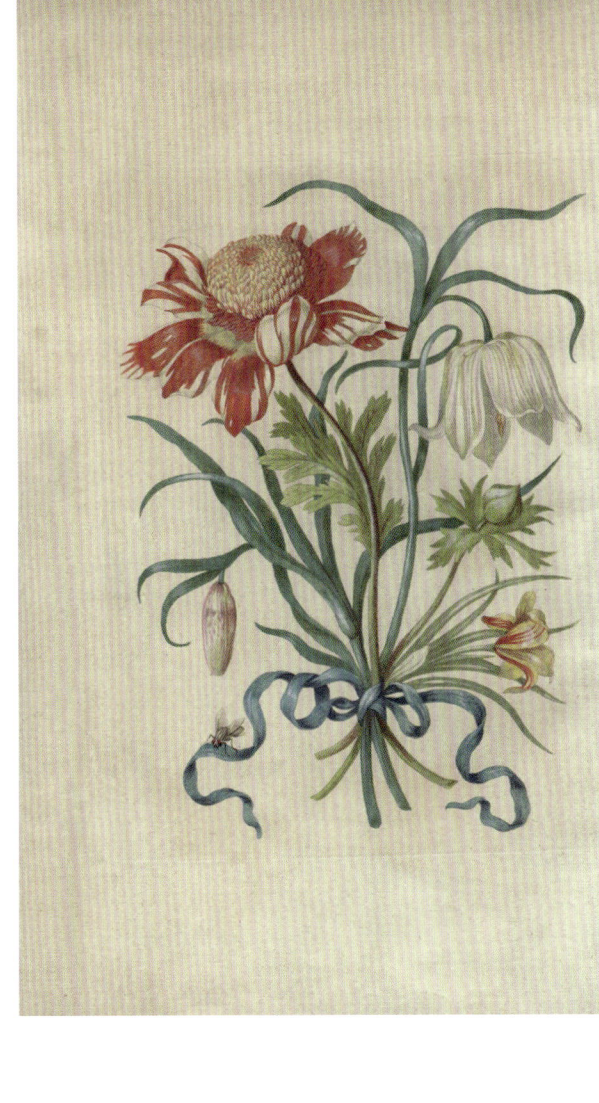

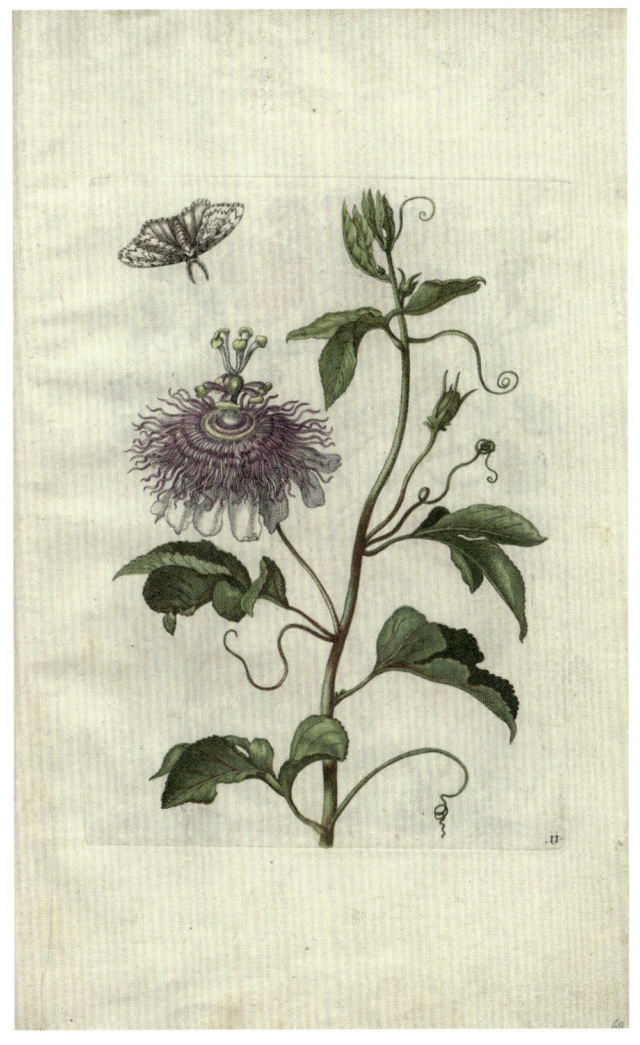

15 Maria Sibylla Merian, 'Passion Flower with Moth', in *Neues Blumenbuch*, part III, Johannes Andreas Graff, Nuremberg, 1680, plate 11, printed book, hand-coloured, Sächsische Landesbibliothek – Staats- und Universitätsbibliothek (SLUB), Dresden

of the fritillaries. Yet, even here, Merian has chosen to include open and closed blooms of the poppy and fritillary, and included a bluebottle fly on the ribbon. In combination with the decaying poppy, the latter could be interpreted as a reminder that beauty is fleeting and death lurks around the corner, or simply as a reflection of the fact that the decaying poppy and strong-scented lily are bound to attract flies. Regardless of the interpretation a viewer of the image adopted, however, they would have immediately been able to identify the types of flowers in the bouquet, because Merian accurately and proportionately represented the characteristics of their stems, leaves and blooms.

THE CATERPILLAR BOOK

The Caterpillar Book (fig.17) reveals an artist who wished to ground her work in her own, first-hand observations. In the preface, Merian sets out how, with great effort and time, she searched and collected 'little animals' (meaning caterpillars) and fed them for days, and sometimes months, so that she could witness and record their metamorphosis. She goes on to state that she had taken the 'utmost care' to depict her observations 'after life', and carefully sets out her choice of nomenclature for the benefit of the reader. As she had with the Book of Flowers and New Book of Flowers, Merian created (and engraved herself) illustrations that featured interesting compositions with multiple visual elements, including flowers and insects, and used the techniques of foreshortening, shadowing and texture to render her three-dimensional observations onto a two-dimensional picture plane as naturally as possible. The pictorial idiom of the Caterpillar Book, however, is markedly different from that deployed in her flower illustrations. Rather than simplified forms and lines and spare compositions, the 100 plates of the two parts of the Caterpillar Book show complexity and dynamism.

As noted in the introduction of this chapter, the Caterpillar Book shifts the relationship between text and image by giving more weight to the text, thereby communicating the primacy of her empiricism. In addition to a preface, each part of the Caterpillar Book includes 102 pages of text for 50 illustrations, plus an index. At first glance, Merian's illustration of the life cycle of a silkworm (fig.18) appears to have more in common with the illustrations from Johannes Goedaert's *Metamorphosis naturalis*, a treatise on the metamorphosis of insects published in 1662–9 (fig.19), than with her own work, previously only known to readers in the Book of Flowers. Both illustrations depict the silkworm resting on a mulberry leaf, thus connecting the insect with its food. Both also depict the pupa (which Merian refers to as a date kernel), and a fully formed moth. In addition, Merian includes two chrysalises, a depiction of a moth laying eggs, clumps of eggs on a mulberry branch, and silkworms of various lengths.

What distinguishes Merian's illustration, however, is not only the completeness of the life cycle of the silkworm, but the detail with which she rendered each stage, from the tightly wound fibres of the chrysalises to the indents on the egg clumps. Her use of fine lines gives texture and volume to the specimens. Yet, it is the manner in which Merian positioned the two moths at the top of the composition, as though they were mirror images of each other; drew a slight overlap between the mulberry leaf and the branch, perpendicular to one another; and made liberal use of shadows, that showcase the breadth of her artistic training and sensibilities and make this scientific illustration into a work of art in its own right. Not relegated to a mere supporting role, as the balance between text and images would suggest, Merian improves upon her descriptions through the inclusion of images.

The other illustrations of the Caterpillar Book support this assertion. In her illustration of a rose from part 1 of the book, for example (fig.20), Merian

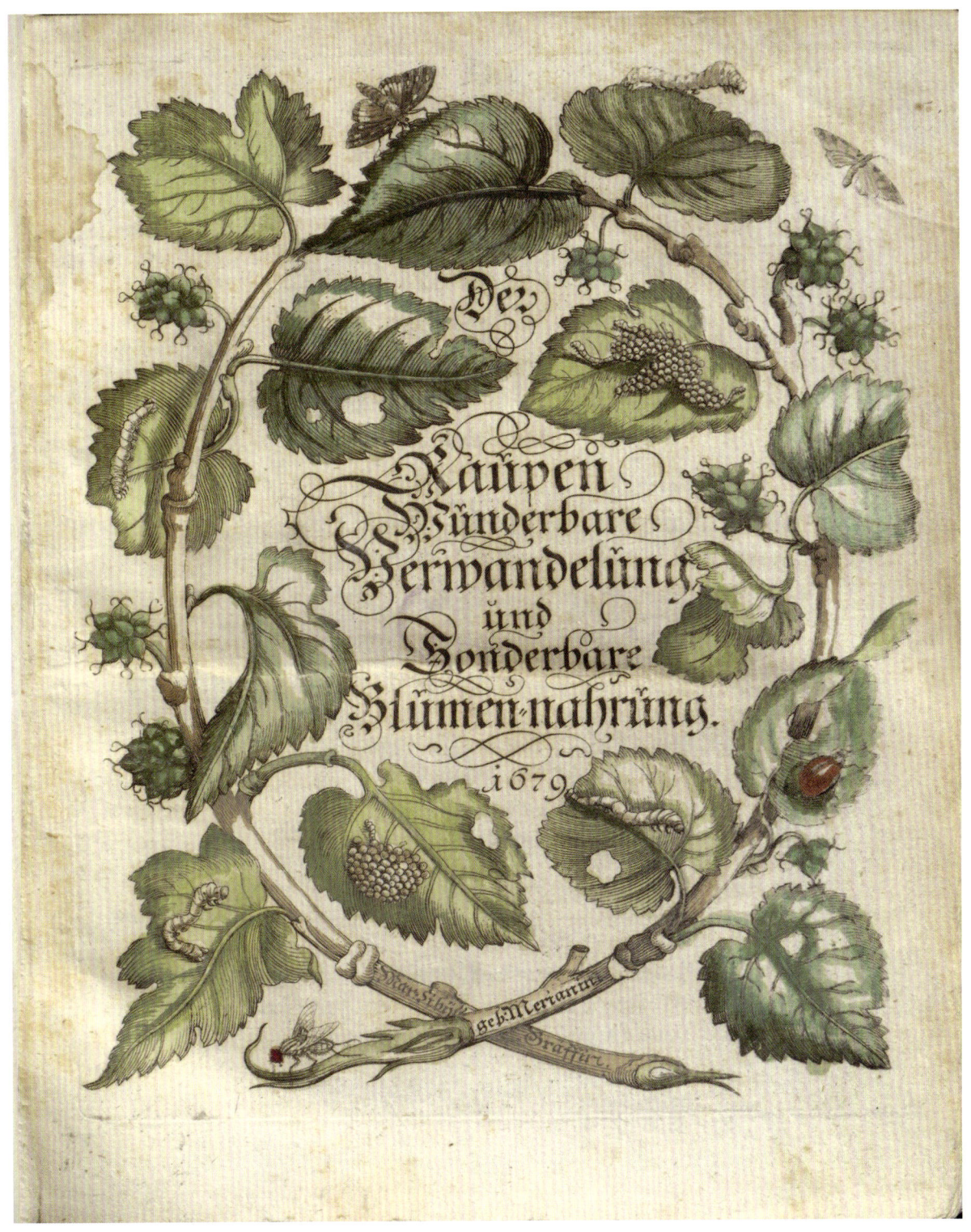

17 Maria Sibylla Merian, 'Frontispiece', in *Der Raupen wunderbare*, part 1, Johann Andreas Graff, Nuremberg, 1679, printed book, hand-coloured, Universitätsbibliothek Johann Christian Senckenberg, Frankfurt am Main

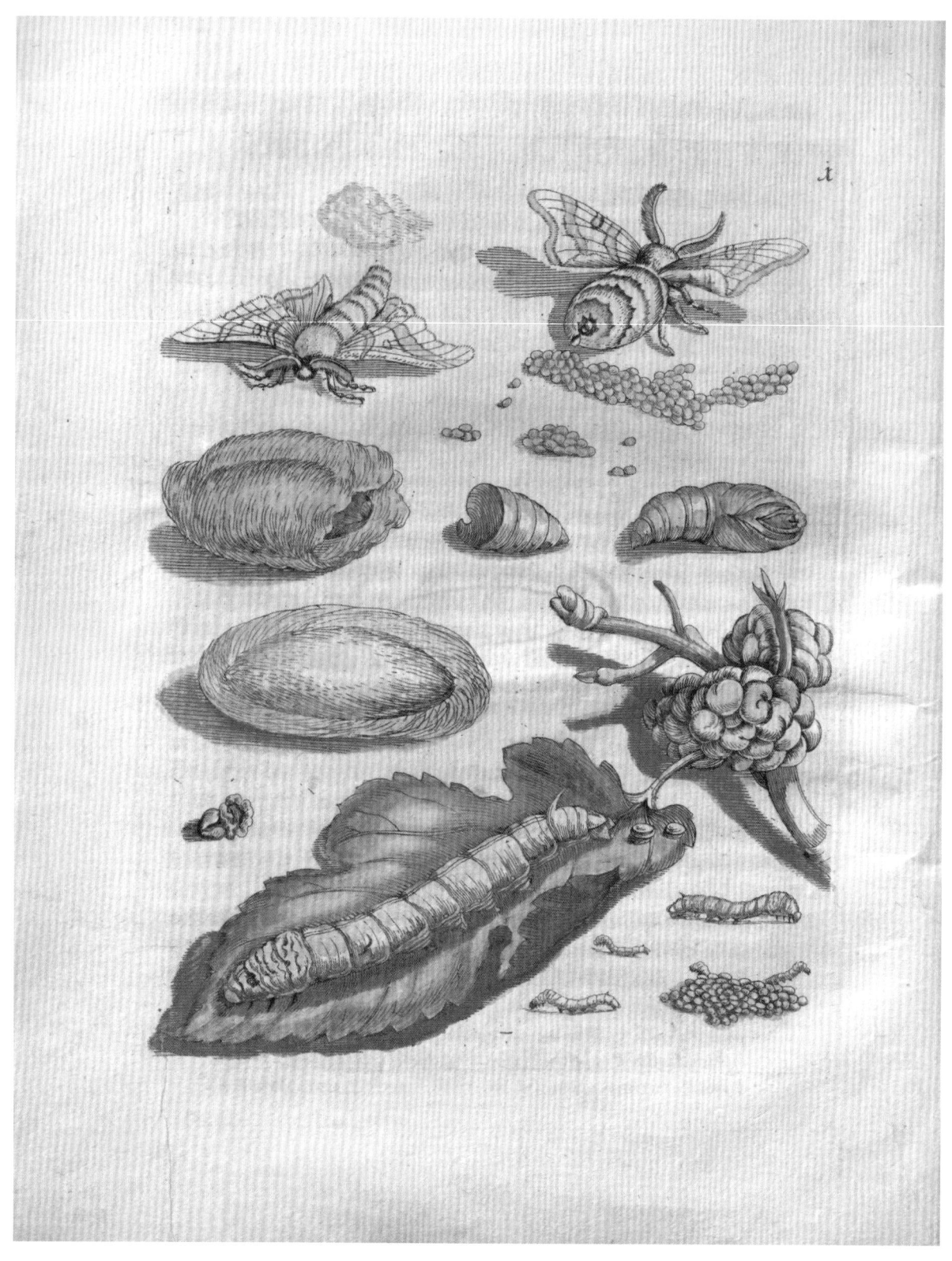

18 Maria Sibylla Merian, 'Life Cycle of a Silkworm with Mulberry Leaf and Branch', in *Der Raupen wunderbare*, part 1, Johann Andreas Graff, Nuremberg, 1679, plate 1, printed book, hand-coloured, Universitätsbibliothek Johann Christian Senckenberg, Frankfurt am Main

cleverly guides the reader's eye along the s-shaped curve of the stem towards the large, open, striated rose at the top of the composition, but not before pausing on the smaller, barely opened rosebud on the right. The weight of the bud is suggested by its slight droop and accentuated by the serrated leaves underneath it, which also point to the ground. These leaves are placed along a diagonal axis that bisects the stem; the upper part of the axis is also graced by serrated leaves. This rather busy composition does not take away from the life cycle of the three insects that are depicted, however: two moths, with their caterpillars and pupae, and one fly, with its eggs.

Merian achieves a similarly unlikely balance of artistic complexity and scientific accuracy with her illustration of blue larkspur, also from part I of the Caterpillar Book (fig.21), and that of carnations, from part II (fig.22). The latter, in particular, renders the acrobatic-like flexibility of the flowers by depicting two stems curving sharply to the right, as if the carnations proved too heavy for their delicate stems. An unopened bud stands nearly erect to the left of the large blooms, unburdened by the crinkled petals that have yet to develop. It may seem as if Merian had decided to forego Fuchs's caution against unnecessary artistic flourishes altogether. Yet, the shape of the leaves and petals and the different growth stages of the flower are all easily recognisable, as are the wasp, ants, moth, caterpillars, eggs and pupa that feast on the carnations. Once again, Merian created an image that met the basic standards for the illustration of nature, while also being a visually arresting artwork.

COLOURFUL TRADITION

With her books, Merian inscribed herself into a rich tradition of illustration of nature. Her focus on the life cycle of caterpillars, spontaneous generation and metamorphosis meant that she was at the forefront of scientific discourse. What distinguished her books from those of her predecessors was her commitment

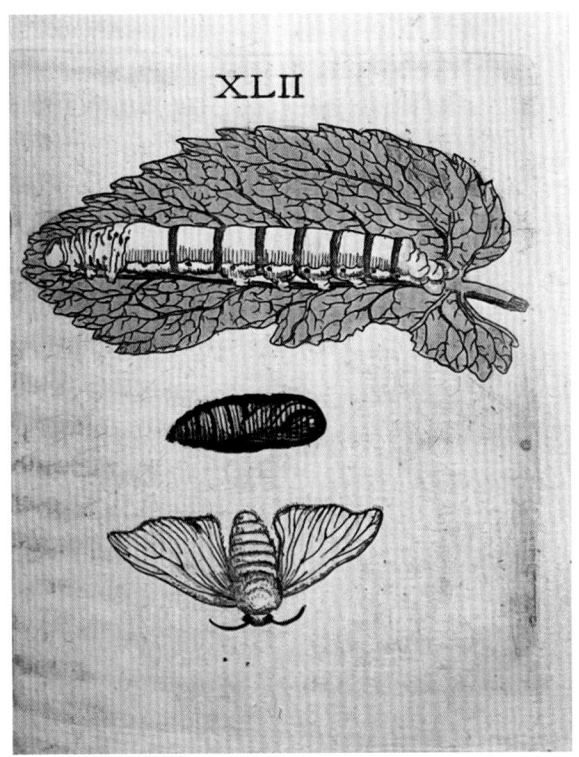

19 Johannes Goedaert, 'Metamorphosis of a Silk Moth', in *Metamorphosis naturalis*, Jaques Fierens, Middelburg, 1662–9, plate XLII, printed book, hand-coloured, Artis Bibliotheek, Amsterdam

to artistic principles and the ingenuity with which she adapted her compositions, lines and forms to meet the demands of other types of visual arts, such as embroidery and decorative painting.

Thanks in part to the training she received in Marrel's painting workshop, Merian could offer her readers something that no other author of *florilegia* or natural history treatises could at the time: colour by her hand. For an additional sum (amounting to four times the 5-guilder price of the Caterpillar Book by 1711), Merian would hand-colour the plates

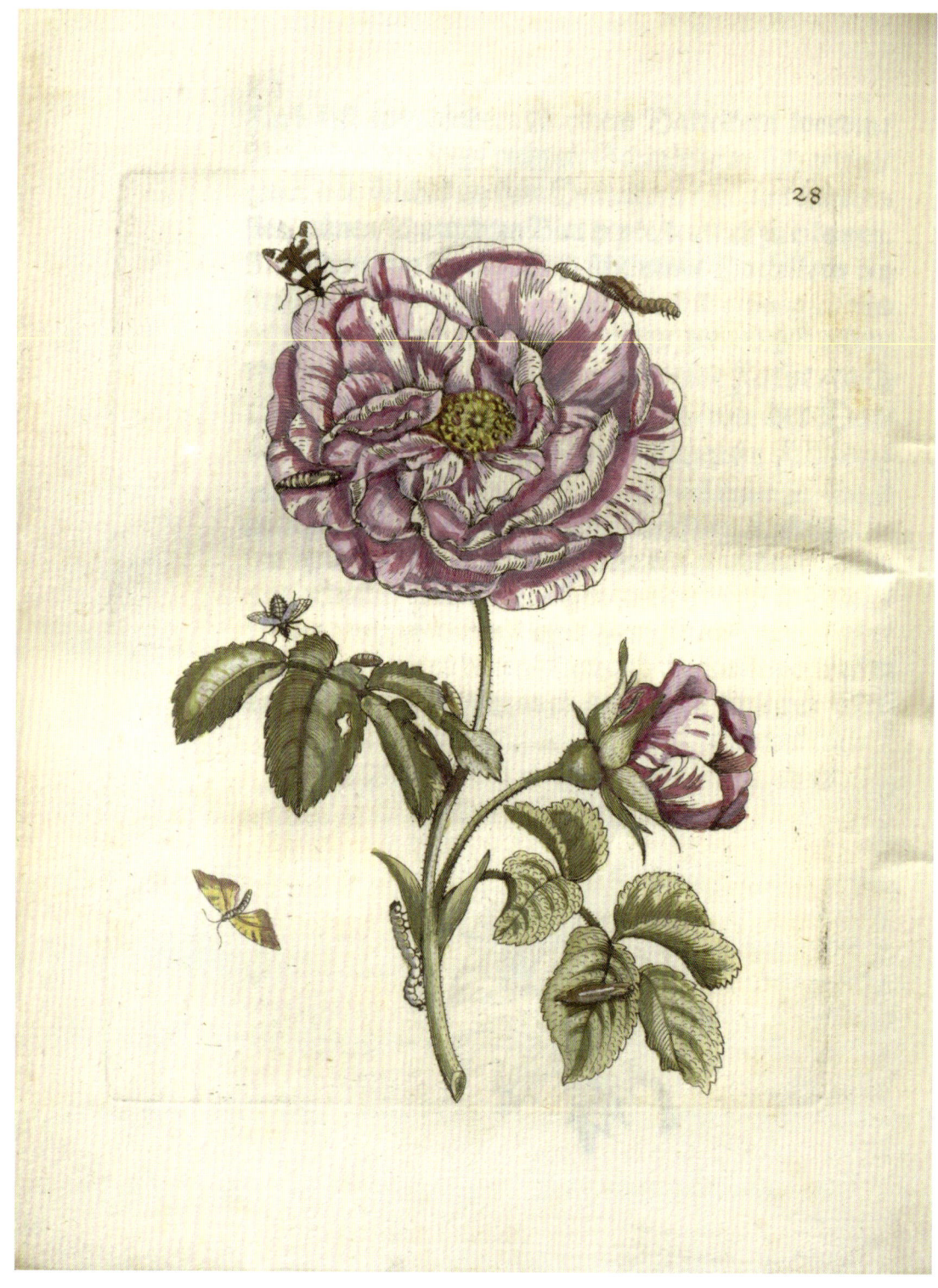

20 Maria Sibylla Merian, 'Gallic Rose', in *Der Raupen wunderbare*, part 1, Johann Andreas Graff, Nuremberg, 1679, plate 28, printed book, hand-coloured, Universitätsbibliothek Johann Christian Senckenberg, Frankfurt am Main

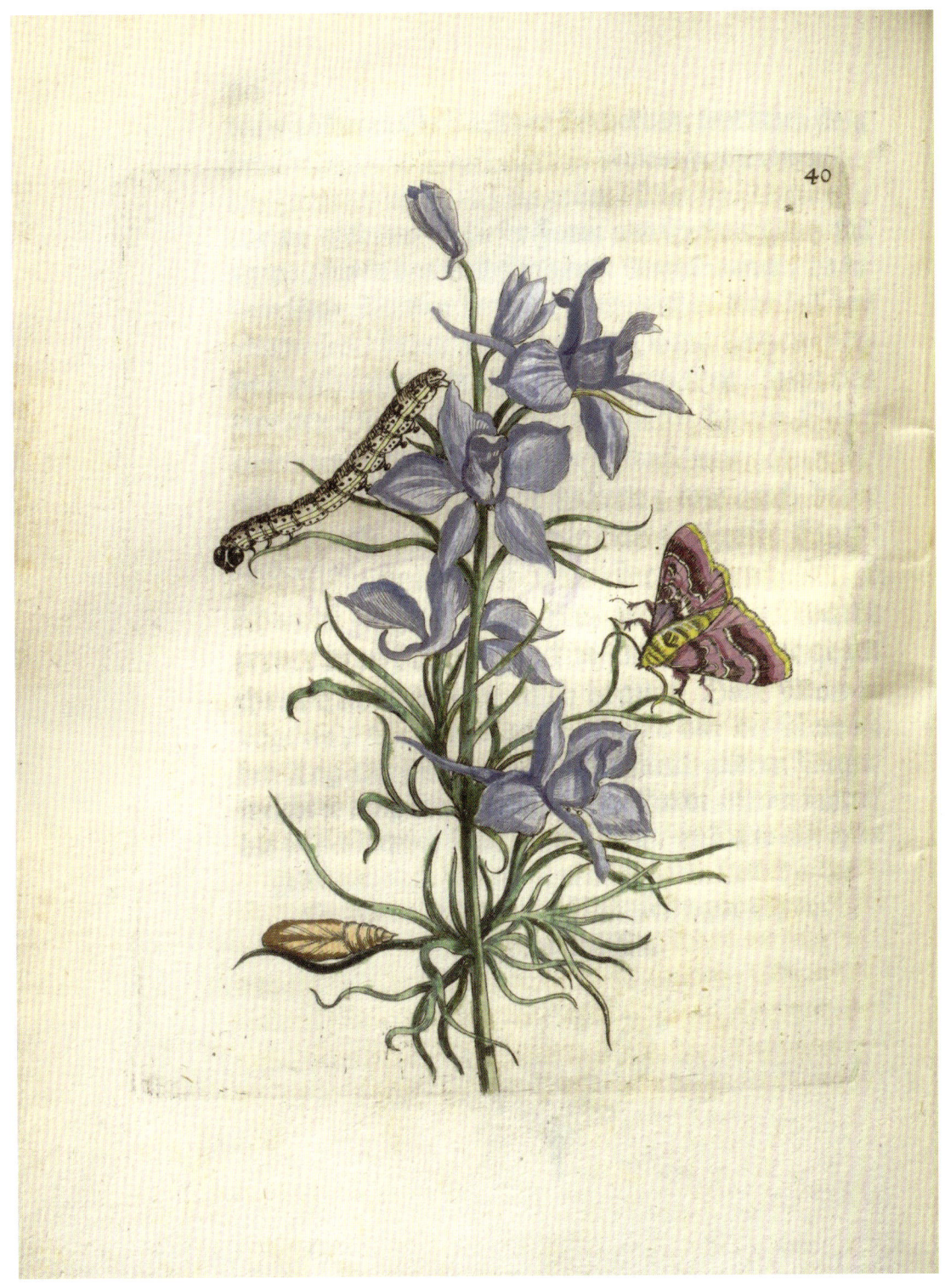

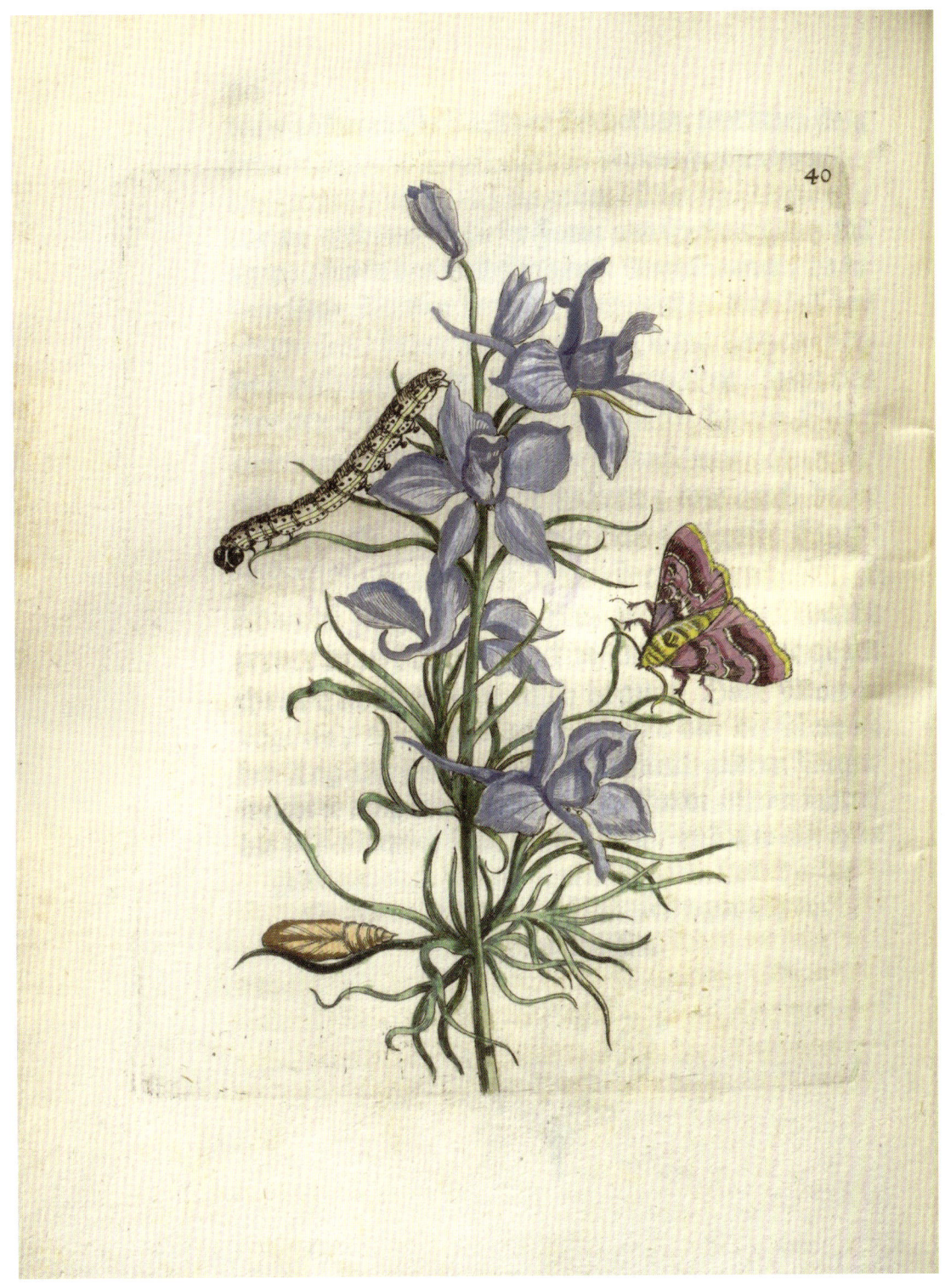

21 Maria Sibylla Merian, 'Blue Larkspur', in *Der Raupen wunderbare,* part 1, Johann Andreas Graff, Nuremberg, 1679, plate 40, printed book, hand-coloured, Universitätsbibliothek Johann Christian Senckenberg, Frankfurt am Main

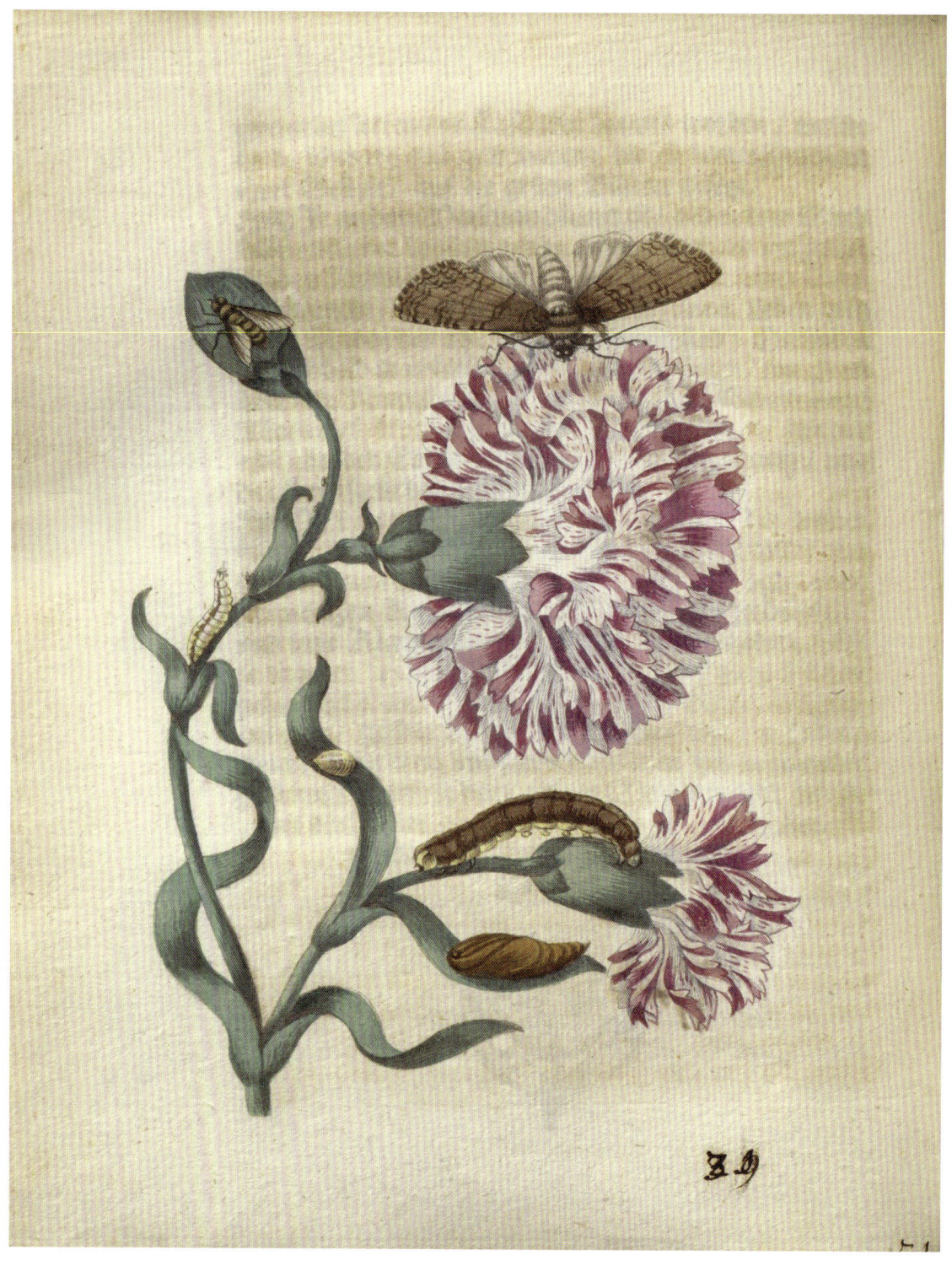

22 Maria Sibylla Merian, 'Carnation and Moth', in *Der Raupen wunderbare*, part II, David Funken, Frankfurt am Main, 1683, plate 31, printed book, hand-coloured, Universitätsbibliothek Johann Christian Senckenberg, Frankfurt am Main

of the Book of Flowers, New Book of Flowers and Caterpillar Book. Although this service was marketed as being 'by her hand', it is likely that she would have had assistance from the young women who were her pupils in Nuremberg, and later in Frankfurt. Very few copies of Merian's original books survive, and it is difficult to determine with certainty which ones were coloured by her. Hand-colouring these books would have required time and patience, access to materials and, above all, skill. At a minimum, rendering their naturalism to insects and flowers would have required a steady brush, the ability to mix pigments to achieve nuanced shades and tones, and the technical knowledge required to prepare watercolours of varying translucence to facilitate layering. In other words, it required an artist. Many of the copies that have survived were hand-coloured by amateurs or lesser artists than Merian. In addition to appearing flat on the page, the colours are frequently incongruous. As well as artistic skills, one needed to have superior skills of observation, which Merian possessed.

As this chapter makes plain, Merian deployed her artistic skills and sensibilities to enhance the aesthetic appeal of the specimens she observed and to direct subtly the relationship between the viewer and the image, for example through the use of foreshortening and by creating dynamic compositions in which flowers, leaves, stems and insects stand in delicate equipoise. With her command of drawing and of engraving, Merian 'matched her optical experience' and conveyed images that were as naturalistic as possible.[27] And, through the combination of her artistic and technical skills and her powers of close observation, Merian's works achieved something that those that preceded them did not: a perfect fusion of art and science, precisely tailored to meet the needs of her readers.

3

Creativity and Innovation in *Metamorphosis*

Merian and Dorothea Maria set off for Suriname in June of 1699, returning to Amsterdam on 23 September 1701. She was 52 years old and was already a recognised artist. Yet it is this trip, and the art she and her daughters produced based on her observations there, published as *Metamorphosis insectorum Surinamensium* (1705), that have most captured the imaginations of readers and for which she is best known. Much has been written about the women's voyage, and about *Metamorphosis*. This was, after all, the first trip taken by a European woman to South America for the purposes of research. These accounts, however, tend to focus on the characterisation of Merian's empirical activities, the results of her research, and the complicated relationship between Dutch colonial expansion and botany. Nearly 320 years after it was published, the beautiful images of *Metamorphosis* continue to awe. Entomologists have examined them for their representation of the life cycle of insects and the plants that they depict; art and book historians have focused on various aspects of the book's production and of its marketing, in addition to the broad aesthetic appeal of its colourful images.

Rather than focusing on the extraordinary adventure that brought Merian and her daughter to South America or the accuracy of Merian's entomological observations and depictions, this chapter proposes to look at *Metamorphosis* as a singularly innovative body of artworks. In addition to representing insects that were new to European audiences, it introduced the concept of ecology as a pictorial genre in a manner that had not been done previously, by combining insects with their food in dynamic compositions. The work also exemplifies Merian's astute business sense in the manner it was marketed, through subscriptions, and produced at various price points and levels of artistic sophistication.

A MONUMENTAL WORK

Merian spent just over two years in Suriname. As she explains in the preface of *Metamorphosis* (and wrote to Johann Georg Volkamer, as set out in Chapter 1), the conditions in the South American colony were extremely difficult; the heat and humidity made it difficult for her to work and she became very ill, prompting her return. The women boarded a ship bound for Amsterdam carrying a multitude of cases and crates containing specimens of plants and insects, live, dried and preserved in alcohol solutions. Equipped with these and the sketches she had made in Suriname, Merian returned to a rented house on the Spiegelstraat and, with the assistance of her daughters, set to work.

Unlike the Book of Flowers or the Caterpillar Book, *Metamorphosis* was an illustration project on a monumental scale, which Merian described herself in the book's preface:

> This work consists then of 60 copperplates, on which some 90 observations of caterpillars, worms and maggots are shown, and also how, shedding their skin, they change colour and form, and ultimately transform themselves into butterflies, moths, beetles, bees and flies. All these creatures have been placed on the same plants, flowers and fruits that they feed on. I have also added the reproduction of the West Indian spiders, ants, snakes, lizards, wonderful toads and frogs, all painted and observed from life by myself in America, except for a small number, which I have added based on the accounts of the Indians.[1]

Not only was the number and size of illustrations and observations considerably larger than in her other projects, but the large illustrations, with one engraving per folio-sized page, were intended to impress. A folio is approximately 56 × 38 cm, equivalent to a large sheet of paper folded in two; in comparison, the Book of Flowers and Caterpillar Book were printed as quarto, meaning that the same large sheet of paper was folded into four, and many books of the period were printed in octavo (8), and even duodecimo (12).

Unlike her earlier books, which she engraved herself, Merian retained the services of three of the best engravers in Amsterdam to translate her designs onto copper. They were Pieter Sluyter (1675–after 1713), Joseph Mulder (1658–1742) and Daniel Stoopendaal (1682–1726), who produced 35, 21, and one engraving, respectively. Three of the engravings are unsigned; it is possible that Merian or her daughters may have prepared those plates. Merian reduced her observations to drawings, which she then passed on to the engravers to transfer onto copper. The engravers would have then returned the prepared plates to Merian, who could inspect them and arrange for them to be printed.

SOPHISTICATED ART

Merian had already begun to illustrate the life cycle of worms and caterpillars accompanied by plants in her earlier works. In *Metamorphosis*, however, the plants and fruits included in the images are the specific ones that provide food for the insects, thereby capturing a slice of their ecosystem. Merian was one of the first authors (if not the first) to do so. The compositions she created for *Metamorphosis* convey a dynamism not seen in earlier illustrations, whether hers or those of other artists or scientists. An illustration of the life cycle of a gaudy sphinx moth (*eumorpha labruscae*) is representative of this artistic feat (fig.23).[2] A multi-segmented brown caterpillar, fangs out, crawls along the stem of a grapevine that divides the composition into two diagonal halves. A reddish-brown pupa rests on a leaf above the caterpillar while, on the other side of the stem, a moth feasts on ripe, blue grapes, its proboscis firmly planted in the underside of a grape while it uses its legs to keep it in place. Through the use of the diagonal vine with its curlicued tendrils, the foreshortening of the leaves at the bottom of the composition, and the slight shadow created on the grapes by the proboscis and antennae of the moth, Merian tricks the viewer into seeing a moth hovering above the grapes and a caterpillar inching along the stem. The grapes, full and heavy, push the vine downwards, just as one would expect. This sense of movement can be seen throughout *Metamorphosis*: moths suck on nectar while fat caterpillars snack on leaves (fig.24); a caterpillar with long, spindly hairs crawls along the surface of a pomelo (fig.25); chrysalises balance on leaves and stems while insects make their approaches (fig.26).

The extraordinary artistic value of the illustrations in *Metamorphosis* is even more astounding when

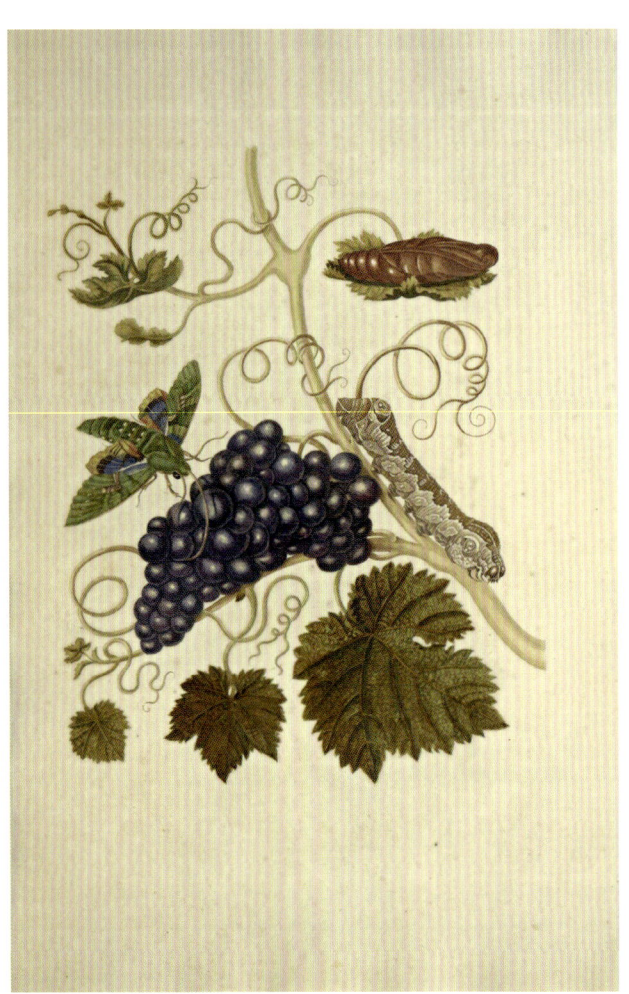

23 Maria Sibylla Merian, 'Gaudy Sphinx Moth with Grapes', in *Maria Sybilla Meriaen Over de voortteeling en wonderbaerlyke veranderingen der Surinaemsche insecten*, Oosterwyk, Amsterdam, 1719, plate 34, printed book, hand-coloured, Getty Research Institute, Los Angeles, CA

24 Maria Sibylla Merian, 'Guava with Moth and Caterpillar', in *Maria Sybilla Meriaen Over de voortteeling en wonderbaerlyke veranderingen der Surinaemsche insecten*, Oosterwyk, Amsterdam, 1719, plate 57, printed book, hand-coloured, Getty Research Institute, Los Angeles, CA

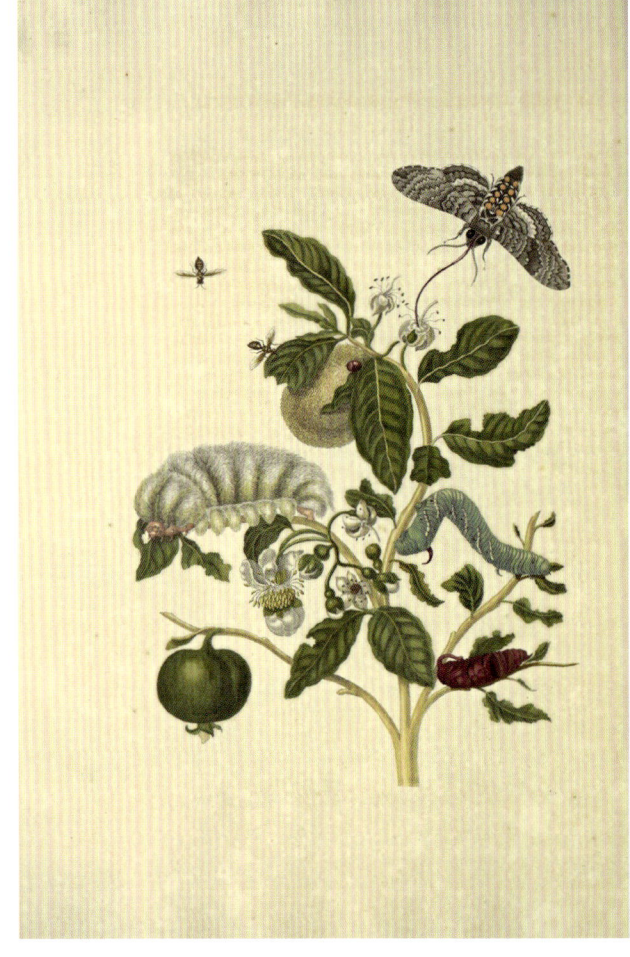

26 Maria Sibylla Merian, 'Lilies with Insects', in *Maria Sybilla Meriaen Over de voortteeling en wonderbaerlyke veranderingen der Surinaemsche insecten*, Oosterwyk, Amsterdam, 1719, plate 22, printed book, hand-coloured, Getty Research Institute, Los Angeles, CA

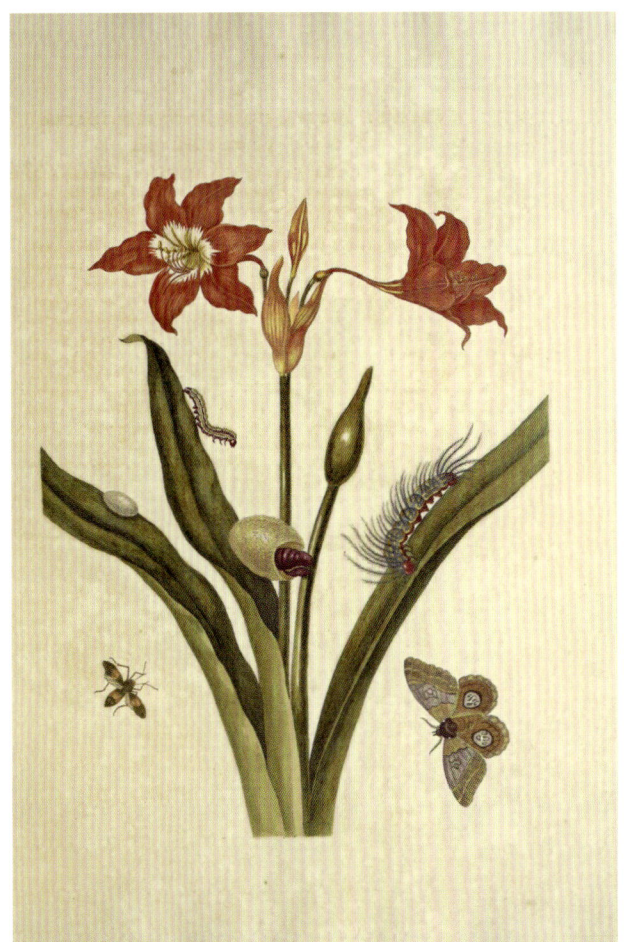

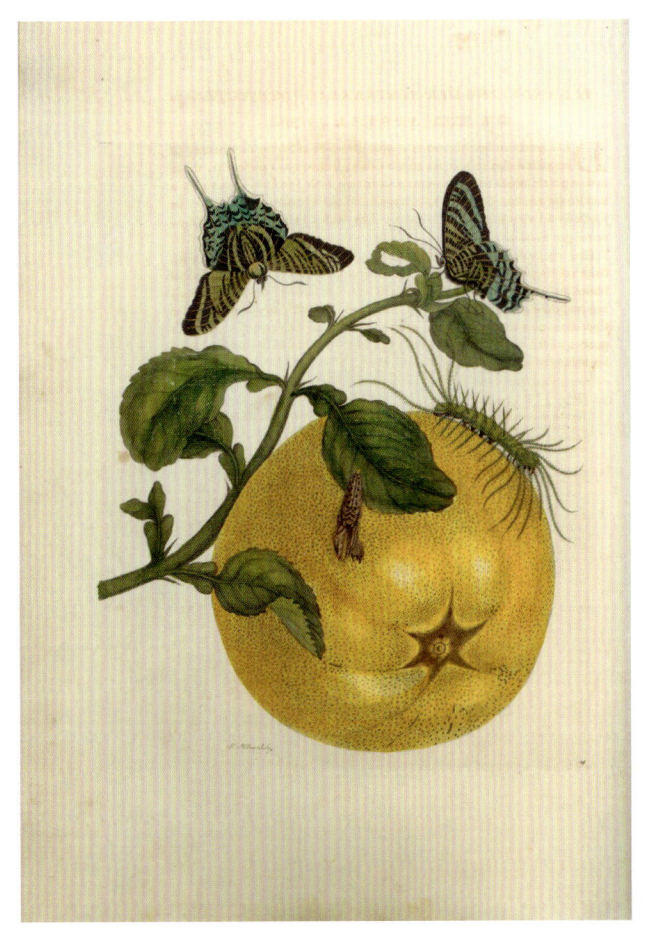

25 Maria Sibylla Merian, 'Butterflies and Caterpillar with Pomelo', in *Metamorphosis insectorum Surinamensium*, by the author, Amsterdam, 1705, plate 29, printed book, hand-coloured, Universitätsbibliothek Johann Christian Senckenberg, Frankfurt am Main

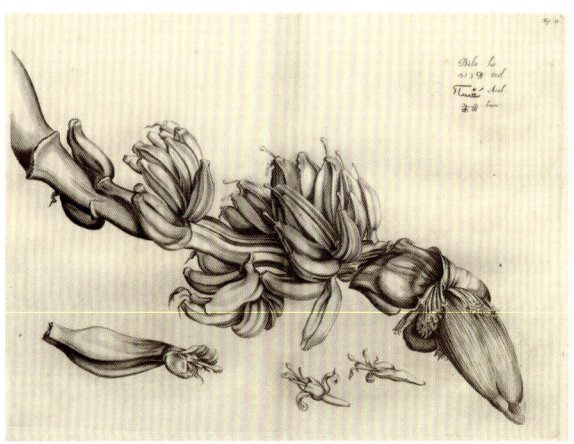

27 Anonymous, 'Banana Flower', in Hendrik van Rheede
    tot Drakenstein, *Hortus Indicus Malabaricus*, vol.1, Joannes
    van Dyck and Joannes van Someren, Amsterdam,
    *c.*1678–9, plate 13, printed book, Biodiversity Heritage
    Library, Washington, DC

ability to depict insects as though they were floating above the page was the result of years of practice. In the preface to *Metamorphosis*, she noted that '[i]n order to practice the art of painting and to be able to draw and paint [insects] from life', she had painted all the insects that she could find from a young age, first in Frankfurt, and later in Nuremberg.[3] In addition, she also relied on empirical methods. In order to produce the lively compositions of *Metamorphosis*, she had to capture, house and feed the insects, and observe them for hours. To appreciate and then reproduce the details of the insects and plants with as much naturalism as possible, she spent a considerable amount of time looking through her magnifying glass – not always a pleasant experience, as she described in the text accompanying her illustration of a type of thistle (*Maccai*):

> Seen through the magnifying glass, both these moths reveal hair like the skins of Hungarian bears. As beautiful as they are when observed without the magnifying glass, they are weirdly bristly and ugly when seen through the latter, having hairs like spikes of barley. I have found that all moths are covered with hairs, all butterflies with feathers, and all translucent or glassy butterflies with scales.[4]

compared to another noted work of colonial botany of the time, the *Hortus Indicus Malabaricus*, published between 1678 and 1693 at the direction of Hendrik van Rheede tot Drakenstein, then Governor of Dutch Malabar. The illustration of the banana flower in the *Hortus Indicus Malabaricus* (fig.27), although well executed, does not compare to that contained in *Metamorphosis* (fig.28). Among other differences, Merian has achieved a greater degree of shading, with darker darks and brighter lights, which better conveys the texture of the plant, in addition to rendering its volume more convincingly. Merian also makes better use of space, giving the reader the impression that the flower might still be attached to the tree; the reader of the *Hortus Indicus Malabaricus* labours under no such pretence.

Merian could achieve three-dimensional, naturalistic effects on a two-dimensional picture plane thanks to her artistic skills. Her unsurpassed

Merian might have felt compelled to undertake the trip to Suriname and to explore its jungles in search of insects and answers to her questions about insect reproduction, habits and habitat, but she maintained a keen eye for aesthetics. Words like 'ugly', 'beautiful' and 'wonderful' pepper the text. Her artistic sensibilities also guided her when it came to the illustrations. While she was strict about representing plants and fruits only with the insects that fed on them, she readily admitted to including reptiles and other animals for the purposes of decoration. This is how a common tegu found itself adorning a manihot plant and a coiled snake appeared to menace a beetle on the root of a cassava

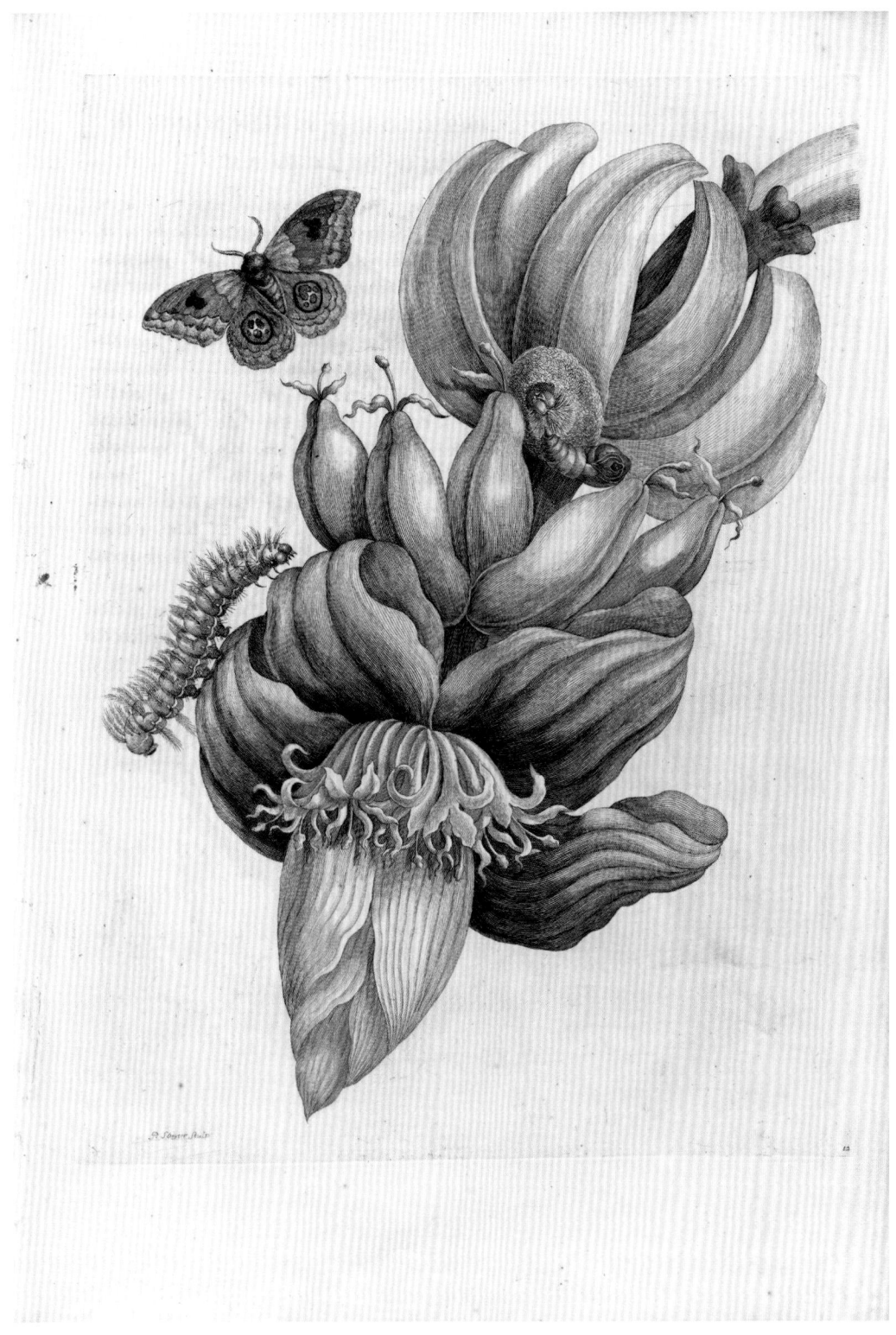

28 Maria Sibylla Merian, 'Banana Flower', in *Dissertatio de generatione et metamorphosibus insectorum Surinamensium*, Joannes Oosterwyk, Amsterdam, 1719, plate 12, printed book, Université de Strasbourg, Strasbourg

plant (fig.29). These animals were real and observed by Merian, and they are presented in a broadly appropriate ecological context. Merian's purpose, however, was not scientific but purely artistic. Of a blue lizard nudging a fruit of the *Baccoves* (Musa) with its head (fig.30), she stated: 'It is mainly to embellish the page that I am here showing the blue lizard with its eggs.' It turns out that the reptile had made its nest in the floor of her house. Merian brought the lizard and its eggs with her on the return journey to Amsterdam; alas, they did not survive.

The Value of Colour

Metamorphosis could be bought in black and white (it was not possible to print in more than one colour until the nineteenth century), or hand-coloured by Merian and her workshop. Those who bought black-and-white copies could attempt to colour them themselves or else retain the services of a different artist. As a close observer of nature, Merian understood the significance of colour not only in the identification of specimens, but also in determining a specimen's life stage. The descriptions that she included with each illustration therefore contained not only the physical description of the plants and insects and their properties, but also detailed explanations of colours and shapes (fig.31):

> *Indiaanse Peper* [Indian pepper] or *Piement* [pimiento] grows to half a man's height. The blossom is white, with violet in the centre. The stem is green and hard, the leaves grass-green and soft. In the beginning the fruit is green, later a beautiful red. [...]
>
> On this pepper I found this lovely big caterpillar which had a red stripe on either side all along its body, and a white stripe all along its back. It had a rose-coloured horn on its hindmost segment, and on each segment a yellow patch rimmed with rose. It ate not only these leaves, but also the pepper itself. On 22 January it became a brown pupa, and on 16 February a

grey moth emerged, having on either side of its body five golden-yellow spots. It flew only at night and by day it was very still.[5]

Stripes, patches, rim, spots; white, violet, green, grass-green, beautiful red, rose, yellow, brown, grey, golden-yellow: more than simple observations, what Merian shared with her readers was her painter's palette.

AN INNOVATIVE APPROACH TO SALES

It was a matter of pride for Merian that she had funded the trip to Suriname herself – an enormous expense. In the months preceding her and Dorothea Maria's departure, she placed an advertisement in the Donderdaegse *Amsterdamse Courant* (a weekly local paper) for the sale of a substantial inventory, which interested purchasers could peruse and buy at her house. The items for sale included 'attractive and curious works by Maria Sibille Merian', consisting of rare plants, flowers and insects – 'all painted in watercolour (after life with extraordinary colour and skill)'; 253 parchment sheets of pictorial observations of plants and insects from the East and West Indies gathered by Merian 'with great expense and effort over the last 30 years' in Germany, Holland and Friesland; two smaller illustrated works by Merian; one complete copy of the *Hortus Eystettensis* (a book by Basilius Besler describing the plant collection of the Prince-Bishop of Eichstätt); and 100 etched copper plates.[6] The same advertisement appeared in the local newspaper in Haarlem, a small town near Amsterdam with a vibrant artistic community and a number of wealthy merchants and collectors.[7]

The sale of prepared copper plates by Merian is particularly interesting: indeed, anyone in possession of engraved copper plates could use them to make prints. As tools with the capacity to generate income, these items were of high value and would have been of great interest to printers and publishers.

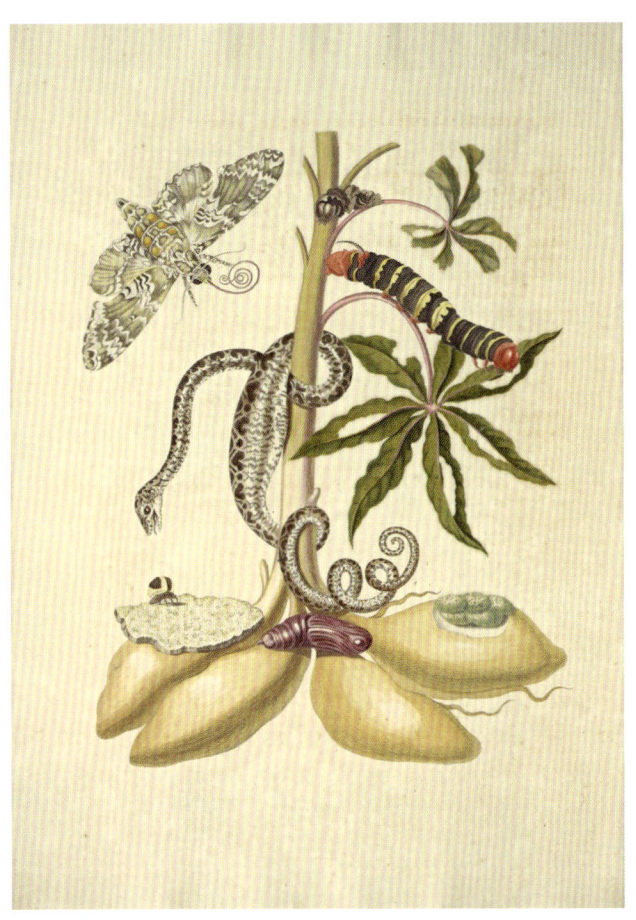

29 Maria Sibylla Merian, 'Cassava with Coiled Snake',
    in *Maria Sybilla Meriaen Over de voortteeling en
    wonderbaerlyke veranderingen der Surinaemsche insecten*,
    Oosterwyk, Amsterdam, 1719, plate 5, printed book, hand-
    coloured, Getty Research Institute, Los Angeles, CA

30 Maria Sibylla Merian, 'Musa with Blue Lizard and Butterfly',
    in *Maria Sybilla Meriaen Over de voortteeling en wonderbaerlyke
    veranderingen der Surinaemsche insecten*, Oosterwyk,
    Amsterdam, 1719, plate 23, printed book, hand-coloured,
    Getty Research Institute, Los Angeles, CA

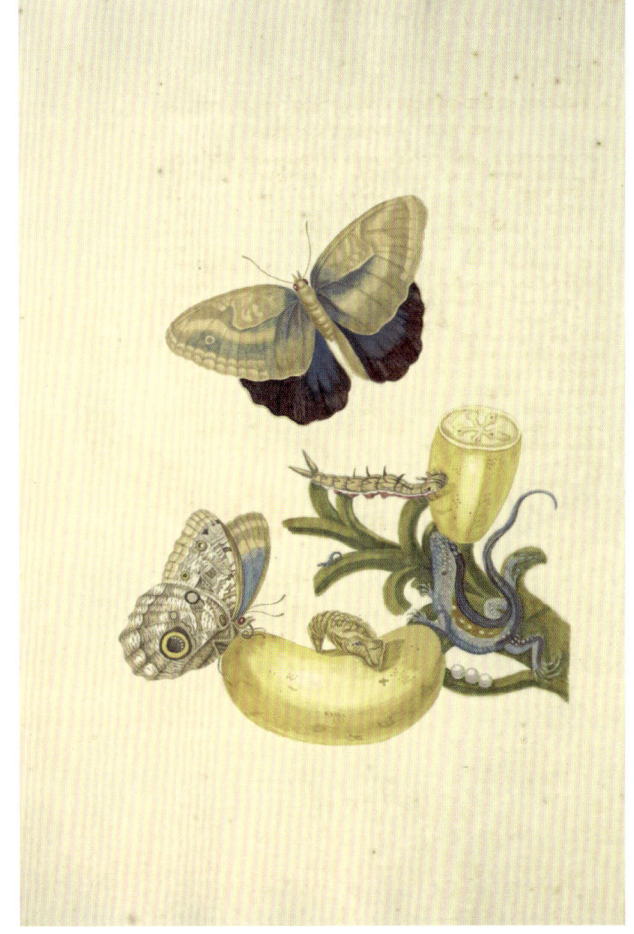

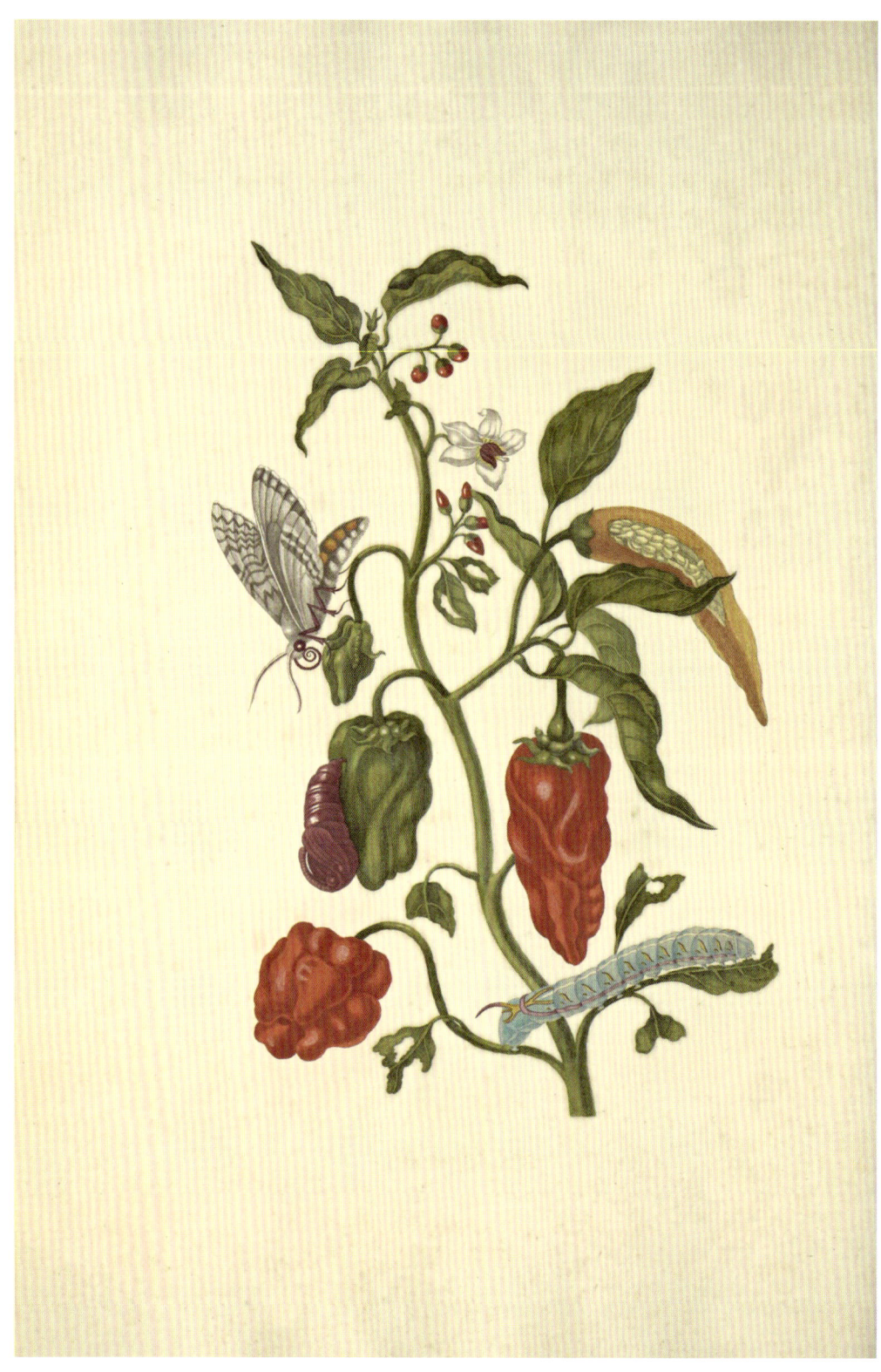

31 Maria Sibylla Merian, 'Pepper Plant with Insects', in *Maria Sybilla Meriaen Over de voortteeling en wonderbaerlyke veranderingen der Surinaemsche insecten*, Oosterwyk, Amsterdam, 1719, plate 55, printed book, hand-coloured, Getty Research Institute, Los Angeles, CA

Furthermore, they could be retooled to produce new blank copper plates, which could be sold. Importantly, their sale meant that Merian was willing to forego a source of potential future income in order to raise funds to travel to South America.

Notwithstanding the sales she conducted prior to leaving for Suriname, however, the need to recover the costs of her two years abroad seems to have been pressing upon her return. In October 1702, Merian wrote to Johann Georg Volkamer to gauge interest in a large, folio-sized book, for which she had apparently already done some of the illustrations.[8] Merian's letter to Volkamer reveals her creativity and awareness of the state-of-the-art both as an artist and as an entrepreneur in two ways. First, she wrote that the book she had in mind would be bigger than the *Horti Medici Amstelodamensis*, part one of which was published by Jan Commelin in 1697 and part two by Caspar Commelin in 1701.

Jan Commelin was one of the founders of the *hortus medicus* in Amsterdam, and Caspar, his nephew, was appointed botanist there in 1696, eventually becoming director. The 1701 volume included engravings (in black and white) of illustrations produced for what is now known as the *Moninckx Atlas*, an illustrated catalogue of the rare plants and flowers in the Amsterdam *hortus medicus* and arguably the most prestigious botanical illustration project carried out in the Netherlands in that period. Jan Commelin was one of the first commissioners for the *Atlas*. With 422 watercolours in total, it required the work of at least six artists, including Maria Moninckx (1673/6–1757) and Alida Withoos, both of whom would have been known to Merian through her work for Agnes Block. Herolt contributed two illustrations.

A city-sponsored commission, the *Atlas* was executed on vellum, the most expensive kind of support for such a catalogue. This was a prestige project, telegraphing the wealth and prosperity of Amsterdam: 'The watercolours bore witness to the vastness of the Dutch trade empire, the richness of the Amsterdam *hortus medicus*, and the talent of the Republic's artists.'[9] As an avid amateur of botany himself, Volkamer would have been well aware of the illustration project underway in Amsterdam, as well as of the *Horti Medici Amstelodamensis*, which he may have owned. Thus, by mentioning her own illustrations and signalling her intention to outdo the work by Jan and Caspar Commelin, Merian was communicating the scale and sophistication of her project.

The second way in which Merian revealed her creativity and sophistication as an artist and entrepreneur is in her mention to Volkamer that she intended to sell her book based on a subscription model, in the same manner as Georg Eberhard Rumphius's *D'Amboinsche Rariteitkamer*, a large, illustrated volume of shells from Indonesia. Merian simply refers to this book as the 'Ambonese work', because it would not be assigned a formal title and published until 1705, the same year as *Metamorphosis*. Merian knew how the most recent, ambitious work of colonial natural history was being marketed, and she was determined to deploy this model herself.

Selling a book through subscriptions would enable Merian to raise funds immediately to finance the publication of *Metamorphosis*. The work was self-published and Merian needed to pay for the services of the engravers she retained, as well as for paper and the cost of the printing itself. Pursuant to this model, subscribers usually benefited from lower prices in exchange for paying up front; the more subscribers a work attracted, the lower the price each subscriber would ultimately have to pay. As Merian explained to Volkamer, *Metamorphosis*, as she envisaged it, was certain to be an expensive endeavour – hence the need to attract as many subscribers as possible. They were offered two options: they could purchase the work for 15 guilders in black and white or acquire a copy hand-coloured by Merian (and her workshop), for 45 guilders. Merian told Volkamer that non-subscribers would have to pay 18 guilders for the book.

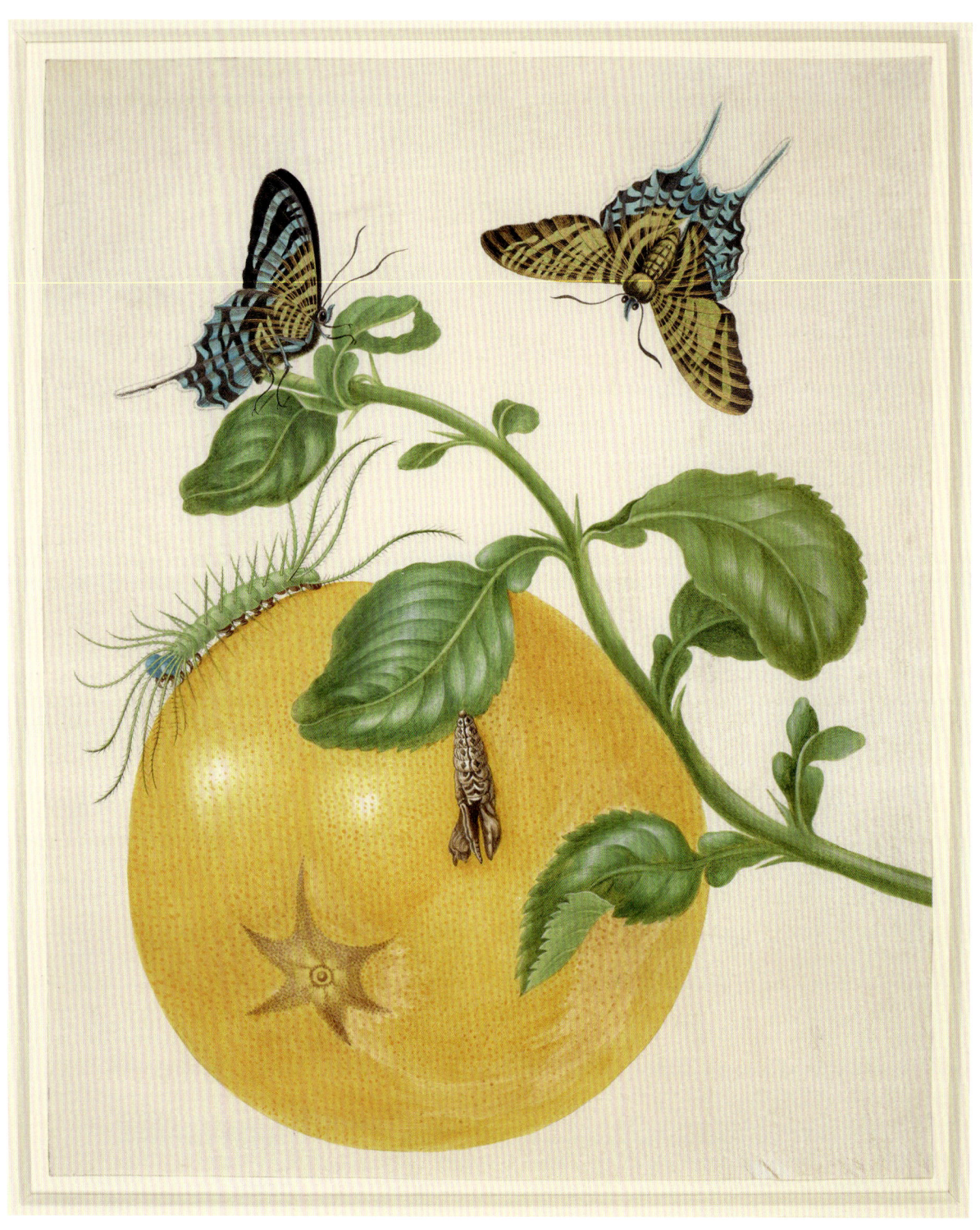

32 Maria Sibylla Merian, *Butterflies, Caterpillar, and Pomelo*, *c.*1702–3, watercolour on parchment, 36.7 × 28.9 cm
(14½ × 11⅜ in), Royal Collection Trust, United Kingdom

In addition to seeking Volkamer's assistance in ascertaining the appetite of German readers for her project, Merian wrote to the London pharmacist James Petiver (*c*.1663–1718) for help in promoting the book in England. Petiver was well connected: he was a member of the Royal Society and a close associate of Hans Sloane, a physician and polymath whose personal collection would become the foundation for the British Museum. Her first preserved letter to Petiver, dated 4 June 1703, introduces *Metamorphosis*. In addition to including the conditions of subscription (in a now lost, separate sheet), Merian attached one print to her letter to Petiver, writing that the image showed that the book was an unequalled, 'utterly consummate' work.[10] In response to Merian's request, Petiver placed an advertisement in the *Philosophical Transactions*, the publication of the Royal Society, which reads in part:

Such Persons as are willing to Subscribe for a work of this Nature, (which for its Curiosity and Performance very well deserves publick Encouragement) She desires the first Payment may be speedily made to *James Petiver* Apothecary in *Aldersgate street*, London, to whom she hath sent several Tables, and some Colours, to shew their Curiosity, and how admirably they are engraved, which may be seen by any that desire it. The work is in great forwardness, and highly approved of by all that see it.[11]

Merian kept up her correspondence with Petiver, determined to make *Metamorphosis* a success. These letters reveal that Merian was commercially astute, for example insisting that interested subscribers or collectors wishing to buy specimens contact her directly and stating categorically that she refused to pay commissions to intermediaries. Merian was also obviously aware of the rare position in which she found herself as a woman, having undertaken a dangerous journey to Suriname and now purporting to publish a book of natural history – the first woman to do so.[12] Boldly, Merian inquired from Petiver whether it would be reasonable to dedicate an illuminated copy of *Metamorphosis* to the Queen, given that they were of the same sex ('du mesme sexe').[13]

For sales closer to home, Merian could rely on local newspapers to spread the word, as she had done when selling materials to raise funds for her Surinamese voyage. She was working fast, and funding appears to have become a pressing issue. An advertisement appeared in the *Oprechte Haerlemsche Courant* on 15 November 1703 in which Merian offered for sale one third of the plates that would constitute *Metamorphosis* (noting that this selection of plates could easily be considered as a completed work in and of itself).[14] By April 1704, half of the anticipated 60 plates were completed and available for sale to buyers and subscribers in Amsterdam, Rotterdam, Leiden, Middelburg and The Hague – but they had to be quick:

Maria Sibylla Merian presents to all curious Enthusiasts her uncommon Surinamese Insect Work, for either Buyers or Subscribers, observed by her in America, consisting of all kinds of worms, how they change into night and day Moths, Beetles, Bees and Flies, each with its own food, like Herbs, Flowers, Fruits, consisting of 60 copper plates, about half of which are ready, and the rest in progress. Whoever would like to subscribe is requested to hurry [. . .][15]

Unfortunately, Merian's marketing efforts abroad were not sufficiently successful and the number of potential subscribers for English or German versions of *Metamorphosis* was too small to proceed with other editions. Merian, ever creative, devised another solution to the money problem: the sale of a luxury, 'painted' edition of *Metamorphosis* for 75 guilders.[16]

PAINTED METAMORPHOSES

Merian clearly intended potential buyers to understand that there existed a difference between the 'regular' edition of *Metamorphosis* that she and

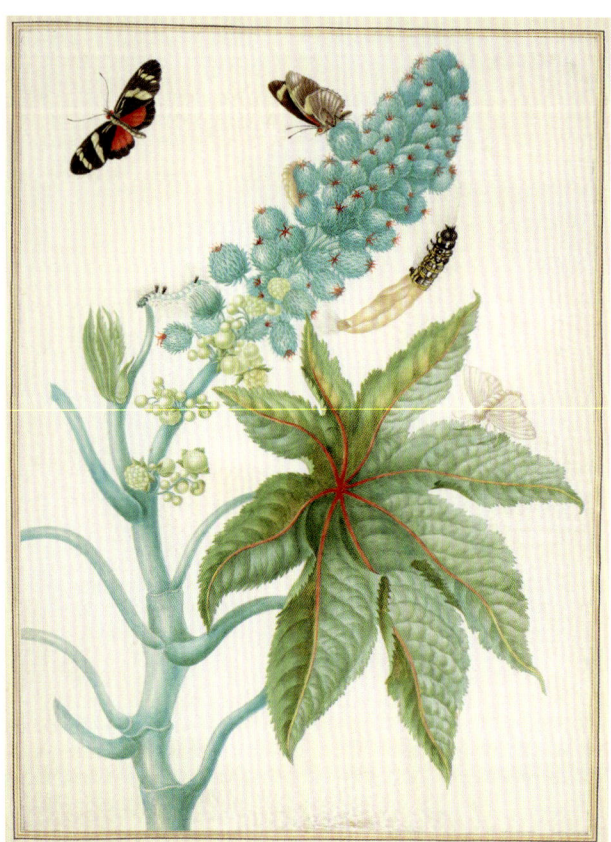

33 Maria Sibylla Merian, *Castor Oil Plant with Ricini Longwing Butterfly*, c.1702–3, watercolour on parchment, 40.4 × 28.5 cm (15 ⅞ × 11 ¼ in), Royal Collection Trust, United Kingdom

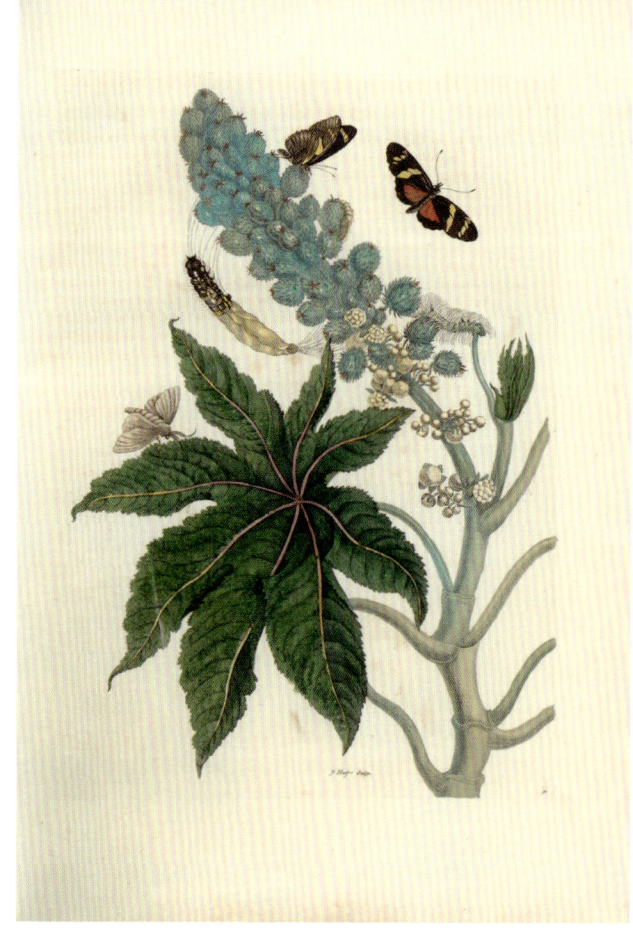

34 Maria Sibylla Merian, 'Castor Oil Plant with Ricini Longwing Butterfly', in *Metamorphosis insectorum Surinamensium*, by the author, Amsterdam, 1705, plate 30, printed book, hand-coloured, Universitätsbibliothek Johann Christian Senckenberg, Frankfurt am Main

her workshop could colour upon request and this special 'luxury' edition. When referring to the former, she used the adjective *illuminated*, whereas she used the word *painted* with respect to the latter. The illumination of manuscripts is an art dating at least to the early Middle Ages and essentially consists of applying water-based colour by hand to decorate or illustrate manuscripts and printed works. When Merian sold coloured copies of the Book of Flowers, Caterpillar Book or *Metamorphosis*, she provided customers images with outlines that had been printed using copper plates that she, her daughters or her pupils filled in with colour.

What allowed Merian to market a valuable edition of *Metamorphosis* as 'painted' was the product of an entirely different process. First, an image would be printed from the copper plate onto a sheet of paper, as would normally be the case. In the second stage, however, rather than hanging the sheet for the ink to dry, a sheet of parchment would be placed directly on top of the still-wet image on paper, thereby transferring a mirror copy of the image onto the parchment, referred to as a counter-proof. Because the printing press was not used and there was a limited amount of ink that remained unabsorbed by the paper that served as the 'original', the lines of the image that appeared on the parchment were faint and incomplete, depending on which elements of the composition Merian chose to reproduce. She could therefore alter the composition of the original image, adding, subtracting or varying the appearance of insects, leaves or blooms. Given the near-total absence of lines, the resulting work was akin to a unique work of art – hence, a painting.[17]

The price of a 'painted' edition of *Metamorphosis* was 75 guilders, or five times the price of a black-and-white edition, and more than one and a half times the price of a hand-coloured, printed edition.[18] A number of factors account for this stark difference in price. In the first place, producing a counter-proof required more time than simply running copies from the printing press. Before the parchment could be placed on top of the still-wet paper, certain elements of the illustration, such as the signature of the engraver and the folio number, had to be hidden, because they would appear inverted on the parchment. In addition, not only did the process frequently result in the waste of the paper copy, which would likely be smudged and therefore unusable, but there was also the cost of parchment, which was higher than the cost of paper. Not least, producing vibrantly coloured illustrations on parchment with minimal guidance from lines would have required a great deal more time than illuminating printed images, which was already a time-consuming activity. Without a doubt, the 'painted' *Metamorphosis* was a luxury item.

As far as is known, Merian was the first artist to rely on the technique of counter-proof with respect to a printed book.[19] Fifteen copies of this luxury edition of *Metamorphosis* have been identified in Europe and America.[20] Their appeal is not surprising. A comparison of the illustration of a caterpillar crawling onto a pomelo in counter-proof on parchment (fig.32) with the same illuminated image on paper (fig.25), for example, reveals the vibrancy of the 'painted' version. Upon close examination, one notices that the only printed lines on the counter-proof are those on the insects; very faint cross-hatching is visible on the body of the pupa, and the outline of the legs of the hairy caterpillar are present, but barely noticeable. The plant and the pomelo, on the other hand, have been drawn freehand before being coloured, and no underdrawing is visible. What is most noticeable is the manner in which Merian created the impression of volume and texture on the fruit by using different thicknesses of yellow watercolour and white highlights, and by dotting the skin with brown specks, thereby conveying the coarseness of the peel. The result is a much brighter and more natural-looking fruit than in the printed image, where the texture has been created by black, printed lines over which watercolour has been applied.

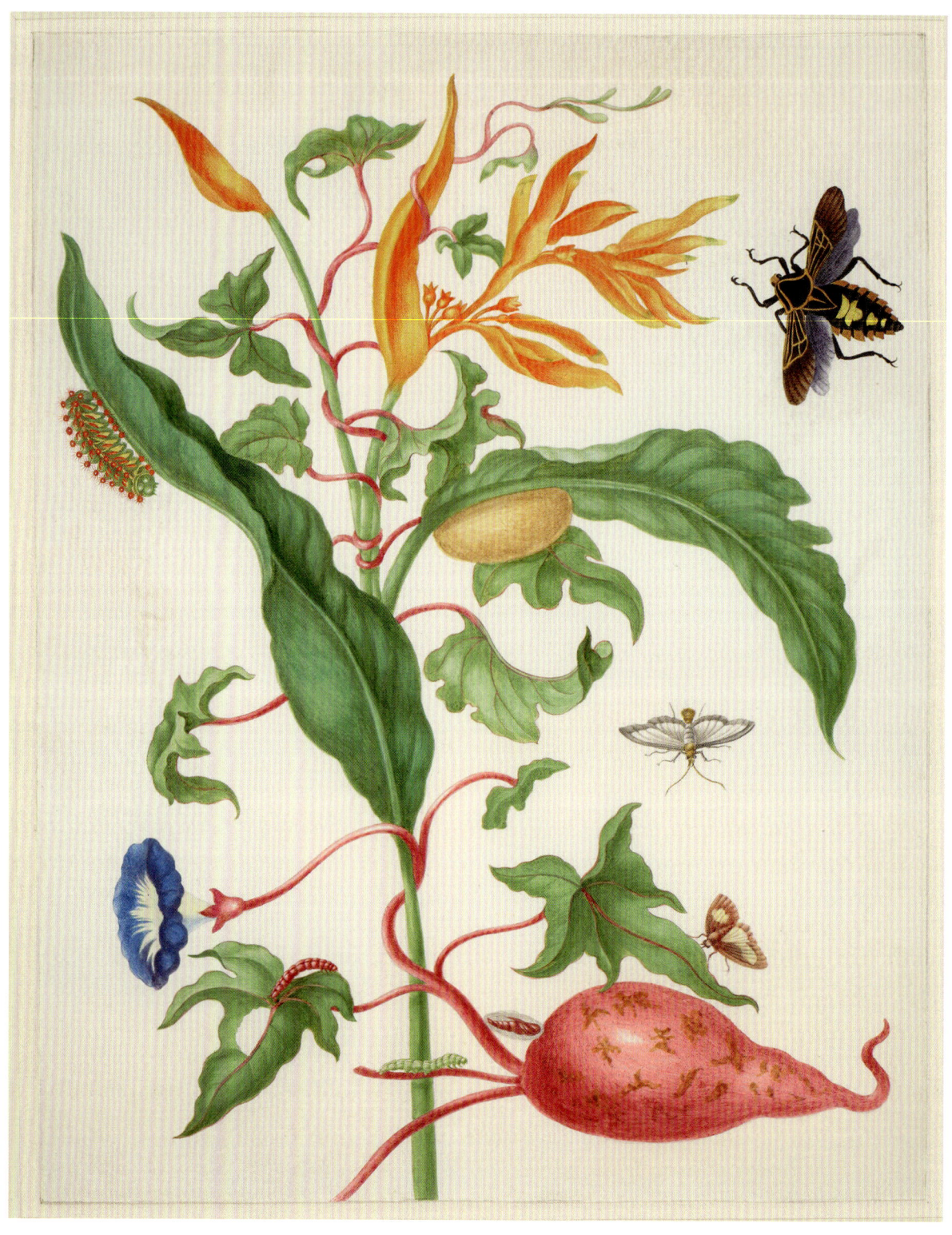

35 Maria Sibylla Merian, *Sweet Potato Plant and a Parakeet Flower with a Leaf-Footed Bug, Melonworm Moth and Pickle Worm Moth*, *c.*1702–3, watercolour on parchment, 39.5 × 29.7 cm (15 ½ × 11 ¾ in), Royal Collection Trust, United Kingdom

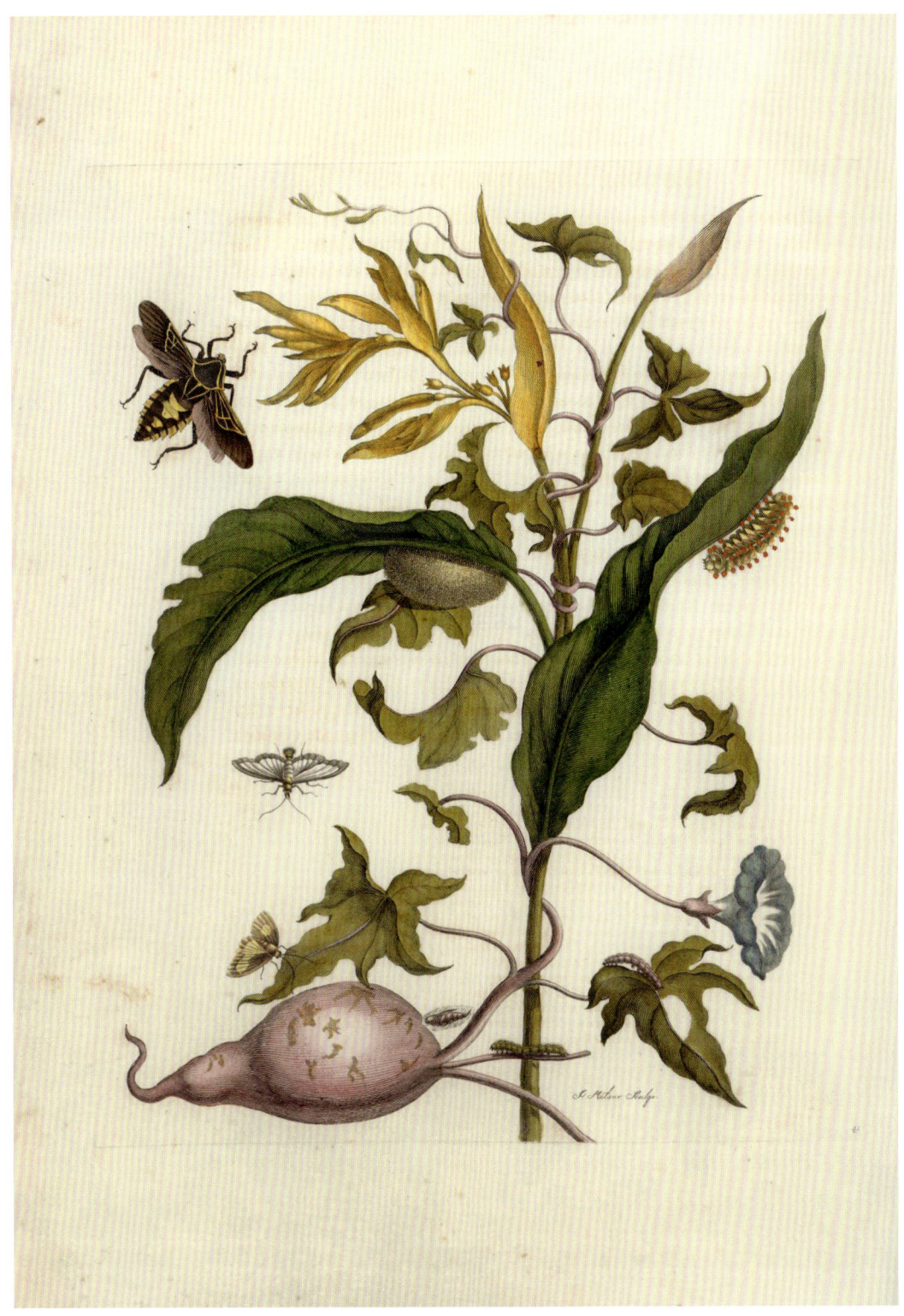

36 Maria Sibylla Merian, 'Sweet Potato Plant and a Parakeet Flower with a Leaf-Footed Bug, Melonworm Moth and Pickle Worm Moth', in *Metamorphosis insectorum Surinamensium*, by the author, Amsterdam, 1705, plate 41, printed book, hand-coloured, Universitätsbibliothek Johann Christian Senckenberg, Frankfurt am Main

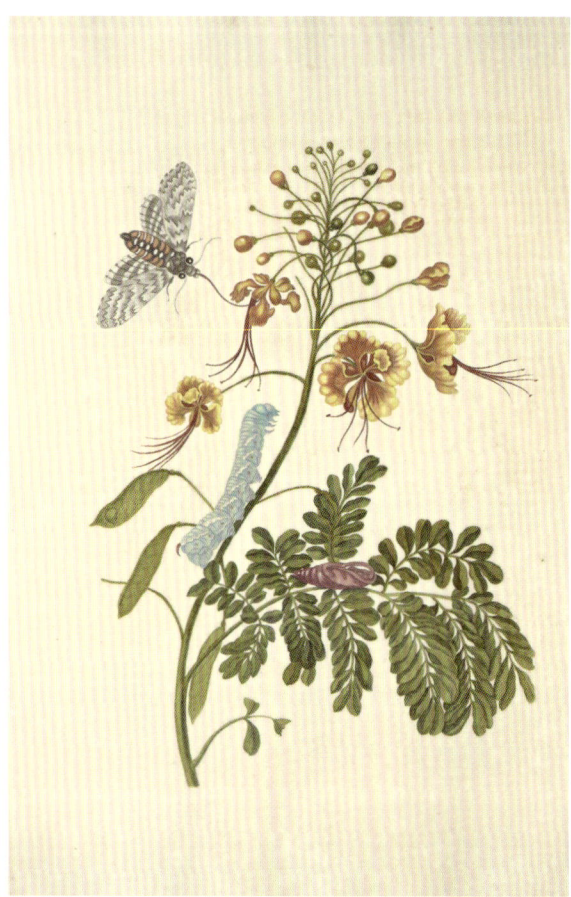

37 Maria Sibylla Merian, 'Flos Pavonis', in *Maria Sybilla Meriaen Over de voortteeling en wonderbaerlyke veranderingen der Surinaemsche insecten*, Oosterwyk, Amsterdam, 1719, plate 45, printed book, hand-coloured, Getty Research Institute, Los Angeles, CA

Similar effects are noticeable on illustrations of a castor oil plant (figs 33 and 34). Compared to the printed, hand-coloured version, the fruits on the plant in the counter-proof are plumper and the slight translucence of their skin is more clearly conveyed. The chrysalis from which a caterpillar is emerging is tethered to the plant by finer threads, and Merian has imparted a ghostly quality to the moth feeding

on the oversized leaf that is absent from the printed image. In another illustration, a fiery orange and red parakeet flower appears freshly cut, and the insects that surround it alive and buzzing (figs 35 and 36).

As the comparisons above demonstrate, the variations in the compositions for the counter-proofs were minimal, and the original designs from *Metamorphosis* are easily recognised; after all, the volumes remained serial works. Nevertheless, the outstanding quality of the illustrations, both in their freehand drawing and in their refined colouring, were undeniably artworks and a type of painting unique to Merian.

VOICING THE KNOWLEDGE OF INDIGENOUS ENSLAVED PEOPLES

Merian was candid about the source of some of the information in *Metamorphosis*. In her preface, she advises that she has 'retained the names of the plants as they are given in America by the inhabitants and the Indians'.[21] Other writers of natural history also relied on local knowledge and acknowledged doing so, albeit frequently legitimising this 'unlearned' knowledge by supplementing it with their own observations. The text of *Metamorphosis*, however, suggests that Merian was confident in the knowledge relayed to her and considered it part of her duty to transmit these details to others. In the text accompanying the illustration of the *flos pavonis* (fig.37), she writes:

> The worm crawling on the stem is orange. It was brought to me by a black female slave who told me that lovely grasshoppers would emerge from it. This one changed into a brown bladder, from which such a green creature would emerge (according to the unanimous account of the inhabitants) which would gradually develop wings like those of the flying grasshopper. I was unable to perceive this observation, because the round pupa died. But since others assured me of having proof of it through their experiences,

I did not want to pass over it in silence, thus giving other amateurs the opportunity to study its certainty.[22]

Throughout the volume, Merian refers to the assistance she received from 'my Indian', such as cutting paths through the thick jungle to facilitate her passage and digging up specimens in the forest so that they could be replanted in her garden. She appears to have been grateful for the knowledge and assistance she received from the local population. Yet, her writing nevertheless evidences the categorisation she made between Europeans and the native and enslaved populations, the latter two of which represented 'the other'. When describing the abortive properties of the peacock flower (*flos pavonis*), Merian acknowledged their lack of freedom and their harsh treatment at the hands of Europeans:

> It bears yellow and red flowers. The seed is used by women giving birth to carry on the labour. The Indians, who are not treated well when in service with the Dutch, use it to abort their children, not wanting their children to be slaves, like them. The black female slaves from Guinea and Angola have to be treated very kindly. Otherwise they do not want children in their state of slavery and will not have any. Indeed, they sometimes even kill them because of the harsh treatment commonly inflicted on them, because they feel that they will be reborn in a free state in the country of their friends, as I heard from their own lips.[23]

This excerpt has given rise to speculation regarding Merian's feelings and attitude towards slavery, motherhood and the female condition.[24] Considering the matter-of-fact quality of the text and its destination for public consumption, it would be inappropriate to pretend to know Merian's mind on these subjects. Her thoughts on Dutch colonial expansion and the resulting abuses and devastation to entire populations, to say nothing of the land, would

have necessarily been influenced by religion and politics, as well as her personal experience; she was a beneficiary of an abhorrent system. What we can take from her writing is that she trusted the knowledge of the native and enslaved populations and listened to their voices: she was aware of their humanity.

LASTING IMPRESSIONS

The figures included in this chapter make it easy to see why *Metamorphosis* was and remains Merian's most popular and admired work. From conceptualisation and creation to production and dissemination, the book testifies to Merian's determination and perseverance in observing some of nature's smallest creatures and to her commercial acumen. She could instruct and evaluate the work of master engravers, in addition to supervising the activities of her daughters and any other assistants she may have retained.

Arguably, however, *Metamorphosis* is first and foremost a monument to Merian's extraordinary skills as an artist. She could draw from life with exquisite detail, devise original and dynamic compositions, and manipulate pigments to render plants, flowers, fruits and insects with great naturalism. As will be discussed in Chapter 6, at least six editions of *Metamorphosis* appeared after Merian's death, each printed using the original plates, which traded hands at least three times. Notwithstanding the impossibility of the claim, booksellers frequently marketed these as having been coloured by Merian herself – proof of the work's (and her hand's) enduring appeal.

4

A Family Workshop: Marketing Matriarchy

From Merian's house in the centre of Amsterdam, Merian and her daughters, Herolt and Graff, formed a family enterprise that functioned much like most artistic workshops of the time. Their situation, however, was markedly different: theirs was a business created and run entirely by women. The women's livelihood depended on the sale of their watercolours and of the books published by Merian, as well as the colouring of engravings of *naturalia*, and trade in pigments and specimens. The women worked together, shared techniques and marketed their works. They relied on model sheets, reused motifs and compositions, and even collaborated on certain illustrations. Merian and her daughters were well aware of the value attached to the Merian name. These artistic practices and production processes, and the manner in which they informed and shaped Merian's oeuvre during her Amsterdam years, are the subject of this chapter.

A SEVENTEENTH-CENTURY DUTCH WORKSHOP

On 5 August 1692, less than two months after the registration of his marriage to the 24-year-old Johanna Helena in Amsterdam, [1] Jacob Hendrik Herolt placed an advertisement in the *Amsterdamsche Courant* for the sale of works by Merian and other 'masters'. The last sentence of the advertisement read: '[...] If anyone wants his daughter to learn to paint flowers or watercolours, she will be faithfully taught [by Maria Sibylla Merian].'[2]

It is unknown whether the advertisement was successful; unlike her Maiden's Company in Nuremberg, Merian does not mention her Amsterdam students, if any, in her correspondence. Having trained her daughters to draw, paint and prepare pigments and vellum, Merian would certainly have been able to teach other young women how to do so. Given the high volume of production of the workshop, Merian and her daughters probably had help, as discussed further below. In addition to providing Merian with a source of income, training pupils also would have assisted with workshop production.

Artistic production in the Dutch seventeenth century was seldom an individual affair. Collaboration, understood in the strictest sense as two artists of equal talent and status working together to complete a work of art, was ubiquitous in the Low Countries of the sixteenth and seventeenth centuries.[3] Other work arrangements that did not necessarily qualify as collaborations existed in workshops, where apprentices and journeymen (trained artists who worked for others, rather than operating their own workshops) made substantial contributions to the artistic production of a workshop master.[4]

In addition to contributing to the reputation of an artist, pupils provided an important source of revenue: families paid considerable sums for a well-known artist to take on their child as a pupil, who then lived with the master for the duration of their apprenticeship. The pupil would be taught to draw and paint, mix pigments, prepare canvasses and clean brushes, amongst other basic tasks. As pupils progressed, they would start contributing to the works of the master – by painting the backgrounds, architectural details, landscapes in compositions – and eventually complete entire works by themselves. Depending on their quality, these works could be sold as workshop copies, or even as works by the master. The larger the workshop, the more productive it could be, and the more financially advantageous it could become for the master.

A master painter was most frequently a man. It was very difficult for women to become registered masters in their local painters' guilds, especially if they were not a daughter or widow of a registered master. Many of the guilds, such as the one in Nuremberg, as discussed in Chapter 1, simply did not allow women painters. Unfortunately, all records from prior to 1750 for the guild of Saint Luke (named after the patron saint of artists) in Amsterdam have been lost, and we do not know with certainty what the status of women artists was in that city.[5] Surviving historical sources regarding commerce and other guilds in Amsterdam from the period 1510–1672 show that women did participate in guild life: they are registered as linen stallholders, keepers of shops for textiles and clothes, yarn spinners and pastry bakers.[6] Griet Claes, a widow, was the owner of a brickworks.[7] We also know that widows carried out the business of their printer and publisher husbands, as did the 'Widow of Dirk Boom' (as she is identified on the frontispiece of the books she published). Based on limited records, however, there appears to have been no woman

registered as a painter with the guild of Saint Luke in Amsterdam prior to 1750.[8] It is likely the case that women artists were not allowed to become guild masters in the city, although they were allowed to do so in Haarlem and The Hague.[9] Certainly, if Merian had been a master, that fact would have been included in the advertisement published in the *Amsterdamsche Courant* in a bid to attract paying pupils.

The inability to become a guild member would have had an impact on Merian's career and opportunities, as discussed in Chapter 1. It did not, however, alter the process of her artistic production: in everything but in name, Merian was the master of a workshop. Herolt and Graff were her apprentices. Unlike the other painters' workshops in Amsterdam, however, theirs was run and staffed by women.

MERIAN AND HER DAUGHTERS

The advertisement placed by Jacob Herolt, mentioned at the outset of this chapter, contains valuable information regarding the production process of Merian's workshop from the very beginning of the women's arrival in the city. Among the offerings on sale are copies of Merian's Caterpillar and Flower Books, offered printed in black and white or hand-coloured.

The colouring of plates in books published by Merian would have been a time-consuming undertaking. When she offered *Metamorphosis* for sale to subscribers, Merian sought 15 guilders for a black-and-white copy, and an additional 30 guilders for colouring, for a total of 45 guilders per coloured copy.[10] The trebling of the price reflected the increased cost of labour and materials, as well as the skill, required to make the 60 illustrations appear as lifelike as possible, as discussed in Chapter 2.

The illumination of books is an example of a task that could have been delegated to the qualified pupils or apprentices who might have answered Jacob Herolt's advertisement, as well as to Herolt and Graff.[11] Indeed, this is the type of artistic practice for which

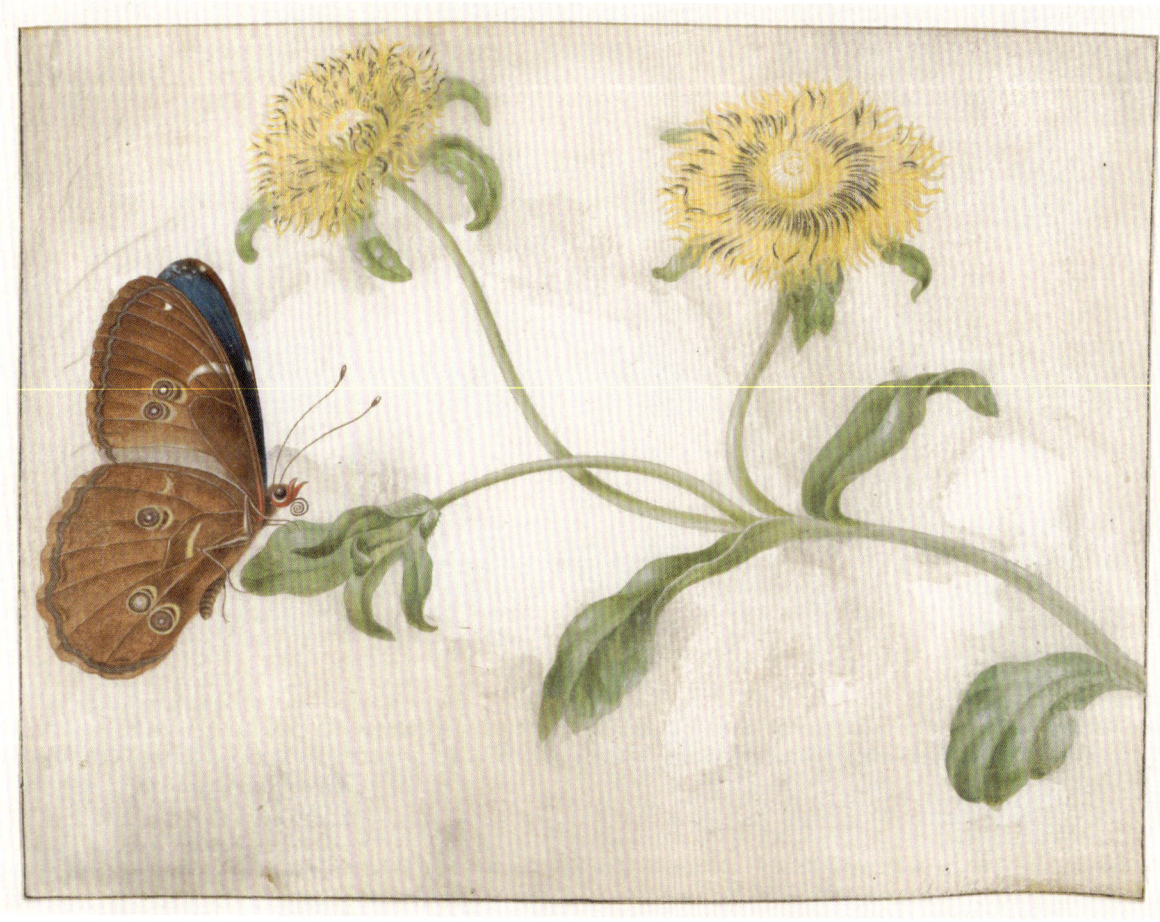

38 Maria Sibylla Merian (attributed to), *Blue Morpho Butterfly with Two Yellow Flowers*, 1696, watercolour on parchment, 29 × 22.5 cm (11 ⅜ × 8 ⅞ in), Rijksmuseum, Amsterdam

Merian would have trained her pupils. In 1682, while in Frankfurt am Main attending to her mother after the death of her stepfather, Merian wrote to a former student, Clara Regina Imhoff, enclosing a floral composition for which she had borrowed models from her Flower Book. Praising Imhoff's talents, Merian encouraged her to colour the composition, specifically advising her that 'the lily must be kept bright blue'.[12] Provided that they had a sample with them, colouring was an activity that pupils, if they did not reside with Merian, could easily take home.

The women would have illuminated the books one plate at a time. Since Merian marketed coloured copies of her Caterpillar and Flower Books (as seen in Jacob Herolt's advertisement), and later of *Metamorphosis*, there would have been considerable work to undertake, and Merian could not have done it by herself. She would have required assistance, at the very least from her daughters. This is so notwithstanding frequent later claims that copies of Merian's books, and especially *Metamorphosis*, had been coloured 'in her hand', which would make them more valuable.[13]

Imparting Technique

The objective, in training pupils and her daughters, would have been to help them become as accomplished as possible and therefore most useful in the workshop. Accordingly, in discussing the contributions of her daughters and possibly of pupils to the colouring of books and printed plates, it is worthwhile to examine a particular illumination technique that Merian likely taught Johanna Helena. In order to create a 'metallic' shine on the wings of butterflies and insects, some artists (for example Otto Marseus van Schrieck, *c.*1620–78) pasted the wings of insects directly onto wet canvas.[14] One negative aspect of relying upon this technique is that the scales from the insect become abraded over time. Merian succeeded in creating a lifelike shine on the wings of insects by layering watercolour of different opacities with gum arabic, a natural resin.

Merian used this technique in an illustration of a *Blue Morpho Butterfly with Two Yellow Flowers* (fig.38). Done very delicately, to view the full effect of the metallic blue of the butterfly's wings one would have to move the sheet to catch the light. Herolt, in her execution of the same subject matter, was more heavy handed (fig.39). The result is a highly shimmering butterfly that looks somewhat less realistic than Merian's.

Florilegium *by Johanna Helena Herolt*

Also listed for sale in Jacob Herolt's advertisement is a *florilegium* (*bloemenboek*) painted on paper by her daughter (assumed to be Johanna Helena, Dorothea Maria being only 14 years old at the time) after observations made 'from life'.[15] We do not know to which *florilegium* the advertisement refers, as no such work dating from 1692 or earlier has been identified. A *florilegium* prepared by Herolt dating from 1698, however, gives us a good idea as to what the work offered for sale several years earlier might have comprised (referred to herein as the '1698 *Florilegium*' or simply the '*Florilegium*').

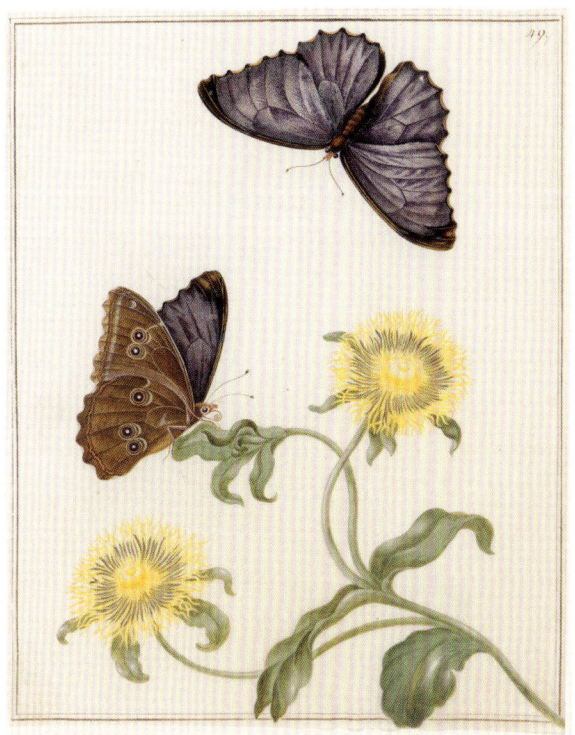

39 Johanna Helena Herolt, *Morpho Butterflies with Two Yellow Flowers*, 1698, watercolour on parchment, 35.8 × 27.4 cm (14 ⅛ × 10 ¾ in), Herzog Anton Ulrich Museum, Braunschweig

The 1698 *Florilegium* is unbound; its only title page is a handwritten table of contents listing 43 plants and flowers, at the top of which is written, in Dutch: 'Register of a florilegium painted by Johanna Helena Herolt, Amsterdam 1698.'[16] The second page of the table of contents continues to illustration number 49, but lines 44 to 49 are left blank, suggesting that either Herolt or the buyer experienced a change of mind.

The first three illustrations included in the 1698 *Florilegium* are bouquets in vases. The very first one consists of a bouquet of assorted cut flowers in a green glass vase set on a ledge, including roses, hyacinth, a pink-and-white carnation, a pink peony,

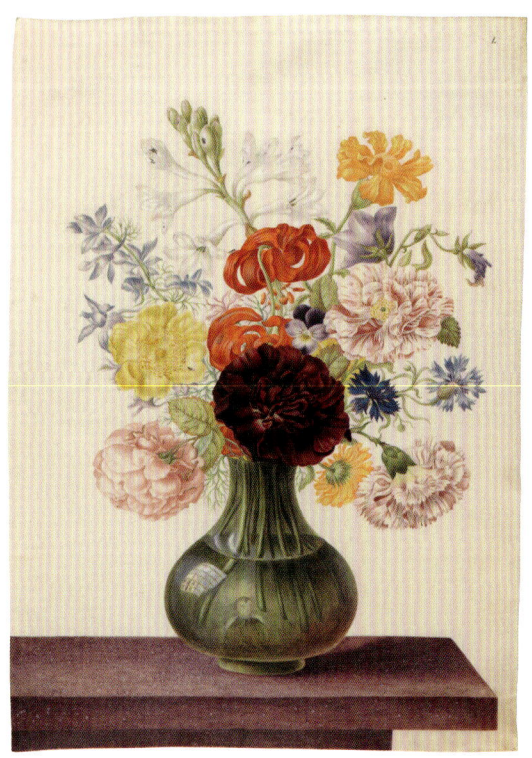

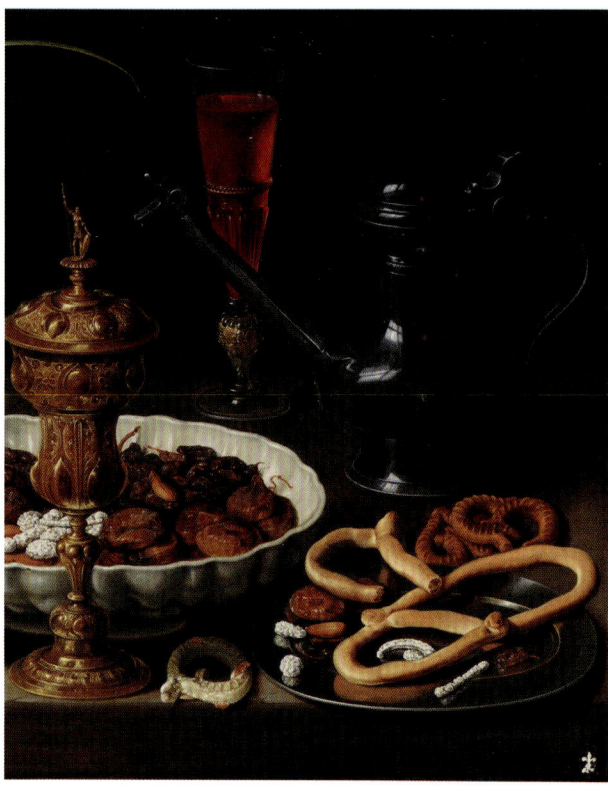

40 Johanna Helena Herolt, *Vase of Flowers with Self-Portrait*, *c.*1698, watercolour on parchment, 46.8 × 32.4 cm (18⅜ × 12¾ in), Herzog Anton Ulrich Museum, Braunschweig

41 Clara Peeters, *Still Life with Flowers, a Silver-gilt Goblet, Dried Fruit, Sweetmeats, Bread Sticks, Wine and a Pewter Pitcher* (detail), 1611, oil on panel, 52 × 73 cm (20½ × 28¾ in), Museo Nacional del Prado, Madrid

orange-red Turk's cap lily, and blue wild larkspur, amongst others (fig.40). The composition is anchored by a dark maroon flower, likely a double rose. Most intriguing, however, is the ostensible self-portrait reflected near the bottom of the green vase, just left of centre. The portrait is not of an identifiable individual: only the vaguest of facial features are included, and the woman's hair is covered by a black cap. In comparison to the depictions of the flowers, with their texture and shading, the portrait seems simplistic, certainly if intended to be a self-portrait. The tradition of integrating such self-reflections into

artworks as a way to advertise artistic skill and engage in self-fashioning was well known and popular in the seventeenth century: the painter Clara Peeters (probably 1587–after 1636) was one of the first women to use the device (fig.41).[17] Unlike a depiction of a woman looking at herself in a mirror, which would have been understood as an expression of vanity, a self-portrait on a carafe, vase or pewter flagon as seen in Peeters's painting, raised no such issues. When creating a self-reflection in a vase or goblet, no detail or resemblance was expected. With this image of a young woman with a modest headdress, positioned near a reflection of a window with a view of a typical Amsterdam house, Herolt asserted her authorship and her place within a specific artistic tradition. It is as if she were stating, 'I, Johanna Helena Herolt, artist, made this in Amsterdam.'

Herolt's illustration of a black iris, listed as number 6 in the table of contents in the *Florilegium*, displays her command of technique (fig.42). Occupying most of the page, the nearly black flower stands tall between two pointed green leaves. The petals are stippled and striped in shades of deep violet, greys, browns and black, giving their scalloped edges an almost mushroom-like, velvety appearance. The clever use of yellow and white highlights, and gum arabic, which creates a shine, allows the artist to convey the volume of the petals. The bottom centre petal, in particular, seems to detach itself from the page. This is the work of a highly proficient artist; Herolt has proudly signed the watercolour in the bottom right corner.

In terms of artistic sophistication, the black iris stands in contrast to the illustration of a pomegranate and its bloom, noted as item 42 in the *Florilegium* (fig.43). As this detailed visual analysis makes clear, there is every reason to believe that the illustration of the pomegranate is not by Herolt. A branch, short and curving upward to the right, with one open bloom and a whole pomegranate, sits in the upper part of the composition. An open, bright red bloom is attached to the branch between two closed blooms. The pomegranate, a moon-like sphere on which sit three insects, rests tangentially to the bloom, and the yellowish-brown fruit is crowned by a calyx with a dark-brown outer skin. The bottom half of the composition is occupied by a pomegranate branch in bloom, which reaches out of the frame on the left.

Upon close observation, the illustration is not as harmonious as one might have expected from the artist who depicted the black iris. The sphere of the pomegranate is awkwardly drawn, and its skin is altogether deprived of texture. The calyx, rather than

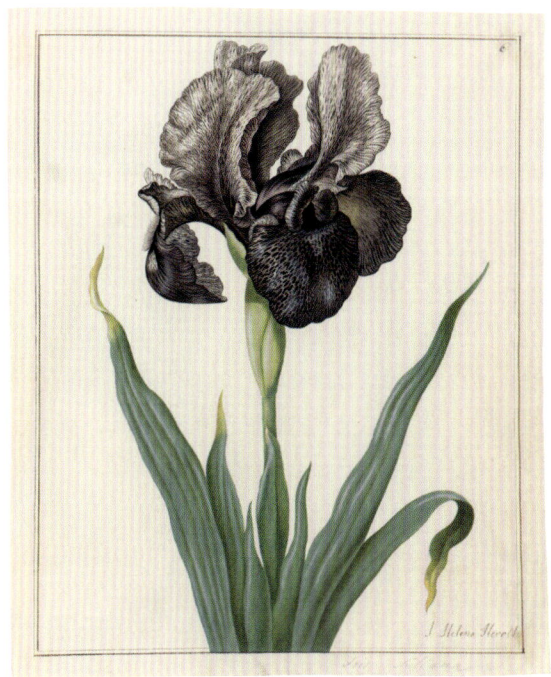

42 Johanna Helena Herolt, *Black Iris* (*Iris Susiana*), *c*.1698, watercolour on parchment, 37.9 × 30.2 cm (14⅞ × 11⅞ in), Herzog Anton Ulrich Museum, Braunschweig

being shown as the organically grown crown that it is, appears to have been deposited on top of the fruit, not quite at the centre. The bloom on the upper branch reflects none of the layering and texture of the blooms below, the petal at the centre being drawn with a heavy, dark brown 'w' rather than being suggested with highlights and shadows, as it is below. Further, the leaves of the top branch are outlined in brown, which does not occur with the leaves below.

The most likely explanation for these discrepancies in quality is that the illustration was completed by two artists. In a workshop context, it would be entirely expected that a more experienced artist would draw a model for a pupil, and leave space for the pupil

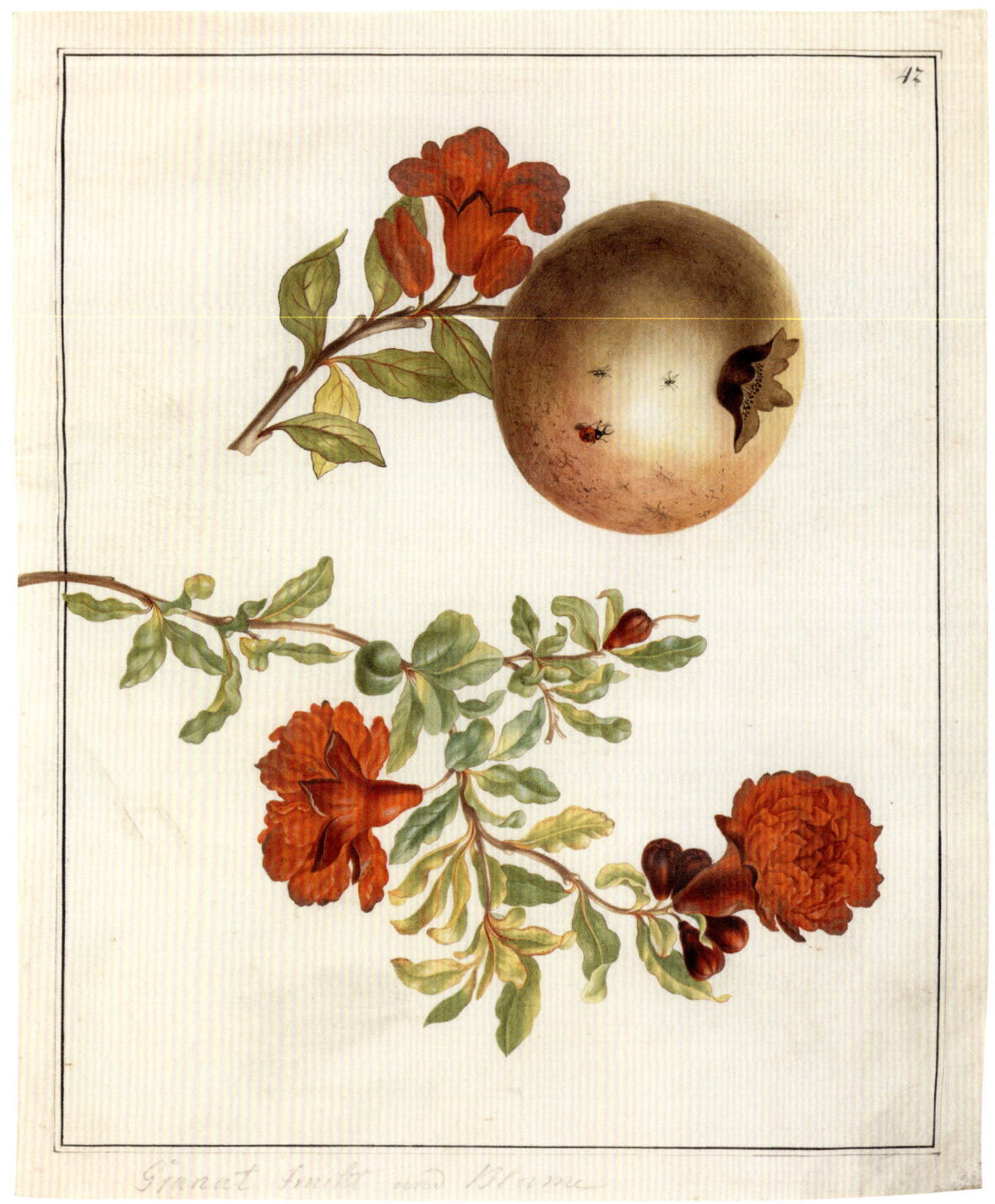

43 Merian workshop (currently attributed to Johanna Helena Herolt), *Pomegranate Fruit and Bloom,* *c.*1698, watercolour on parchment, 37.8 × 30.5 cm (14 ⅞ × 12 in), Herzog Anton Ulrich Museum, Braunschweig

to copy or complete the work. This is what occurred in the Merian workshop, and it is likely that Herolt carried out this practice as well. A careful observation of the 1698 *Florilegium* reveals that the quality of the illustrations varies considerably, ranging from exquisite to merely competent. That an artist should produce lesser works, or that her work should improve over time, is to be expected. A more compelling explanation, however, is that there were several hands at work, notwithstanding Herolt's claim on the title page that she made the watercolours.

Workshop Production, Models and Copies

A feature of the workshop is the presence of models for illustration that inspired artists as they worked. Models came in the form of sheets depicting individual flowers, originals or copies of completed works by the master or other artists, as well as books and actual objects. When working in the studio, artists could look to these models. In some instances, artists copied the models with exactitude; other times, they borrowed elements or else simply were inspired by what they observed. Ella Reitsma and Sandrine Ulenberg have referred to the practice of copying and borrowing motifs from models as 'collage'.[18] This is how the Merian family workshop operated.

Thus, the pink rose to the right of the composition of the *Vase of Flowers with Self-Portrait* (fig.40) and the wild blue larkspur on the left can be traced to figures that appeared in part I of the Caterpillar Book (figs 20 and 21), and the carnation appeared in part II (fig.22). Herolt would have had access to a copy of the Book of Flowers, New Book of Flowers and Caterpillar Book hand-coloured by her mother to guide her.

'Collage' also explains the inclusion of two works by different hands in the illustration of the *Pomegranate Fruit and Bloom* (fig.43). The branch depicted in the lower part of the composition appears in at least two other works, the first by Merian and the other by a member of the workshop

(figs 44 and 45). Here, the branch of pomegranate blooms is not only used as a guide or a source as part of a more complex composition – it has been reproduced with exactitude. A different but similar branch appears in a composition by Merian featuring lantern flies and a moth (fig.46). In the ultimate collage, all are variations on some of Merian's earliest motifs, including the pomegranate tree (fig.4) and a pomegranate branch in bloom dating to 1677 (fig.47).

In the case of the illustration included as part of the 1698 *Florilegium*, it is likely that Merian herself or Herolt drew the pomegranate branch in the lower half of the composition, leaving it to a younger member of the workshop to complete the sheet, based on the model. The model for the fruit itself might have come from the very early drawing by Merian of a shoot from a pomegranate tree, which includes three fruits at various stages of ripening (fig.4). Merian subsequently refined the motif of the fruit that has burst from ripeness, disgorging its glistening seeds, and included it as plate 9 of *Metamorphosis*, where it is accompanied by blue morpho butterflies (fig.48). A counter-proof of the pomegranate branch, printed on vellum (fig.49), was then sold as a unique work of art (likely stand-alone, as discussed in Chapter 5) by Merian, although it was probably by the workshop.

The theory that it was the practice in the Merian workshop to have a more experienced artist complete part of a work and for a less experienced artist to finish it is supported by the existence of one unfinished work attributed to Merian (fig.50). Here, the large leaves of the vine, finely veined and slightly mottled, their curled tendrils and part of the stem have been completed. Two caterpillars and one pupa have been added; the brown caterpillar, in particular, is exquisitely detailed. Yet, the centre of the composition remains blank, without a focal point, awaiting – a passion flower? Grapes? A melon-like fruit? All we know is that this sheet was awaiting the brush of someone in the workshop.

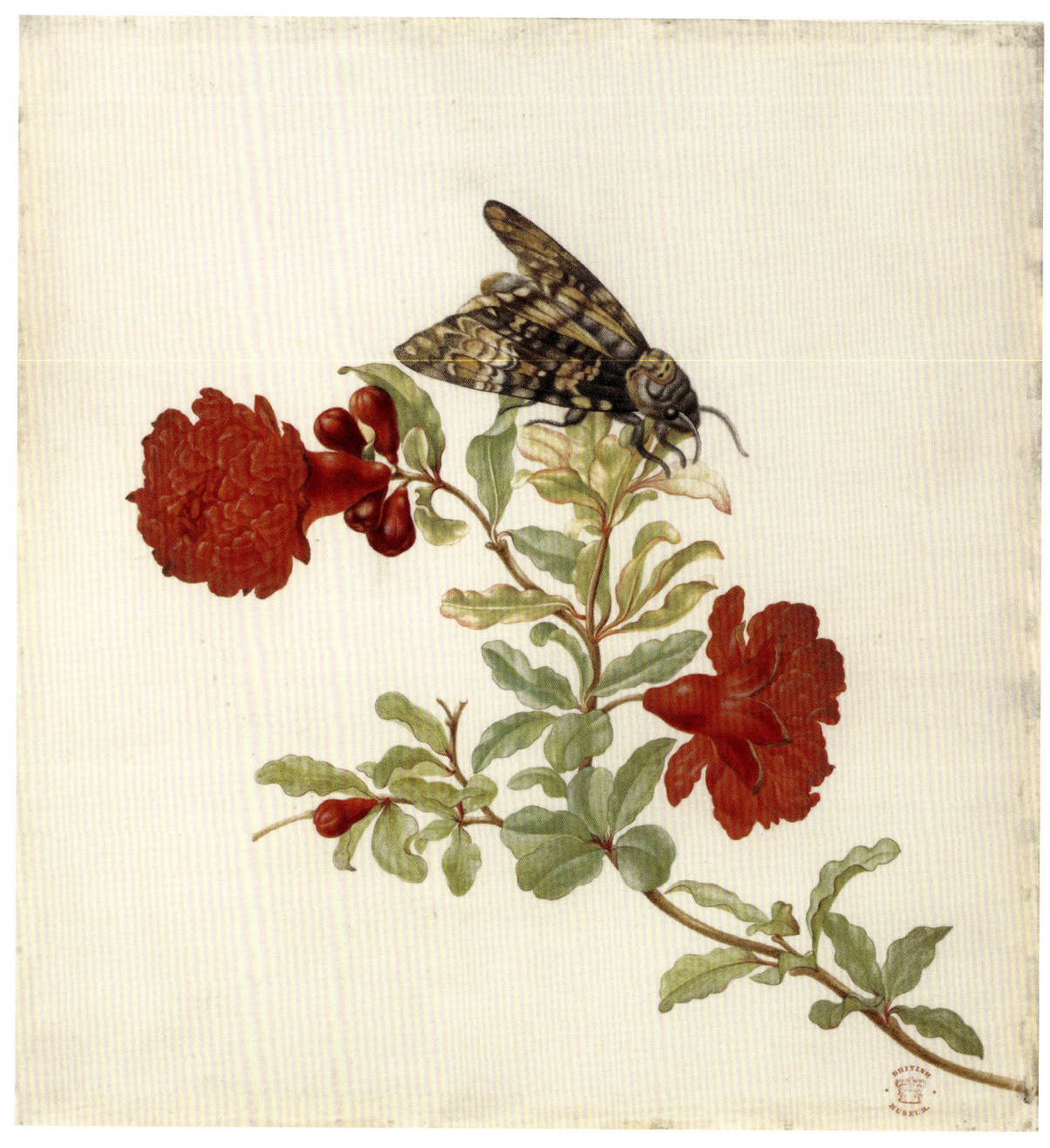

44 Maria Sibylla Merian, *Pomegranate Flowers with Moth*, c.1691–9, watercolour on parchment, 29.6 × 27.2 cm (11 ⅝ × 10 ¾ in), British Museum, London

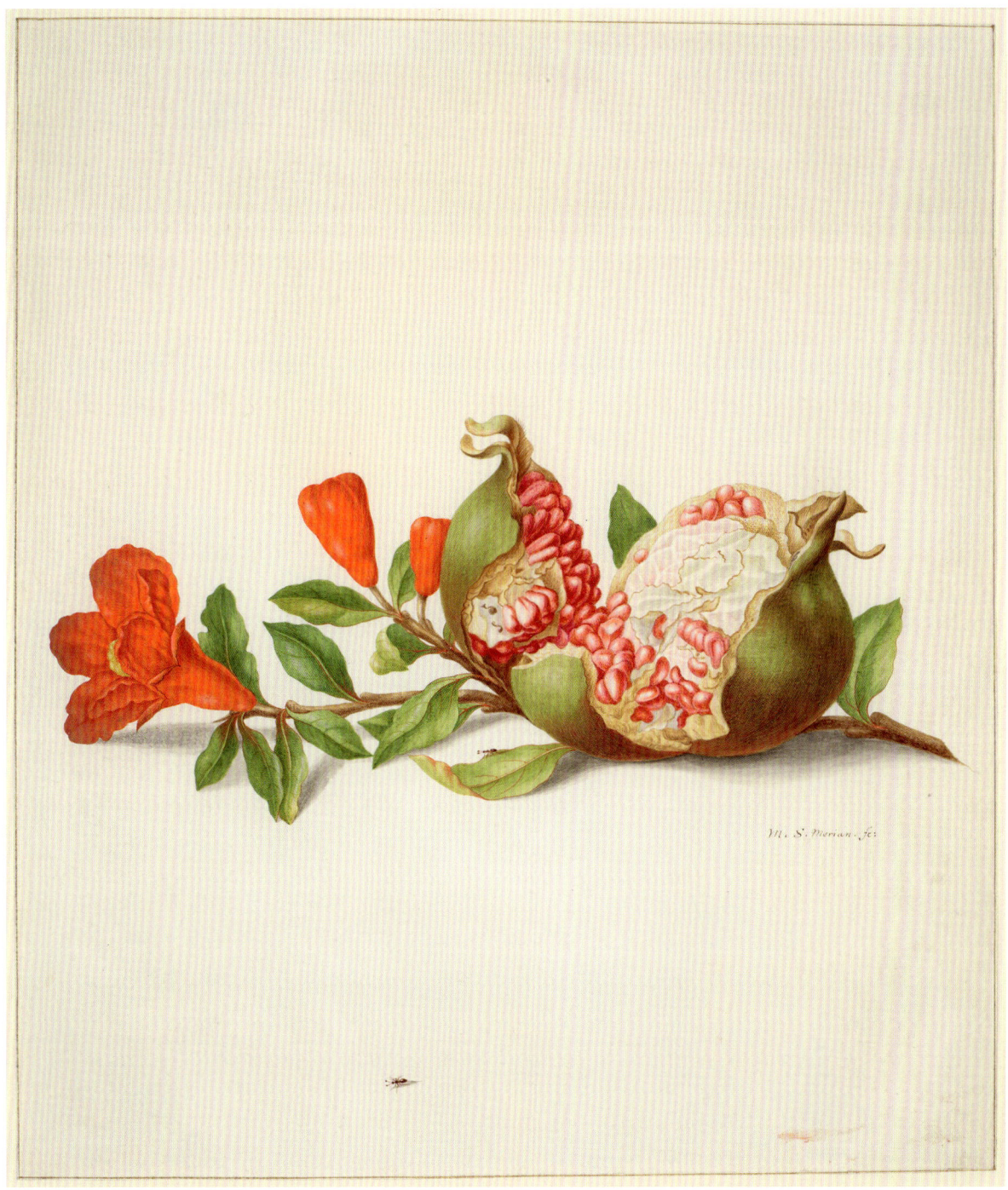

45 Merian workshop, *Branch of Pomegranate with Insects*, *c*.1705, watercolour on parchment, 34.9 × 27.3 cm (13 ¾ × 10 ¾ in),
Royal Collection Trust, United Kingdom

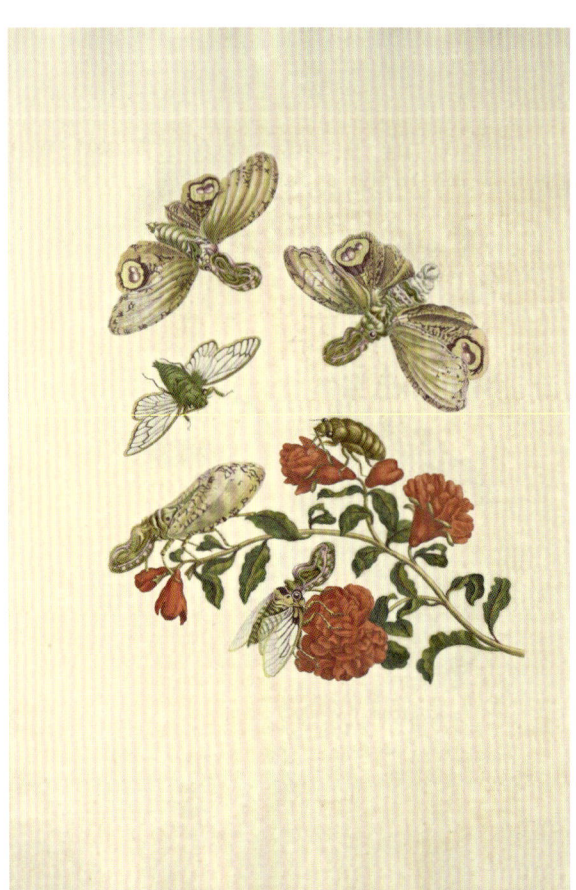

46 Maria Sibylla Merian, 'Lantern Flies with Pomegranate Flowers', in *Maria Sybilla Meriaen Over de voortteeling en wonderbaerlyke veranderingen der Surinaemsche insecten*, Oosterwyk, Amsterdam, 1719, plate 49, printed book, hand-coloured, Getty Research Institute, Los Angeles, CA

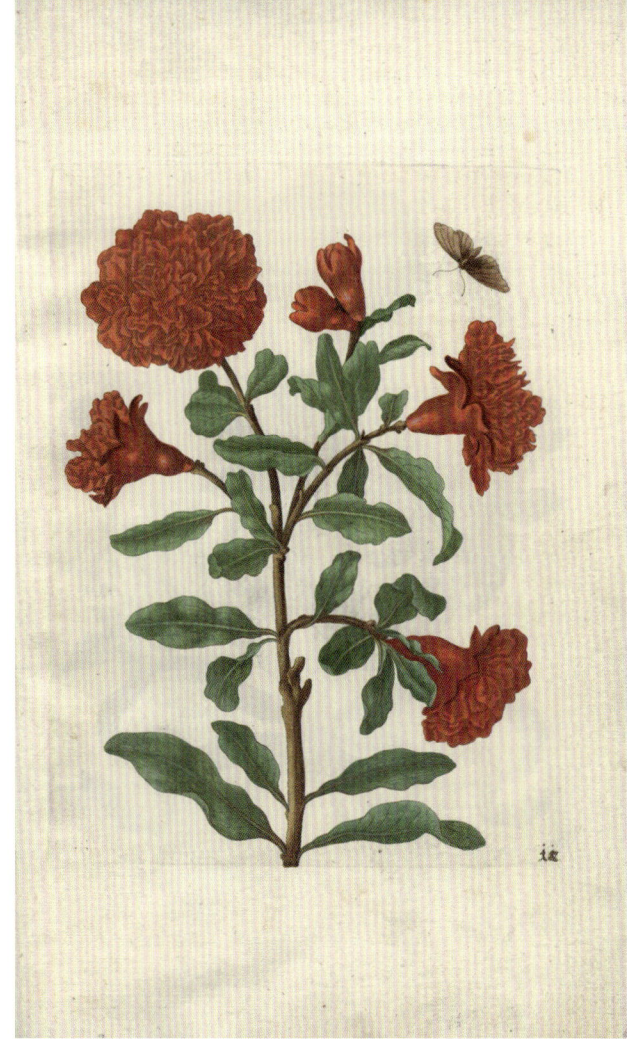

47 Maria Sibylla Merian, 'Pomegranate Branch in Bloom', in *Neues Blumenbuch*, part 11, Johannes Andreas Graff, Nuremberg, 1680 (originally published 1677), plate 11, printed book, hand-coloured, Sächsische Landesbibliothek – Staats- und Universitätsbibliothek (SLUB), Dresden

49 Merian workshop, *Branch of Pomegranate*, *c.*1705 (?),
watercolour on parchment, 32.3 × 27 cm (12 ¾ × 10 ⅝ in),
Royal Collection Trust, United Kingdom

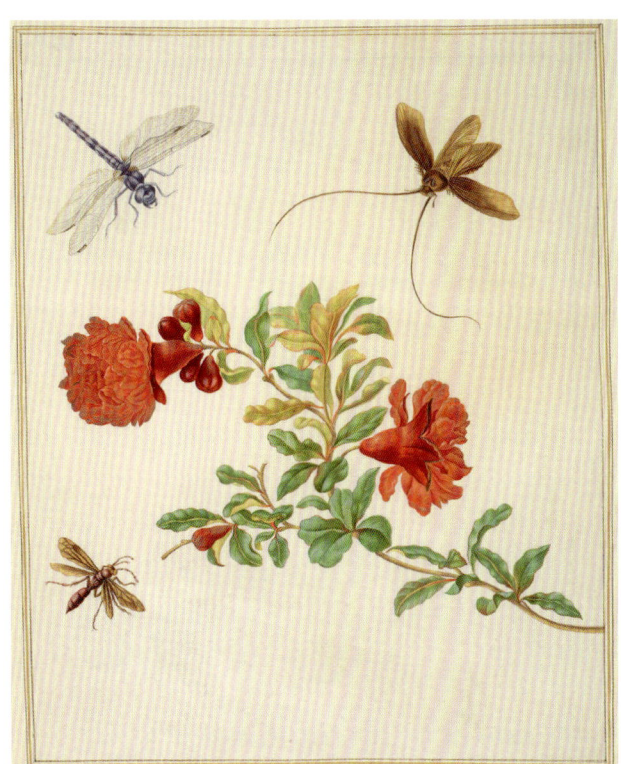

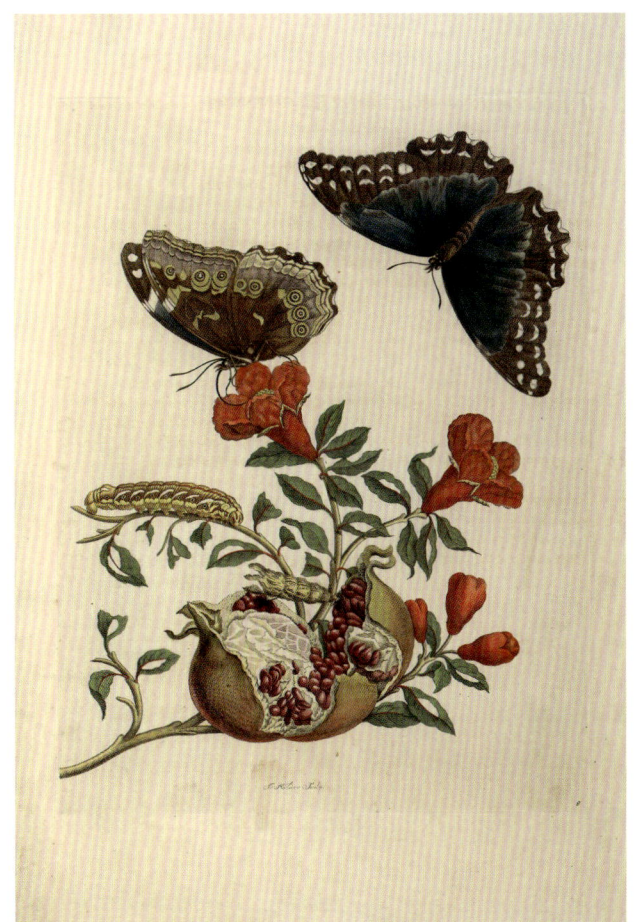

48 Maria Sibylla Merian, 'Morpho Butterflies with
Pomegranate Fruit and Flower', in *Metamorphosis insectorum
Surinamensium*, by the author, Amsterdam, 1705, plate 9,
printed book, hand-coloured, Universitätsbibliothek Johann
Christian Senckenberg, Frankfurt am Main

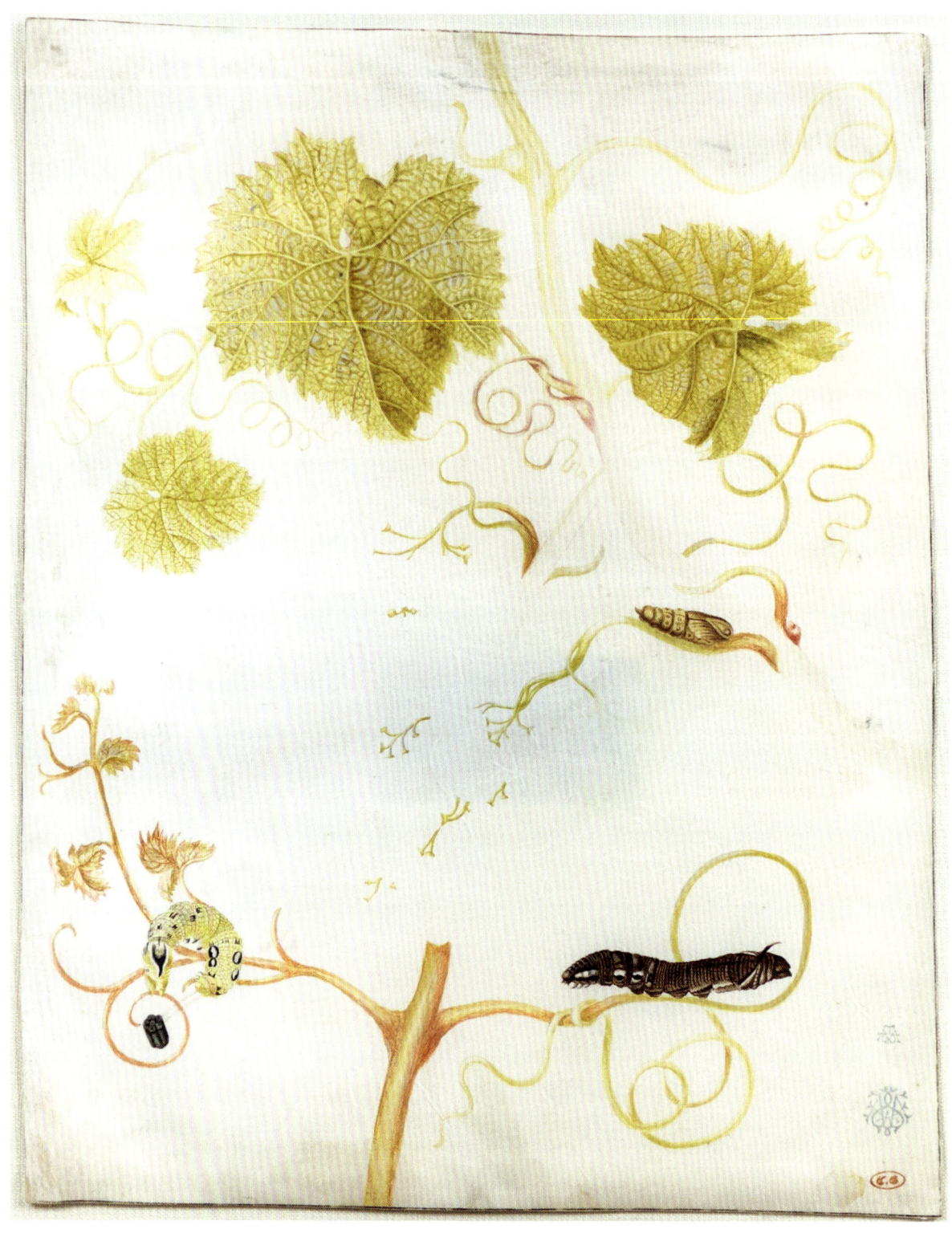

50 Maria Sibylla Merian (attributed to), *Study of Vine with Caterpillars*, c.1690–1717, watercolour on parchment, 24.8 × 31.9 cm (9 ¾ × 12 ½ in), Arader Galleries, New York

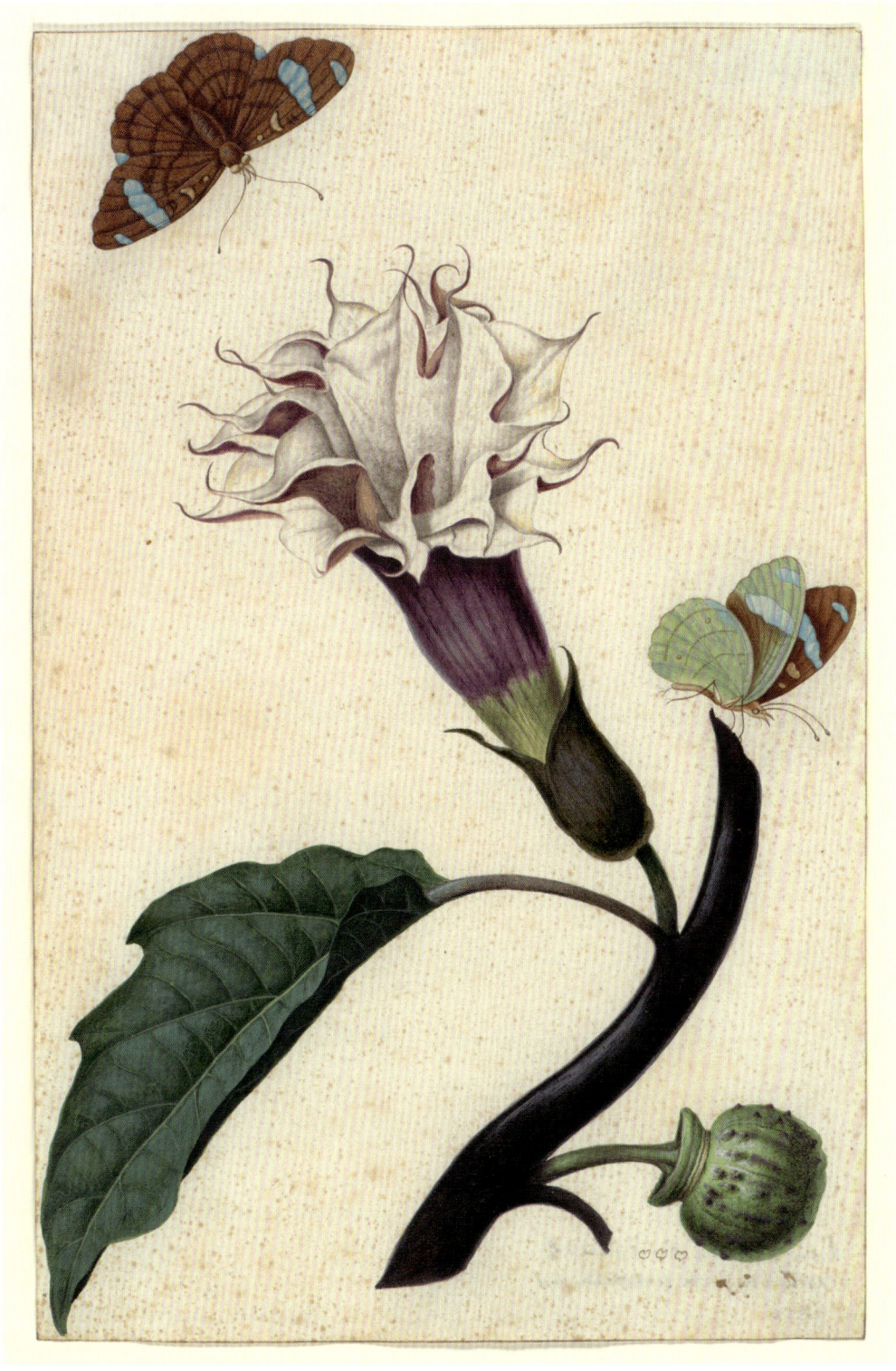

51 Willem de Heer and Mara Sibylla Merian, *Datura with Butterflies*, c.1679/95, watercolour on paper, 33.3 × 21 cm (13 ⅛ × 8 ¼ in), The Morgan Library & Museum, New York, NY

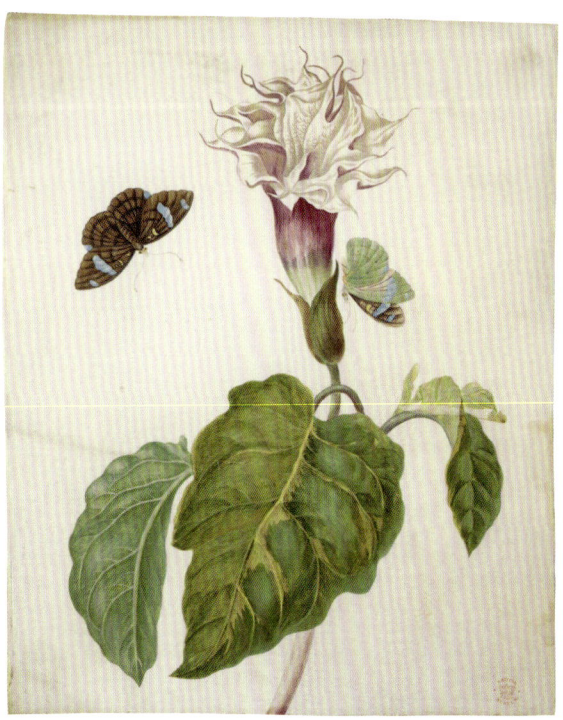
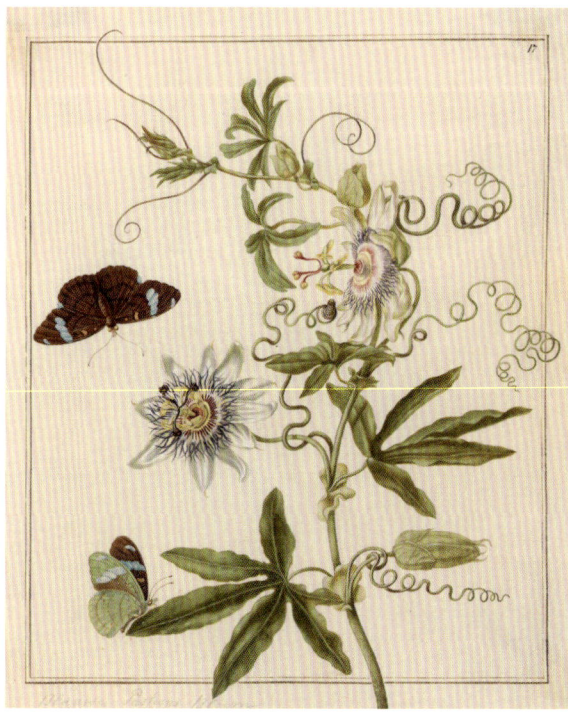

52 Johanna Helena Herolt (attributed to), *Datura with Butterflies*, *c.*1690–1700, watercolour on parchment, 37.8 × 29.7 cm (14⅞ × 11¾ in), British Museum, London

53 Dorothea Maria Graff (new attribution; Johanna Helena Herolt, current attribution), *Blue Passion Flower with Two Butterflies*, *c.*1698, watercolour on parchment, 37.5 × 30.3 cm (14¾ × 11⅞ in), Herzog Anton Ulrich Museum, Braunschweig

The copying from models could be nearly perfect, as was the case with a pair of blue-brown butterflies, probably Gulf fritillaries, that fluttered from one drawing to another in the workshop.[19] First, the butterflies came to rest on the illustration of a Datura completed in 1679 by Willem de Heer (1637/8–81) for Agnes Block (fig.51). One butterfly flies in from the left, wings open flat; the other rests on the thick branch, to the right of the composition, as though it were on its way to the bottom of the page. Its wings are nearly closed, showing the viewer its watery green scales. The same butterflies, displaying the same wing positions, appear in a drawing of a Datura attributed to Herolt (fig.52), and on a drawing of a passion

flower which I attribute to Graff on the basis of the quality of its execution (fig.53). Merian's daughters have copied the butterflies, down to the asymmetrical antennae of the open butterfly. In this case, it might even be that the women traced the butterflies. This would have been an acceptable way to add visual interest to their compositions. Merian herself would go on to reuse the motif in or about 1705 (fig.54), in a small drawing that might have been intended for an *album amicorum* (friendship album), which was a common way to memorialise friendships and networks at the time.[20]

A close examination of the body of work from the Amsterdam period reveals that members of

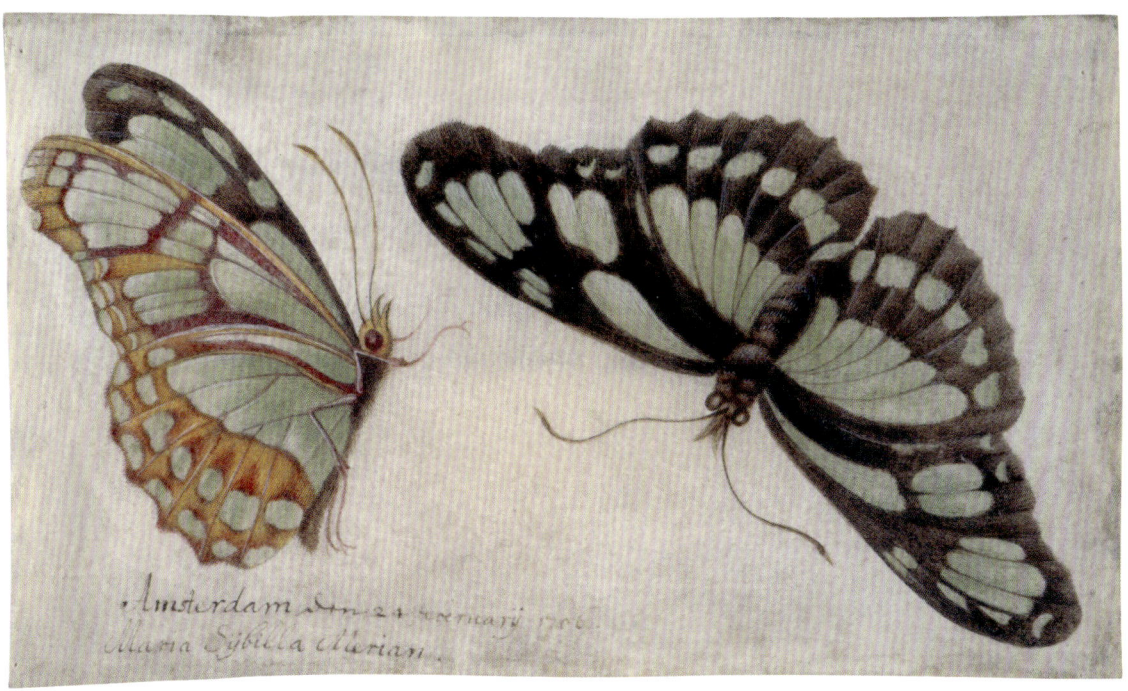

54 Maria Sibylla Merian, *Two Butterflies*, before 1705, watercolour, white ground on vellum, 9 × 14.5 cm (3 ½ × 5 ¾ in),
Germanisches Nationalmuseum, Nuremberg

the Merian workshop frequently used the practices of borrowing, copying and refining. Reitsma and Ulenberg, for example, have observed that most of the stone fruits and branches from the 1698 *Florilegium* are modelled after drawings by Merian. Indeed, one can trace the genesis of Herolt's *Branch with Apricots* (fig.55) to Merian's watercolour of *Fruits in a Chinese Bowl* (fig.57).[21] Importantly, these practices were not limited to Herolt and Graff's artistic output. Anyone leafing through the *album amicorum* of the engraver Peter Schenck (fig.58), for example, would have come across Merian's thoughtful inscription, accompanied by a lantern fly, which also appeared on an illustration of pomegranate blooms (fig.46). Similarly, many of the sheets included in an album of Merian drawings from the Hans Sloane collection dating to 1691–9, now in the British Museum, are in fact reproductions

on vellum of works from the Caterpillar and Flower Books (see Chapter 5 for a discussion about the collection of Merian's artworks).[22]

None of the foregoing suggests that Merian and her daughters lacked in creativity or were lesser artists, or that Herolt and Graff inappropriately plagiarised their mother's work – quite the opposite. This overview of the practices of the workshop demonstrates that the women operated a business in the same manner as would have any master with apprentices in Amsterdam. Merian gave those who worked with her the necessary instruction and tools to enable the workshop to produce works of high quality efficiently, for the purpose of earning an income. And, as Merian seems to have realised, the workshop's ability to earn income was intimately tied with her name.

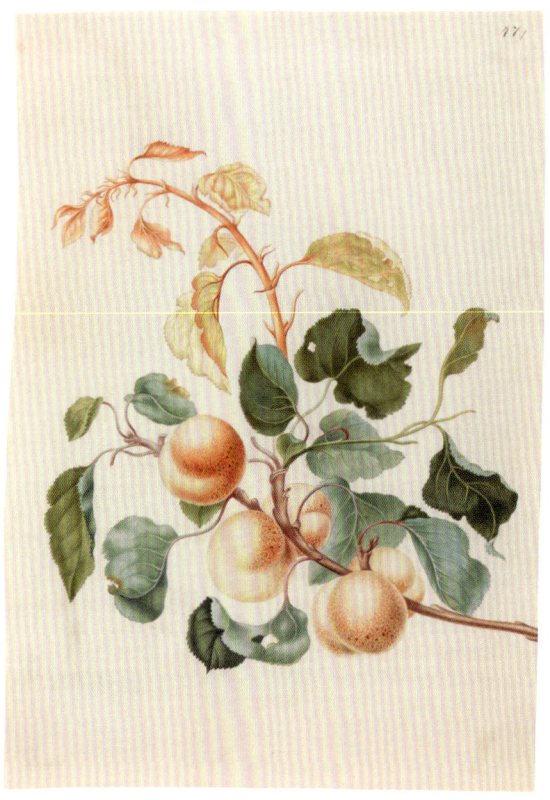

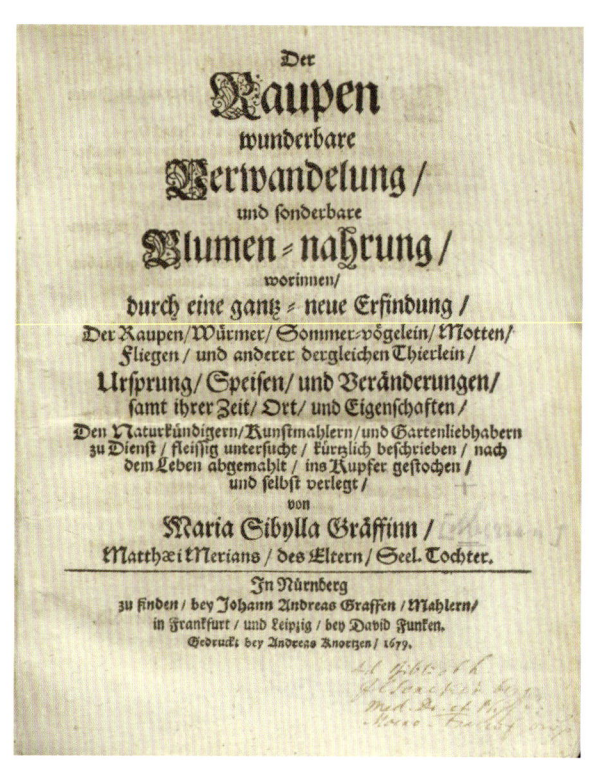

55 Johanna Helena Herolt, *Branch with Apricots*, *c.*1698,
watercolour on parchment, 38.1 × 25.8 cm (15 × 10⅛ in),
Herzog Anton Ulrich Museum, Braunschweig

56 Maria Sibylla Gräffin, 'Title Page', in *Der Raupen
wunderbare*, Johann Andreas Graff, Nuremberg,
1679, printed book, Friedrich-Alexander-
Universitätsbibliothek, Erlangen

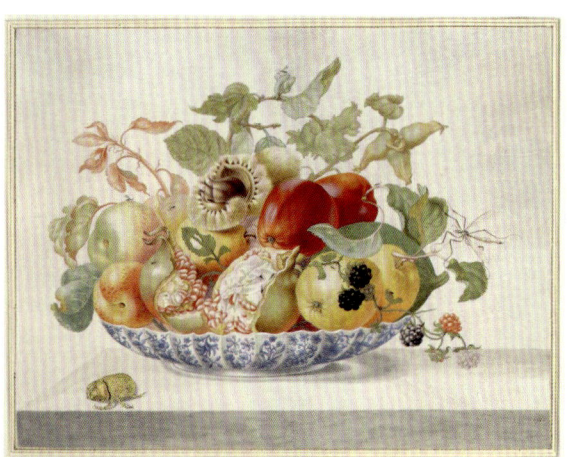

57 Maria Sibylla Merian, *Fruits in a Chinese Bowl*, 1695,
watercolour on parchment, 29.9 × 38 cm (11¾ × 15 in),
Albertina, Vienna

A ROSE IS A ROSE . . . UNLESS IT IS A MERIAN ROSE

Merian appears to have understood early on the artistic significance attached to her name. Her father, Matthäus Merian the Elder, was the owner of one of the most important publishing houses in Germany, having married into the family of the engraver and publisher Theodor de Bry. It was her stepfather, Jacob Marrel, and his apprentices, Abraham Mignon and Johann Andreas Graff, who provided Merian with her artistic training. Yet, when she signed the vellum bearing her illustration of a shoot from a pomegranate tree (fig.4), she wrote 'Maria Sibylla Gräffin geb. Merianin fecit.' – meaning 'Maria Sibylla Graff, née Merian, made this'. The title page of her first book on caterpillars, published in 1679, notes the author of the work as Maria Sibylla Gräffin, daughter of Matthäus Merian the Elder (fig.56). Merian might well have taken notice of the fact that the commentator Joachim von Sandrart had done the same in referring to her in his directory of great German artists, as discussed in Chapter 6.[23]

Most of the autograph drawings that post-date 1691 are signed in the name of Maria Sibylla Merian. As Reitsma and Ulenberg have observed, the signature can vary considerably.[24] There is a compelling argument that many of the drawings that are signed with Merian's name were in fact authored by Herolt and Graff. Not only did Merian almost certainly sign works that had been made by her daughters, but a study of the various signatures found on the works reveals that it is also highly probable that they imitated their mother's signature on their own works.

Once again, in a workshop context, this practice is not controversial. The fact that the three women adopted this strategy confirms that Merian was familiar with the workings of an artist's studio and its marketing strategies. Critically, it signals that the women were aware of Merian's reputation and of the value attached to her name. This hypothesis is supported by the fact that, in some instances, both Merian and Herolt signed an artwork. One such instance is a watercolour of three mice munching on leaves and acorns dating from *c.*1710, signed by Herolt at bottom left, and Merian at bottom right (fig.59). Interestingly, a related drawing has been attributed to Herolt alone (fig.60). Other drawings from the same period are also signed by the two women.[25]

The practice of double signature was not new. It was, however, unusual. Working approximately one hundred years earlier, Joris Hoefnagel and his son, Jacob, both signed a drawing of Diana and Actaeon (1597).[26] Jacob illustrated the principal scene from Ovid's *Metamorphoses*, while Joris executed flowers and various insects around the borders. For the Hoefnagels, the double signature served two purposes: to tell the viewer that both artists contributed to the work of art, and to formally establish the heritage in the family line. There was no better way to ensure that the father's patronage would pass to his son.[27]

The same is arguably true of the drawings signed by both Merian and Herolt. Having recognised Merian's name as a mark of value, the practice testifies to the need that the women perceived to highlight the relationship between them. The double signature served to place Herolt firmly in her mother's legacy and make her an heir to the Merian reputation. The fact that the works bearing the double signature all appear to date from after 1710 – nearing the end of Merian's career and before Herolt departed for Suriname in 1711 – supports this interpretation. Historian Natalie Zemon Davis noted that Merian seemed to have imparted to her daughters a strong sense of matriarchal loyalty and that one name, Merian, mattered more than the others: 'One suspects that [Merian] passed on to her daughters, at the expense of their father, the feeling that they were Merians first and foremost.'[28]

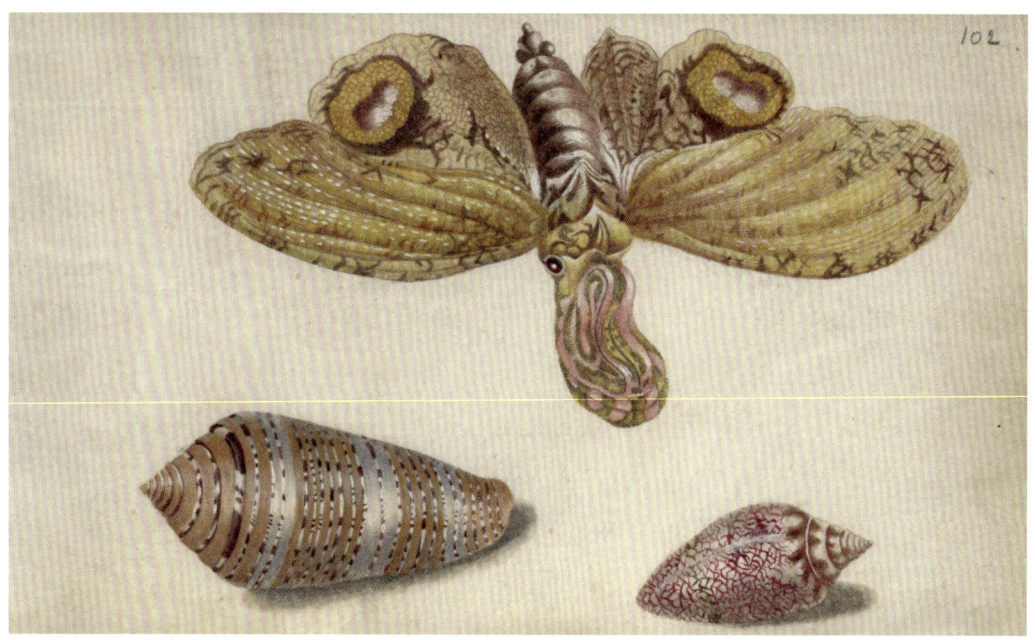

58 Maria Sibylla Merian, 'Lantern Fly and Two Shells', in *Album Amicorum of Petrus Schenk*, fols 101ᵛ–102ʳ, 1709, watercolour on paper, 11.8 × 19.3 cm (4 ⅝ × 7 ⅝ in), Bibliotheek Universiteit Leiden, Leiden

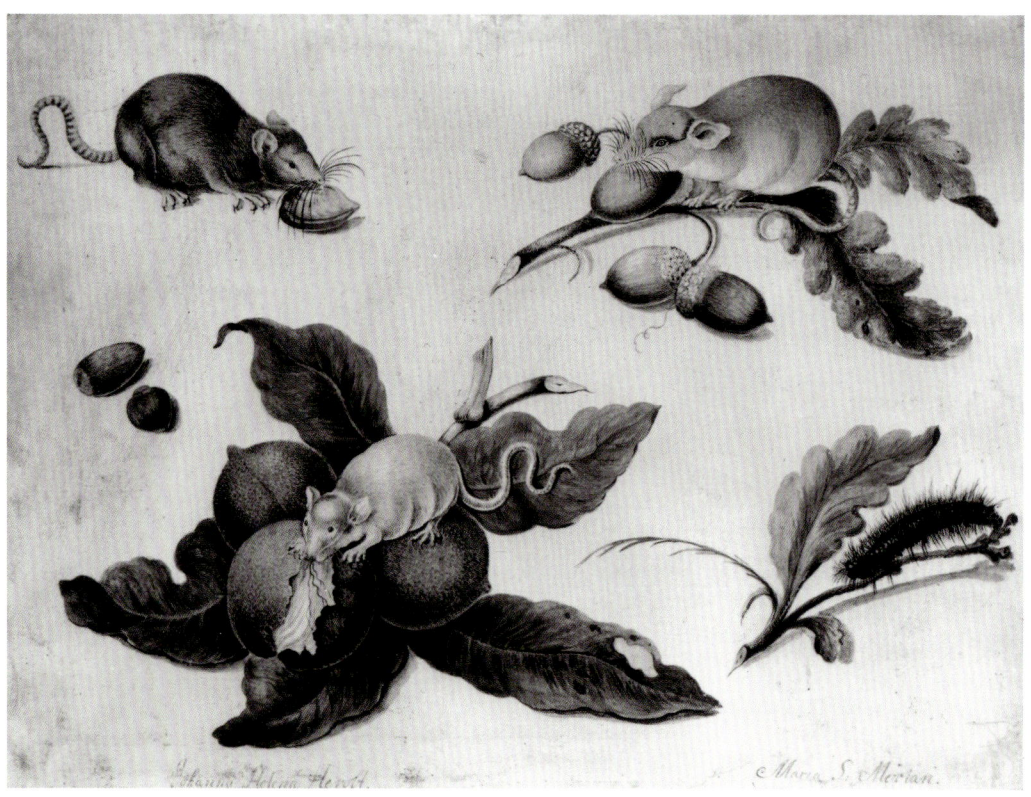

59 Maria Sibylla Merian and Johanna Helena Herolt, *Three Mice with Caterpillars, Limes, and Nuts*, c.1710, photograph of watercolour on parchment, 26.3 × 34.8 cm (10 ⅜ × 13 ¾ in), RKD, The Hague

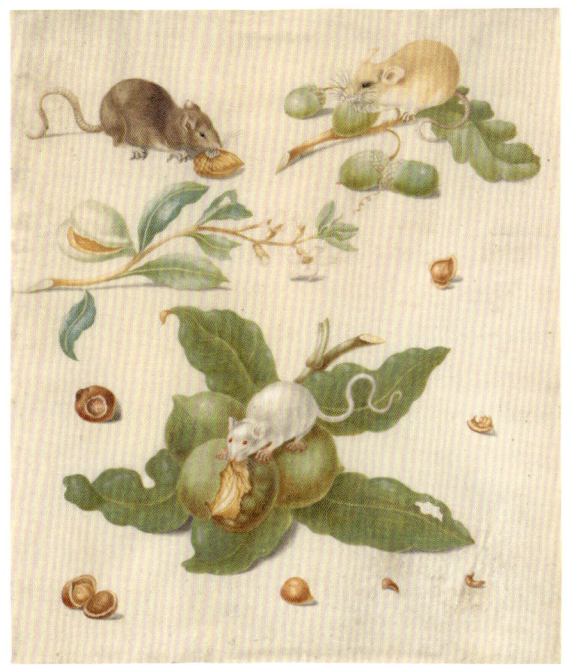

60 Johanna Helena Herolt (attributed to), *Three Mice Nibbling Fruit*, c.1710–17, watercolour on parchment, 32.6 × 26.8 cm (12 ⅞ × 10 ½ in), The Morgan Library & Museum, New York, NY

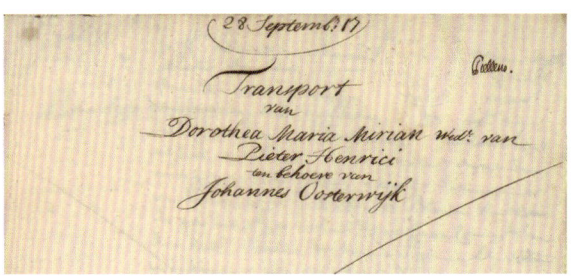

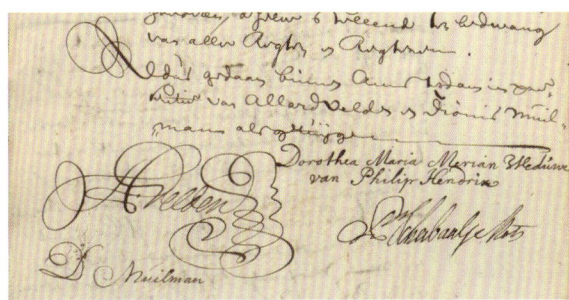

61 Agreement between Dorothea Maria Merian, widow of Pieter Henrici, and Johannes Oosterwyk, 28 September 1717, Gemeente Archief, Amsterdam

THE ULTIMATE MARKETING OF MATRIARCHY

After Merian's death, it was Graff who arranged for the publication of the third instalment of the volume on caterpillars, as Herolt had departed for Suriname by then.[29] That volume is believed to contain unattributed engravings by Graff and Herolt. Between her two marriages, Dorothea Maria reverted not to the name Graff, but rather to her mother's maiden name, Merian. While she used the Latinised name of her first husband on the title page of the book, Merian was the name she used when negotiating the publication of the third volume of the Caterpillar Book (fig.61).[30]

The final part of the Caterpillar Book was a collective production. A metaphor for the workshop and the artistic practices of the three women, it features insects from Europe and from the Dutch colonies. Some of the plates are by Merian, while others could be by Graff or someone else; the explanations that accompany the images have been related by Etheridge to observations recorded in the Study Book over more than three decades.[31] The images vary in style and in quality. The depictions of a branch of celery (fig.62) and a carnation (fig.63), for example, are far less detailed and finely executed than the illustrations from the first two parts of the Caterpillar Book. In comparison, the depiction of the life cycle of a moth on a thistle (fig.64), also from this posthumous edition, is much closer in style and quality to the hand of Merian. Regardless of the hand, however, all of the illustrations in part III of

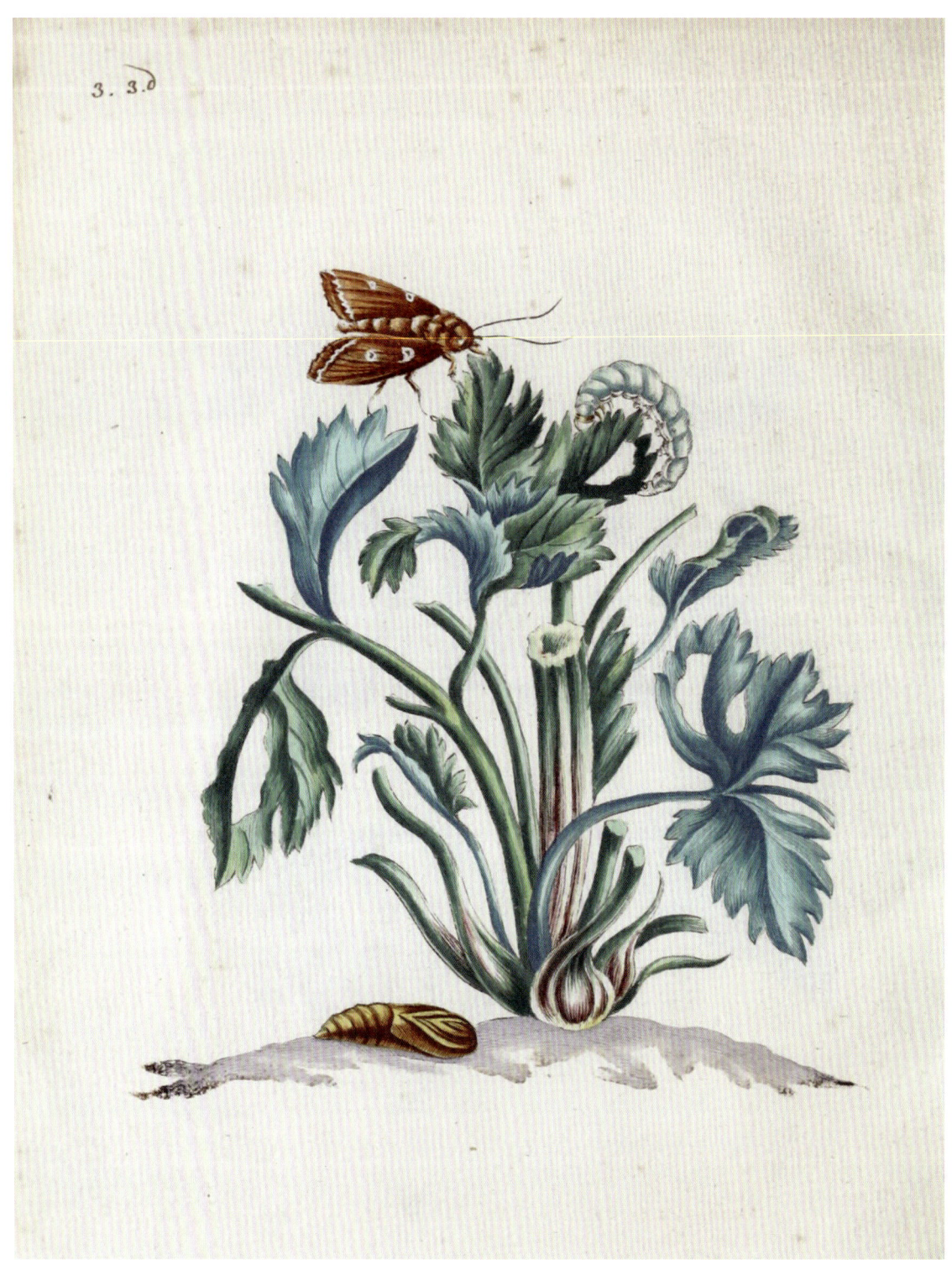

62 Maria Sibylla Merian (attributed to), 'Celery', in *Der rupsen begin*, part III, for and sold by the author, Amsterdam, 1717, printed book, hand-coloured, Getty Research Institute, Los Angeles, CA

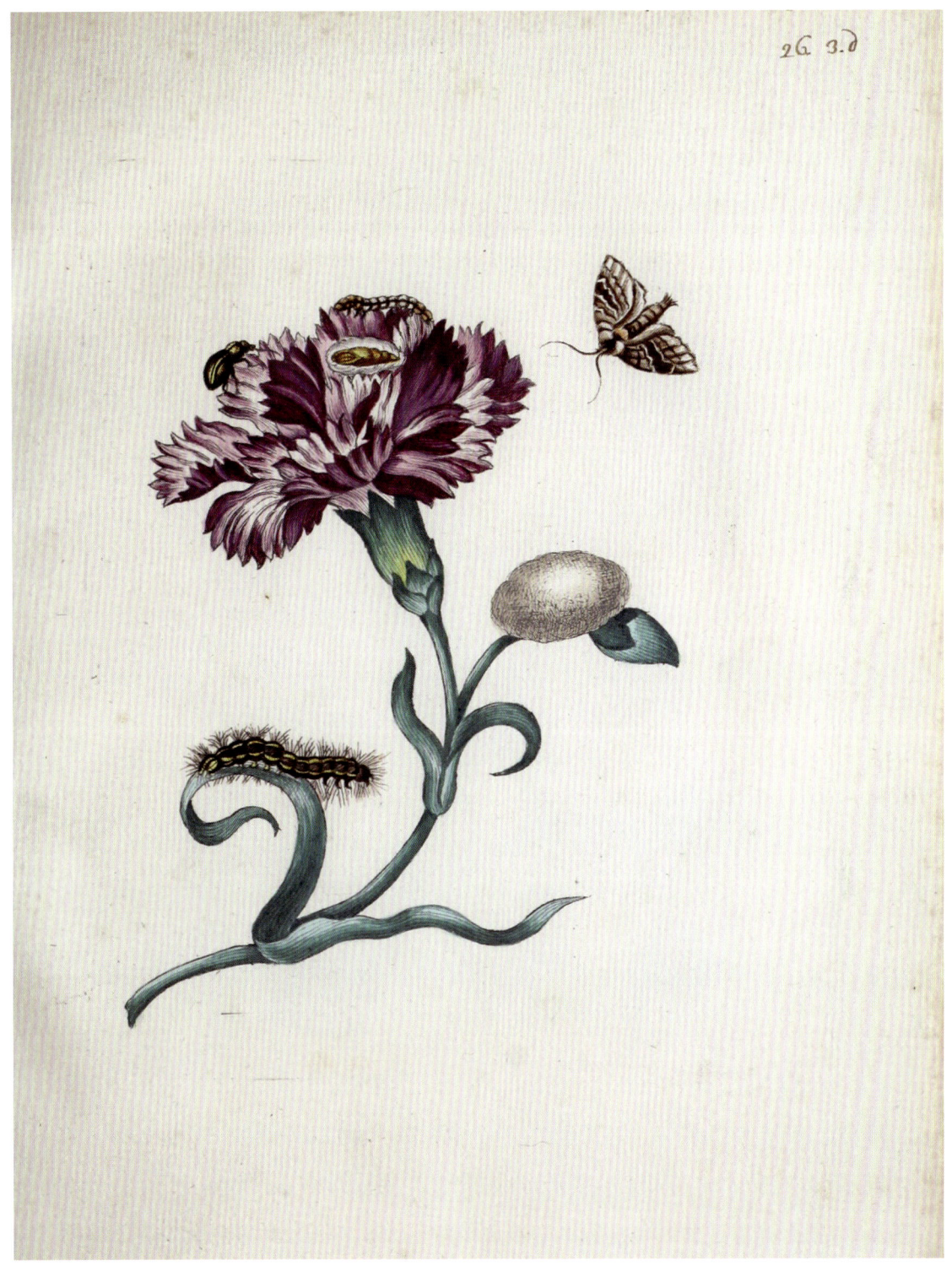

63 Maria Sibylla Merian (attributed to), 'Carnation with Life Cycle of a Moth', in *Der rupsen begin*, part III, for and sold by the author, Amsterdam, 1717, printed book, hand-coloured, Getty Research Institute, Los Angeles, CA

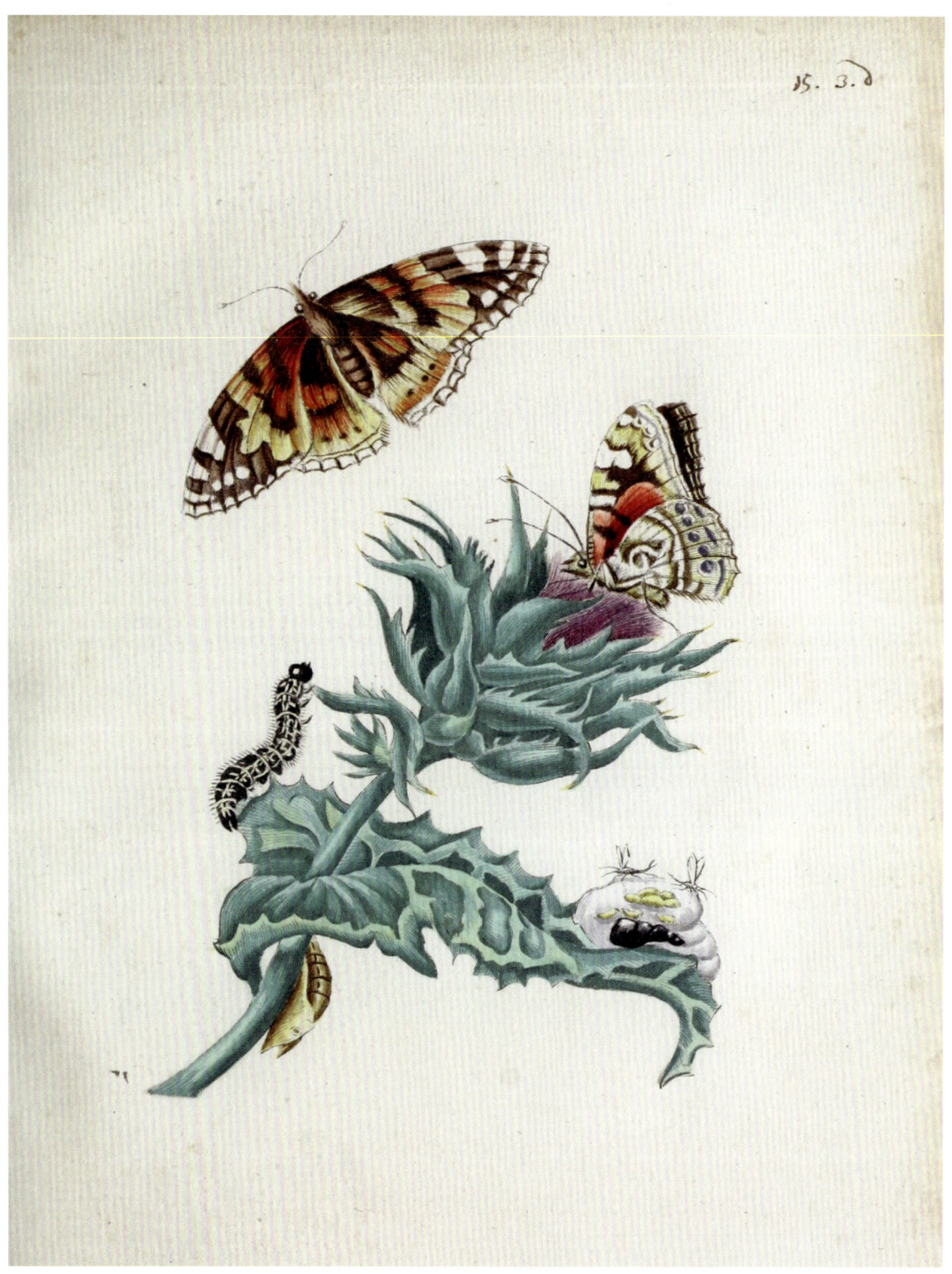

64 Maria Sibylla Merian (attributed to), 'Life Cycle of a Moth and Thistle', in *Der rupsen begin*, part III, for and
sold by the author, Amsterdam, 1717, printed book, hand-coloured, Getty Research Institute, Los Angeles, CA

the book are unmistakably in the pictorial idiom
of Merian.

MERIANS

While she faced obstacles due to her gender both in
becoming an artist and with respect to her reception
(as discussed particularly in Chapter 1 and Chapter
6), Merian nevertheless succeeded in establishing her
own business and earning a reputation. Conceiving
of Merian not only as an individual artist, but also
as the master of a workshop, provides a much better
understanding of her oeuvre and its magnitude. It
enables us to gain a sense of the popularity of Merian
and her daughters, and of their work. Organising as
a workshop, the women could produce more, faster,
and with fewer resources. The repetition not only
of elements from compositions but also of entire
compositions suggests that there was a market for the
sale of these works, and that the women understood
this to be the case.

The Merian 'brand' continued to hold currency
long after Merian's death. Tsar Peter the Great, who
appeared to admire the Netherlands and visited the
country twice, collected her works, as discussed in
the next chapter. The Tsar had ambitious plans for
Russia, which included the creation of the Academy
of Sciences in St Petersburg and the decoration
of his palaces. After the death of Merian, the Tsar
invited Georg Gsell and Graff to assist with both
endeavours. Graff became a drawing and painting
instructor, passing her mother's teachings on to
Russian pupils. When she moved to St Petersburg,
Graff brought with her an inventory of works by
Merian. In bringing over Merian's material legacy and
in hiring her daughter, Peter the Great was essentially
attempting to buy a reputation, and a mark of quality.

While Merian began by trading on her father's
name, her daughters traded on hers. They were, in
effect, marketing matriarchy. In doing so, arguably,
Merian and her daughters exhibited the emergence of
a feminist consciousness.[32] In this context, this means
that the women conveyed that they were aware of
the limitations imposed upon them by their gender,
and that they took the steps to overcome or at least
compensate for these limitations. Merian inculcated
in her daughters an excellence in art and a dedication
to the pursuit of knowledge, as well as the value of the
family business she had begun.

The third part of the Caterpillar Book, published
in 1717, *Erucarum ortus*, a Latin translation of the
three Caterpillar Books, published in 1718, and four
editions of *Metamorphosis* published between 1719
and 1730 were all published in Merian's name. In
Suriname, Herolt continued to study and paint
insects and nature, as well as to collect specimens for
sale to collectors in Europe, most likely in part to
fulfil orders communicated by her mother and, after
the latter's death, on her own. In St Petersburg, Graff
continued to disseminate her mother's teachings at
the newly formed Academy of Sciences.[33] They might
have been wives, but they were 'Merians first and
foremost'.

5

Flowers, Art and Collectors

The passion for collecting and nature introduced in Chapter 2 undoubtedly spurred the popularity of Merian's Caterpillar Book and *Metamorphosis*, in particular. As we have seen in earlier chapters, these books were addressed to specific audiences: enthusiasts, and lovers of art and nature. The extensive textual observations on the origins, nature and properties of the specimens depicted in the two works were aimed at a public interested in learning. This passion for nature and natural history, moreover, created yet another public for the works by Merian and her daughters: art connoisseurs. Indeed, as collectors amassed shells, dried insects and plant specimens, they also started adding landscape and flower paintings and drawings to their collections in larger numbers than ever before. Notwithstanding Merian's commitment to scientific principles and without regard to the rarity of the specimens or the accuracy of their representation, her illustrations of flowers and plants on parchment, on which this chapter focuses, were works of art in and of themselves and held great appeal to collectors at home and abroad.

LANDSCAPE AND FLOWER PAINTINGS

During the first part of the seventeenth century, patrons and collectors in Northern Europe prized history paintings in the form of scenes from the Bible or from mythology. According to contemporary art theorists and commentators, this genre required the most skill and ingenuity, and was therefore at the top of the hierarchy of painting. Next were portraits, followed by landscapes. Still lifes (including flower still lifes) were last, as authors such as Karel van Mander found that they required little skill and no ingenuity – all that was required was to copy nature. In the Low Countries during the second half of the seventeenth century, however, the balance shifted: whereas history paintings had previously dominated inventories, they were now far behind landscape paintings. In Amsterdam during the last quarter of the seventeenth century, landscape paintings accounted for 36 per cent of holdings of all paintings, while history paintings constituted just under 12 per cent.[1]

The sheer number of artists specialising in flower paintings during the same period suggests that a similar shift took place with respect to this 'lowly' genre. We know that collectors owned both flower paintings and albums of flower and other natural history drawings; the vast inventories of such works in museum collections today confirms that quantities of these works were produced by both well-known artists and anonymous ones.

Over time, flower painting developed an association with 'femininity' and 'feminine art'. This was partly due to the association of nature with women, whether as healers and providers of herbal remedies or as mythological figures like Flora and the Hesperides.[2] It was also in part because flower painting, as a subgenre of still life, was a popular artform among wealthy female amateurs not only in the Low Countries, but also in England and France.[3] The view that flower painting was particularly well suited to the female hand was not new. From the sixteenth century, an often repeated trope was that flowers, insects and birds were a subject matter particularly appropriate for women artists, the argument being that 'they called not so much for creative imagination as they did for patience and the "precise application of colors or a delicate touch [...] appropriate to the feminine hand"'.[4]

Some authors voiced a similarly gendered opinion with respect to the use of watercolour, as opposed to oil paint. The Dutch author Willem Goeree, writing in 1670, emphasised that watercolour was well suited to women, as it could be undertaken without the need for much drawing instruction, especially if one 'tackled such unchallenging subjects as fruits, flowers, and birds'.[5] The reality, as is frequently the case, was otherwise. Notwithstanding Goeree's condescension, it is evident that women like Merian and her daughters elevated the art of watercolour and mastered artistic techniques and the use of equipment such as microscopes and magnifying glasses. As the earlier chapters have demonstrated, Merian's illustration of nature was anything but simple or unchallenging, but rather was aesthetically complex and scientifically accurate.

Furthermore, women *and* men specialised in the production of flower still lifes. Anna and Rachel Ruysch (fig.65) worked at the same time and for many of the same patrons as Jan van Huysum (1682–1749), for example. Women *and* men found inspiration (and a brisk trade) in the depiction of fruits and

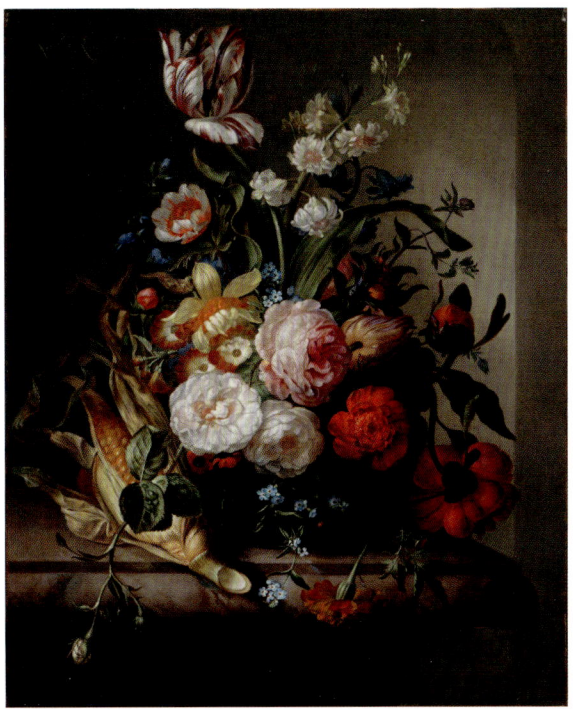

65 Rachel Ruysch, *Vase of Flowers with an Ear of Corn*, 1742, oil on canvas, 50.6 × 40.2 cm (19 ⅞ × 15 ⅞ in), National Gallery of Ireland, Dublin

flowers, insects, plants and animals using watercolour, from Alida Withoos and Maria Moninckx (fig.66) to Herman Henstenburgh (1667–1726; fig.67) and Pieter Holsteyn (1614–73). Thus, it seems, at least some contemporaries believed that there was nothing 'feminine' in the art itself. Rachel and Anna Ruysch, Alida and Pieter Withoos, Maria and Jan Moninckx, Henstenburgh and Holsteyn all belonged to the same artistic circle as Merian. Among other patrons, all of them, with the exception of Anna and Rachel Ruysch, worked for Agnes Block, whose collection is discussed below. Alida Withoos and Jan and Maria Moninckx also worked with Herolt on the *Moninckx Atlas*, mentioned in Chapter 3. Anna and Rachel

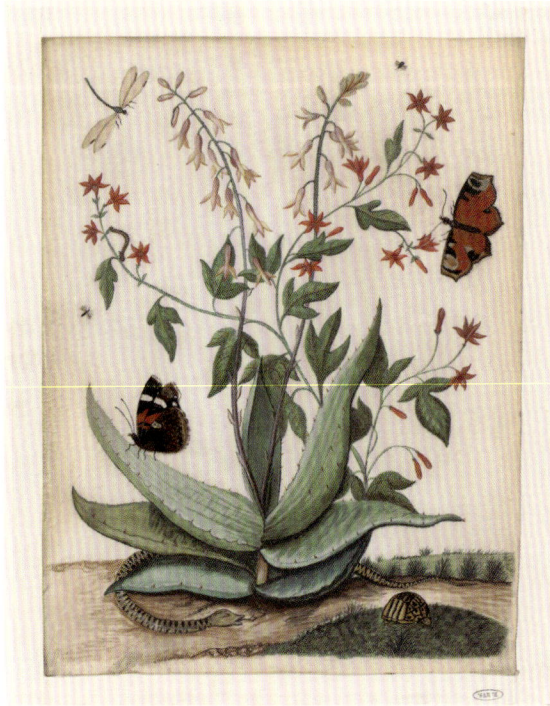 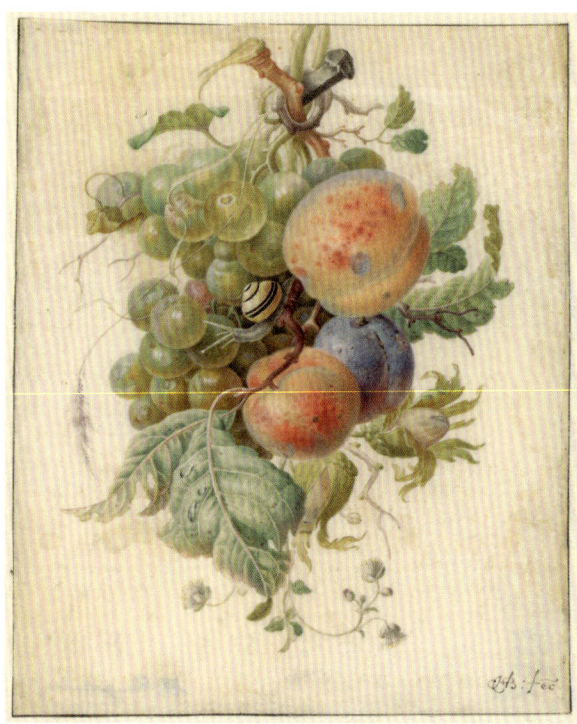

66 Maria Moninckx, *Butterflies and Dragonfly around an Agave in Bloom, with Snake and Turtle*, 1686–1757, gouache on vellum, 39.8 × 29.7 cm (15 ⅝ × 11 ¾ in), Rijksmuseum, Amsterdam

67 Herman Henstenburgh, *Festoon with Fruit*, 1677–1726, gouache on vellum, 23.5 × 18.8 cm (9 ¼ × 7 ⅜ in), Rijksmuseum, Amsterdam

Ruysch were the daughters of anatomist and botanist Frederik Ruysch, with whom Merian visited the Amsterdam medical garden and exchanged views on botany and entomology. He was also one of the individuals named in the preface of *Metamorphosis*; it seems highly likely that Merian and Anna and Rachel would have known each other and been at least aware of each other's work.

(RE)INVENTION

It is against this background that Merian (and her workshop) adapted her artistic practices to reach a new audience of art collectors. In addition to creating counter-proofs from *Metamorphosis* that were sold as the entire set of 60 plates plus text (the 'painted' *Metamorphosis* discussed in Chapter 3), Merian and her daughters also created individual counter-proofs of the images to be sold as separate artworks. Because books were sold unbound, and in the intervening 300-plus years many bound volumes were taken apart, it is impossible to know which illustration on parchment was produced as an independent work and which was part of a set. Based on the frequency of their appearance in collections, however, it is apparent that certain illustrations were highly popular and were likely printed more times than others. This is the case, for example, with respect to an illustration of two Menelaus blue morpho butterflies with a bursting pomegranate fruit (fig.48). Brightly coloured with

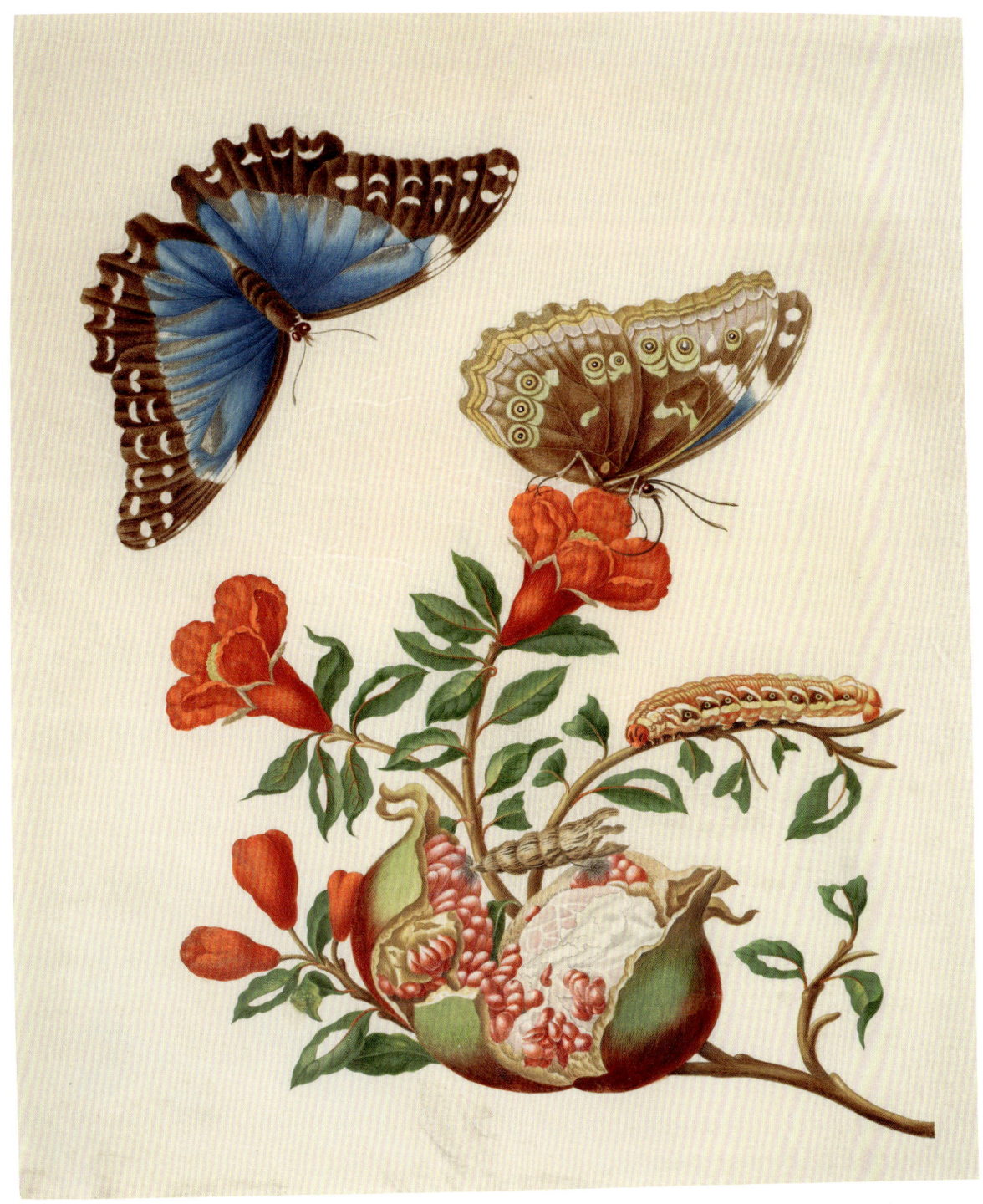

68 Maria Sibylla Merian, *Pomegranate and Menelaus Blue Morpho Butterfly*, *c.*1702–3, watercolour and silver paint on parchment, 37.3 × 30.2 cm (14 ⅝ × 11 ⅞ in), Royal Collection Trust, United Kingdom

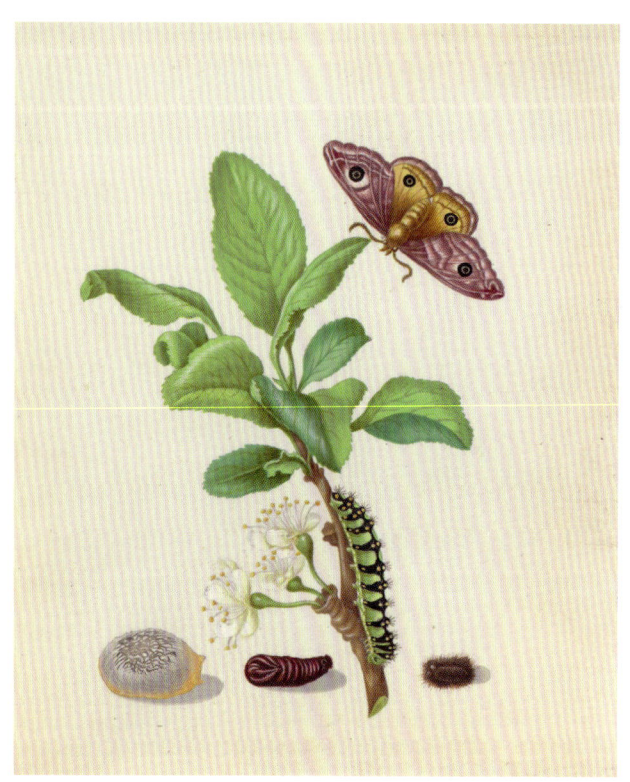

69 Maria Sibylla Merian, *Metamorphosis of a Small Emperor Moth on a Damson Plum*, 1679, watercolour on parchment, 18.7 × 14.9 cm (7⅜ × 5⅞ in), J. Paul Getty Museum, Los Angeles, CA

70 Maria Sibylla Merian, 'Small Emperor Moth on Damson Plum', in *Der Raupen wunderbare*, part 1, Johann Andreas Graff, Nuremberg, 1679, plate 13, printed book, hand-coloured, Universitätsbibliothek Johann Christian Senckenberg, Frankfurt am Main

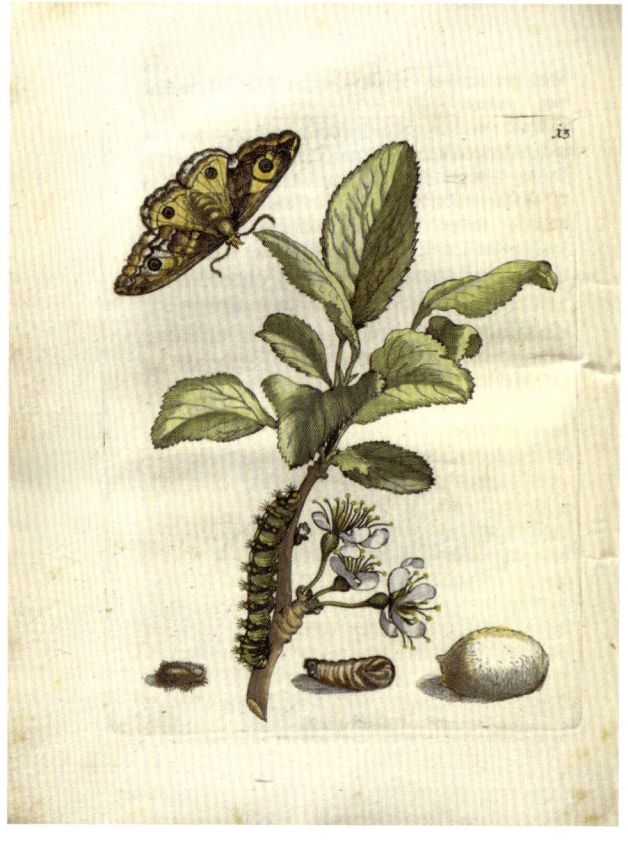

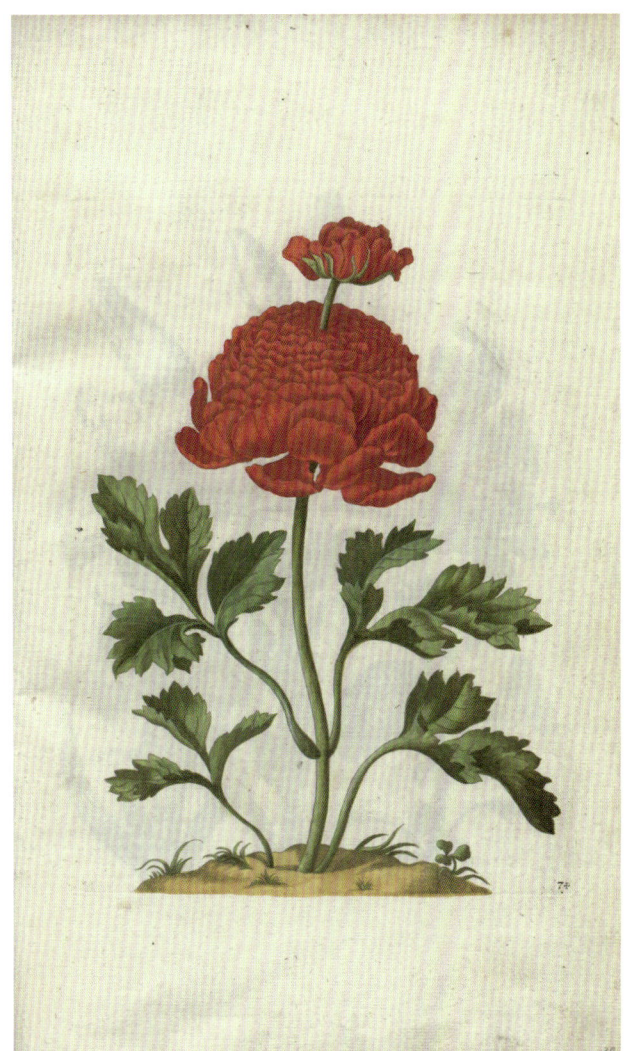

72 Maria Sibylla Merian, 'Double Ranunculus', in *Neues Blumenbuch*, part 11, Johannes Andreas Graff, Nuremberg, 1680 (originally published 1677), printed book, hand-coloured, Sächsische Landesbibliothek – Staats- und Universitätsbibliothek (SLUB), Dresden

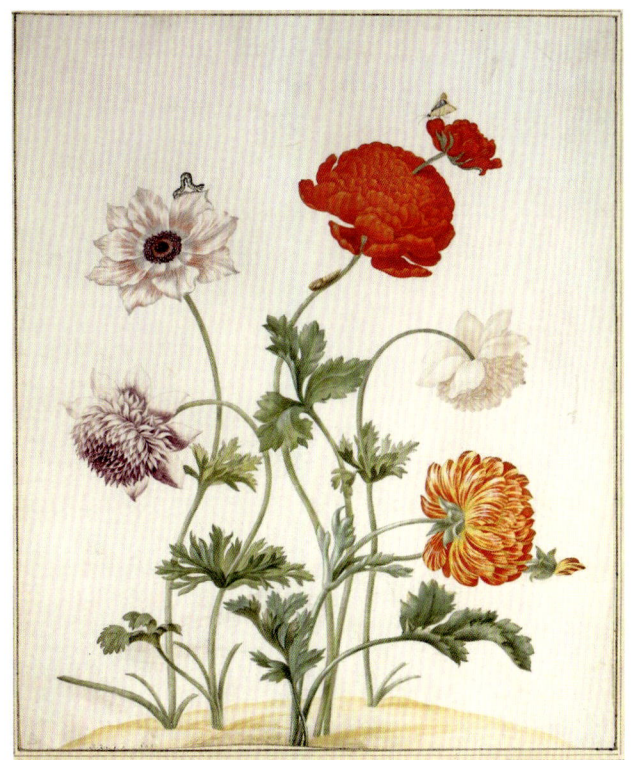

71 Maria Sibylla Merian, *Anemones and Ranunculus*, 1695, watercolour and tempera on vellum, 38 × 30.6 cm (15 × 12 in), Albertina, Vienna

watercolour and with the addition of silver paint to convey the shimmering of the butterflies' scales, as in a version from the Royal Trust, this work on parchment needs no textual context to appeal to a viewer (fig.68).

Counter-proofs showing the same compositions that appear in the Caterpillar Book also emerged from the workshop. In these instances, the focus seems to have been in producing artworks that would be as vibrant and pleasing to the eye as possible, as was the case with the blue morpho butterfly. A good example of this approach is the counter-proof illustration of a small emperor moth on a damson plum (fig.69), made using plate 13 of the Caterpillar Book (fig.70). Although this is not a particularly complex composition, the use of bright colours applied with great detail demonstrates that exceptional artistic skill could elevate a scientifically accurate illustration of the life cycle of a moth into a luxurious work of art.

In addition to repurposing exact compositions from her books as individual works of art, Merian also created new works that incorporated elements of the compositions from her Book of Flowers, New Book of Flowers and Caterpillar Book. A 1695 illustration on parchment in watercolour and tempera (pigment mixed with egg as a binding agent) of anemones, double ranunculus and poppy, for example, is inspired by an earlier image (fig.71). The striking, red double ranunculus first appeared in part II of the Book of Flowers in 1677, and again as part of the New Book of Flowers in 1680 (fig.72). The simplified design of the flower, with its nearly straight stem and well-spaced, non-overlapping leaves, which make the image ideal for embroidery, has now been transformed into a flower with a sinuous stem that is in part obscured by overlapping leaves from other flowers and that anchors the composition by providing a point of focus. The anemones, for their part, can be traced to a bouquet composition from the third part of the New Book of Flowers (fig.73). Although Merian was inspired by and reused some elements of earlier works, the result is a different, and unique, artwork.

Merian created a composition that is freer than those of the New Book of Flowers, with intertwining stems and overlapping leaves, and even adding shadows. Not all of the flowers are easily identifiable, but identification and study were not the intended use of this illustration. This was a work to handle and display: when the light hit the surface at a certain angle, the addition of tempera would have produced a glass-like sheen. Kept in an album or a portfolio, the work could have been passed around when entertaining guests, a sure way to impress. Indeed, by owning such a work, a collector would telegraph their knowledge of art and nature, their interest in collecting and, of course, the fact that they were able to afford works of art by Merian.

Not all of Merian's individual works on parchment were inspired by her early books or by *Metamorphosis*. A still life of fruit in a blue and white porcelain bowl of the kind wealthy collectors imported from China (fig.57) seems to have no direct precedents, although elements of its composition are familiar: Herolt painted a branch of apricots (fig.55), and the bursting pomegranate is a recurrent motif in Merian's body of work (for example fig.48), as are hazelnut branches. Once again, this still life by Merian was intended for display. Indeed, it is reminiscent of a painting featuring a porcelain bowl, fruits and insects by artist Jan van Kessel (1626–79; fig.74). Van Kessel's work, which preceded Merian's by approximately 25 years, is painted on copper and of small size. This would have been a precious work that the owner might have kept in a drawer and handled on occasion. Merian's own porcelain bowl with fruits, branches and insects would have served the same purpose.

Works on parchment by Merian were intended for the discerning eye of art lovers and collectors. Merian sometimes used more fragile media, such as tempera, on these works. She also used precious metals, as she did with the Menelaus blue morpho butterflies, which are dotted with silver paint (fig.68). Merian even used shell gold on some occasions, for example

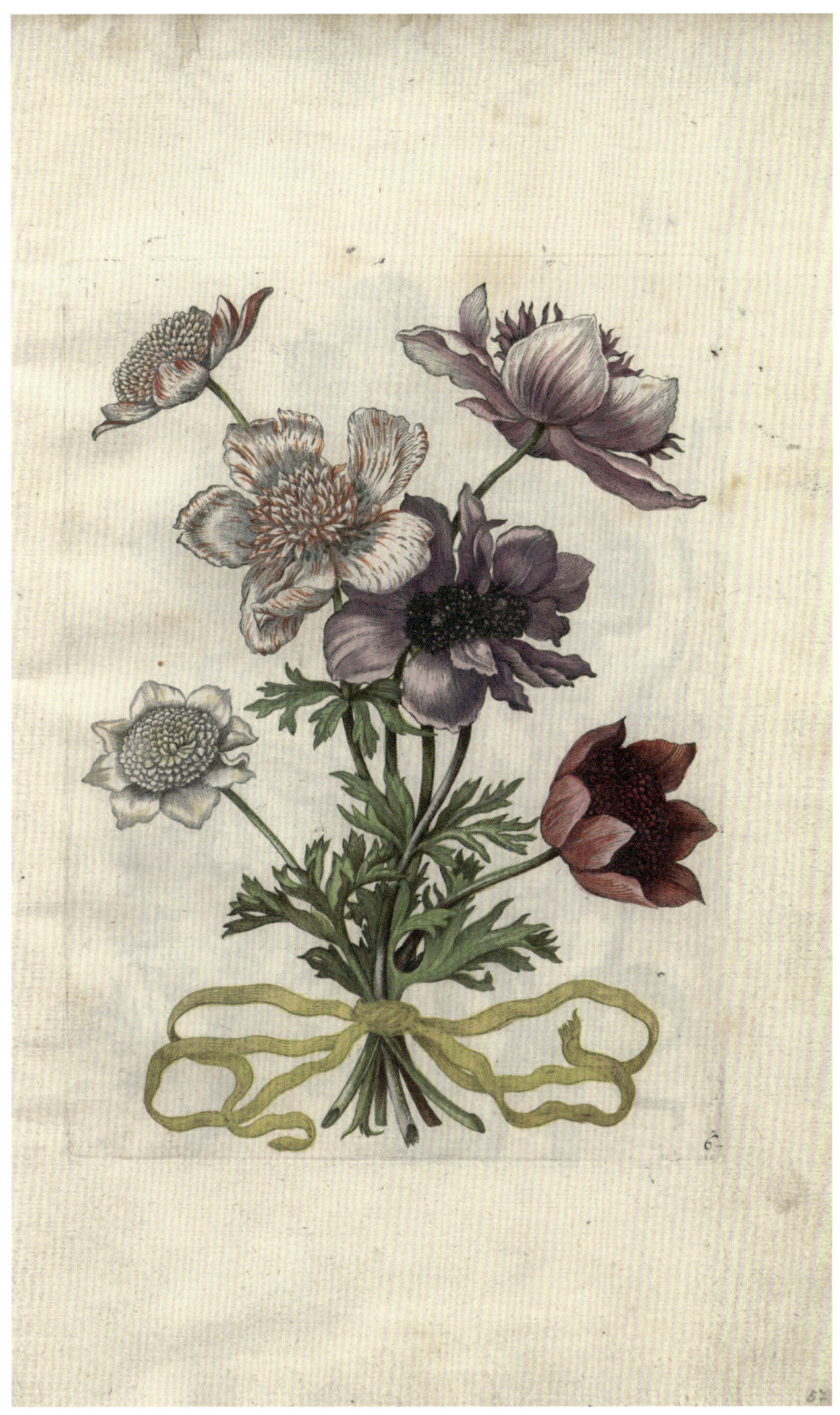

73 Maria Sibylla Merian, 'Anemones', in *Neues Blumenbuch*, part III, Johannes Andreas Graff,
    Nuremberg, 1680, printed book, hand-coloured, Sächsische Landesbibliothek – Staats- und
    Universitätsbibliothek (SLUB), Dresden

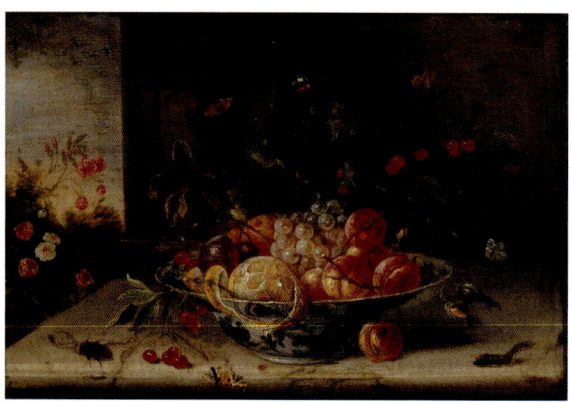

74 Jan van Kessel the Elder, *Decorative Still-Life Composition with a Porcelain Bowl, Fruit and Insects*, 1650–79, oil on copper, 14 × 20 cm (5 ½ × 7 ⅞ in), Ashmolean Museum, Oxford

with respect to a depiction of the moth *noctua comes* (fig.75), thereby evoking not only the shimmer of the scales on the wings of the moth, but also the visual richness of the artwork.

SOME COLLECTORS AT HOME AND ABROAD

Merian's artworks held great appeal for collectors at home and abroad. Some would have been primarily collectors of art. Petronella de la Court (1624–1707), for example, was a wealthy widow in Amsterdam who ran a brewery with her sons after her husband passed away.[6] Today, she is best known for the luxurious doll's house that she assembled (fig.76). Far from being a toy, the doll's house, which included miniature artworks by Frans van Mieris and Frederik de Moucheron, amongst others, was an art and curiosities collection in miniature in and of itself.[7] At the time of her death in 1707, De la Court held a vast collection of paintings, including two flower paintings: one by Maria van Oosterwijck (1630–93), and one by David de Heem (1663–after 1701). She also

owned multiple albums of drawings, including many of flowers, butterflies and other animals. Among the artists identified in the inventory taken in 1707 are Alida Withoos and Herman Henstenburgh. Many albums are simply identified as containing works 'by the best masters'. Although we cannot know if De la Court in fact owned works by Merian, they would have been at home in these albums.

Other collectors would have been enthusiasts of science, who were attracted both to Merian's books and to her more exclusive, individual works on parchment. This was the case with the Dutch collector Agnes Block, the German polymath Zacharias Conrad von Uffenbach and Tsar Peter the Great. Their respective relationships with the work of Merian are explored briefly below.

Agnes Block

Agnes Block (1629–1704) was a collector, art patron and amateur botanist who divided her time between a house in a wealthy enclave in Amsterdam and her riverside country estate outside of Utrecht, which she named Vijverhof (meaning 'pond court') (fig.77).[8] Over the years, she developed the property to include ponds, hedges, orchards, flower gardens and a combination of an orangery and greenhouse. Block was a highly knowledgeable horticulturist whose contributions to public gardens were recognised in botanical treatises of the period. She acquired seeds and roots from Indonesia, Africa and the Americas. She became part of a network of expert and amateur botanists in the Dutch Republic (including Caspar Commelin), Italy, England and France. In 1687, Block achieved a feat nobody else in Northern Europe had done previously: she grew a pineapple.

Block was not only passionate about botany, she was also an avid collector of art. The inventory compiled after her death lists more than 20 paintings, many of them landscapes. Her life's project, however, was her collection of watercolours. Block retained

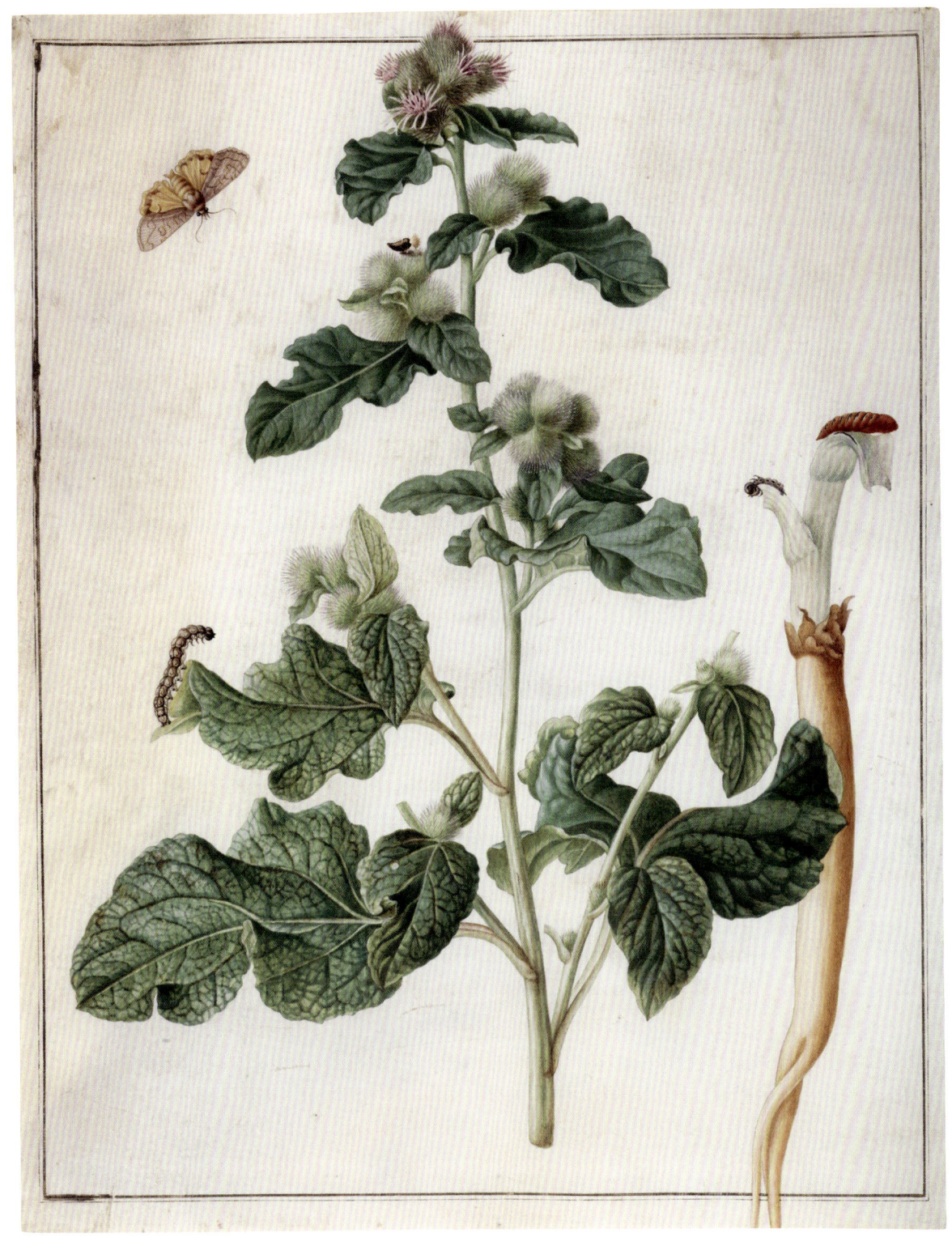

75 Maria Sibylla Merian, *Arctium lappa (?) with Noctua comes*, undated, watercolour on parchment, 37.1 × 27.9 cm (14½ × 11 in), The Fitzwilliam Museum, Cambridge

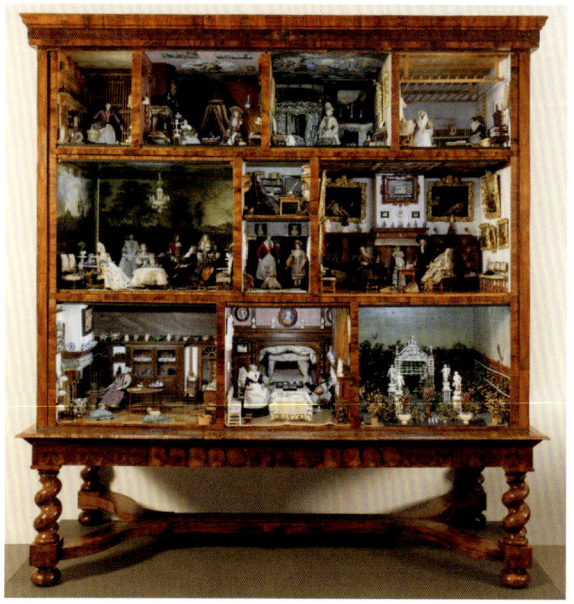

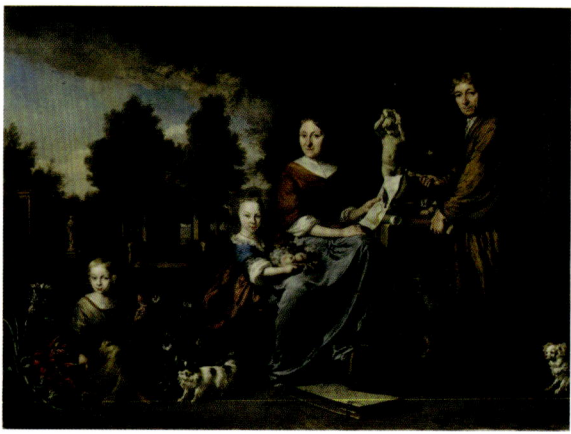

77 Jan Weenix, *Portrait of Agnes Block, Sybrand de Flines, and Two Children in Front of Vijverhof*, c.1693, oil on canvas, 84 × 111 cm (33 ⅛ × 43 ¾ in), Amsterdam Museum, Amsterdam

76 Anonymous artists, components assembled by Petronella de la Court, *Doll's House of Petronella de la Court*, c.1670–90, multimedia, 208.5 × 189 × 79 cm (82 ⅛ × 74 ⅜ × 31 ⅛ in), Centraal Museum, Utrecht

the best artists of the time to produce 'portraits' of her plants – likely well over 500 of them. Block's collection has been dispersed and it is difficult to know exactly what it contained. Fortunately, one volume of watercolours belonging to her has been preserved intact (fig.78). It contains 194 paginated leaves with illustrations of plants and flowers. Furthermore, we know from the inventory of Valerius Röver, who purchased a portion of Block's collection, that the artists who produced watercolours for her included Herman Henstenburgh, Alida Withoos, Maria Moninckx and Pieter Holsteyn, as well as Merian and Herolt.[9]

One illustration identified in the inventory is a depiction of a double Datura, a highly poisonous flower, by Willem de Heer, with two butterflies (Gulf fritillaries) by Merian (fig.51). Block's handwriting is on the back of the work, indicating

that De Heer painted the flower in 1679 and that Merian added the butterflies in 1695. Thanks to Block's patronage, Merian and De Heer could 'meet' on the page, and their individual work become part of a beautiful whole. Given the time lapse between the two artists' respective contributions, we can assume that Block admired Merian's work and thought that the work of De Heer, a very well-known painter, could only be improved by the addition of her famed butterflies. As noted in Chapter 4, the same butterflies would reappear multiple times in the works of Merian and her daughters, from which we can deduce that Merian agreed with Block: this representation of two Gulf fritillaries was particularly successful.

Based solely on the inventory of Valerius Röver, Merian made 25 watercolours for Block, while Herolt made three, making the pair favourites among the artists to whom Block extended her considerable patronage. In all likelihood, they made many more. Their relationship is an example of the ability of early modern women, in certain circumstances, to exercise agency and shape the course of their lives – as patrons and as artists.

Zacharias Conrad von Uffenbach

Merian's appeal transcended Dutch borders. Collectors of her works included, for example, the customers of English art dealer and merchant Solomon Gautier, who travelled throughout Europe to acquire works of art to resell at home. A sale held on 8 February 1725, consisting of more than 550 works of art, included examples by artists such as Jan Brueghel the Elder, Rembrandt and Rubens. On offer were also two illustrations by Merian, one of a 'foreign plant' and one of a coral tree, both painted on vellum.[10]

The German Zacharias Conrad von Uffenbach (1683–1734) was another of Merian's admirers and a collector of her works. A true polymath, Von Uffenbach was a bibliophile, a book collector and an antiquarian; his interests included architecture, science and travel. Between 1709 and 1711, he and his brother undertook a journey in which they visited Lower Saxony, England and the province of Holland, in the Dutch Republic. Von Uffenbach kept a travel diary, which was published in three volumes in 1753 and 1754. His account of his travels tells us that he visited James Petiver when in London. Although he found the apothecary hopelessly disorganised, he was able to admire works by Merian, which Von Uffenbach described as depicting beautiful insects.[11] During his stay in London, Von Uffenbach also visited Hans Sloane, and similarly examined the works by Merian that were in Sloane's possession, about which he seemed less impressed, noting that although her book of insects and plants 'was very well illuminated by her, but in comparison with the others [in Sloane's collection] it was of no account'.[12]

It seems that whatever reservations about Merian's work Von Uffenbach may have had, they did not keep him and his brother from spending time with her in Amsterdam, where they visited her on the morning of 23 February 1711. During their visit, she told them about herself and showed them her life's work. Von Uffenbach carefully recorded his impression of

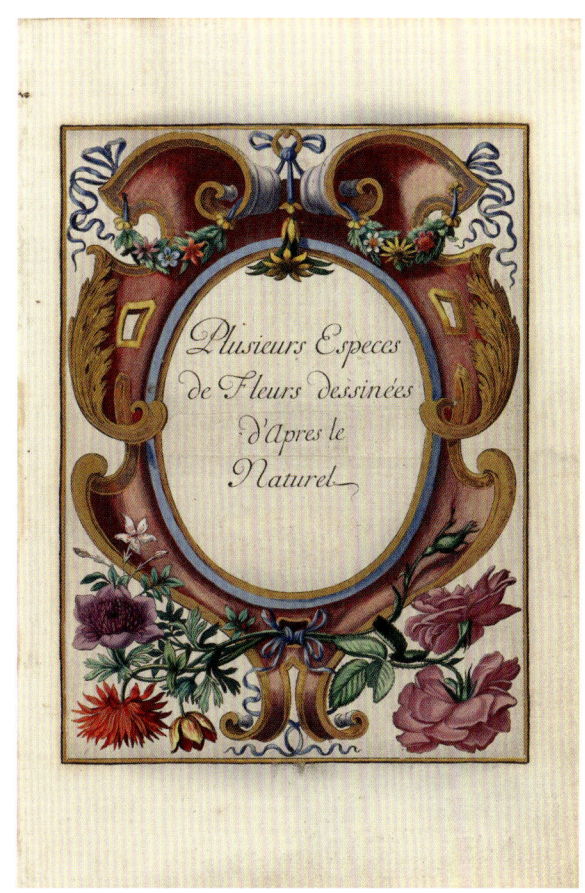

78 Anonymous, 'Plusieurs especes de fleurs dessinées d'apres le naturel', in Agnes Block, *Bloemenboek*, c.1680–90, manuscript, 33 × 21 cm (13 × 8 ¼ in), Rijksmuseum, Amsterdam

Merian and noted his purchases. Notwithstanding the few inaccuracies in his account, Von Uffenbach conveys his admiration for Merian, and was obviously taken by the quality of her work:

> She is about two and sixty years old, but still quite lively, and a very polite and mannerly woman, very skilful in water-colouring, and quite industrious. She showed us

the rest of a book with about fifty figures on parchment, painted with water-colours after life in an incomparable manner. They were all animals that she had seen in Surinam […] as well as the originals of her own work on insects. Thirdly, a very large volume, more than a handful thick, in which all sorts of plants and fruits, both foreign and European, were also painted from life, all on parchment. Fourthly, she showed us her own work of Surinamese insects, which she herself illuminated very neatly after life; as well as her two small works in quarto of insects, most of which she edited in Frankfurt, and the rest in Nuremberg, also illuminated. For these, this industrious woman engraved all the plates herself. I bought these works of hers from her, and had to pay her five and forty florins for the large one, which cost only fifteen florins, because she illuminated it herself with great diligence, and twenty florins for the two smaller ones, which otherwise cost only five florins. She had to write her name on it in her own hand. I also bought several originals from her.[13]

Tsar Peter the Great

Merian's popularity abroad also reached the highest echelons of the nobility. As noted in Chapter 4, Tsar Peter the Great of Russia was one of her admirers. Although it does not appear that the Tsar met with Merian personally during his visit of 1716–17 to the Dutch Republic, he tasked his physician, Robert Areskin (1677–1718), to acquire some works on his behalf at that time. An account book related to the Tsar from 1717 notes that Areskin had purchased 253 sheets of parchment on which were depicted 'with all the skill of the art of painting all manner of flowers, butterflies, flies, and other creatures'.[14] Merian is believed to have been in poor health for several years before her death in 1717.[15] In all likelihood, Areskin made an agreement with Graff and her husband for the artworks.

Areskin himself had a collection of watercolours by Merian, which he might have bought at the same time. A jewel of Areskin's collection was Merian's Study Book, replete with her sketches and annotations – a total of 133 leaves with text and watercolours. The Study Book and Areskin's watercolours by Merian entered the collection of the Academy of Sciences in St Petersburg upon his death in 1718. In 1736, a further 35 works by Merian entered the collection of the Academy. In all likelihood, these were artworks that Graff brought with her to St Petersburg after a return visit to Amsterdam.[16] While Merian herself never set foot in Russia, it may be there that her legacy is strongest.

A LASTING ARTISTIC LEGACY

This chapter offers a window into the multitude of artworks that Merian and her workshop produced. Her command of drawing and composition, and handling of watercolour and pigments, allowed flexibility in her approach to art and enabled her to appeal to a public that appreciated her art for its technical refinements and beauty. The works on parchment frequently reused images from her books and employed familiar motifs. Yet they were painstakingly produced one at a time, making them unique artworks that collectors would have proudly displayed and shared with guests.

Merian's own pursuit of nature coincided with a thirst for knowledge of the natural world, including the depiction of landscapes, flowers, fruits, insects and animals. These subject matters found favour with a number of artists, including decorative painters, furniture makers, textile makers and embroiders, and painters, whose works are listed in contemporary inventories. Because she worked on parchment and paper, and because she depicted flowers and insects, Merian's individual works would have been costly but nevertheless more affordable to a broader segment of society than most paintings would have been. Thus, they found a place in a large number of collections, from merchants to the highest echelons of civic service and the nobility, at home and abroad.

6

Reception and Legacy

It is here, Reader, that I ask you to stop with me for a little while, so you can be amazed [...][1]

Artist, author, naturalist – Merian does not fit neatly into any single category. This has posed a challenge in determining the reception of her work and, consequently, her legacy. Whether admired or dismissed for her independence and pursuit of nature, however, Merian's exceptional artistic abilities were consistently acknowledged during her lifetime, with only one known exception, noted below. Merian received praise from different strata of society and succeeded in selling books and in shifting the course of natural history, which is more than most early modern women could expect. Her readers, however, were never allowed to forget that she was a woman, engaged in men's work. She was remarkable – for a woman.

IN HER OWN WORDS: NOT FOR MY SAKE

It is fitting to begin a section on the reception of Merian by looking at the manner in which she presented herself – in other words, how she wished or hoped to be received.[2] Her unconventional path for a woman of the seventeenth and early eighteenth centuries brought her considerable attention, but it is not to say that she sought personal fame.

As noted in Chapter 2, publishing technical or scientific texts was not the norm for early modern women.[3] In his expansive nineteenth-century *History*

of the Natural Sciences, George Cuvier referred only to one female author for the sixteenth and seventeenth centuries – Merian.[4] Although he wrongly believed that *Metamorphosis* had only appeared in 1719, Cuvier described it as having 'magnificent' plates. From this perspective, as Natalie Zemon Davis remarked, 'For the seventeenth century, Maria Sibylla Merian is a sample of one.'[5] The women who did write, in any field, found themselves having to manage gender expectations that enshrined their domesticity at the same time as publicity.[6] It would have been deemed poor taste to be seen to court publicity overtly, and doing so would have placed a woman at risk of being considered lacking in virtue, or worse. It is in that light that we must consider Merian's self-presentation in her publications.

In the New Book of Flowers and the Caterpillar Book, Merian is careful to maintain her image as a modest, respectable woman by readily adopting a 'rhetoric of modesty', emphasising that her work was not published for her own sake, but rather for that of the public and, always, to the glory of God.[7] Her self-representation as a reluctant author is particularly explicit in the preface of the Caterpillar Book:

All of which then finally so moved me and caused me – especially having often been urged and encouraged by learned and respected persons – to present such Divine marvels to the world in a modest book. Therefore, seek herein not mine, but God's glory alone, and glorify Him as Creator of even these smallest and least of worms, for they have their origin not in themselves, but from God [...]

The beginning has been made, and if it is your wish, / I will pursue this work in service to my readers, / that I may keep their interest keen with art / and earn the praise and favor of great men.[8]

It might seem that her last line, in which she explicitly hopes to earn the praise and favour of great men, is immodest. Arguably, however, it is entirely consistent with Merian positioning herself at a level much lower than that of the men who published scientific treatises, and the 'great men' – the prince-bishops and other wealthy patrons who might judge her work of sufficient value as to support it.

Merian was bolder in her self-representation in the preface of *Metamorphosis*, in which she explicitly set out to improve upon existing knowledge, having found that the collections of the renowned men of Amsterdam that she had visited (including those of the Burgomaster Nicolaas Witsen and anatomist and botanist Frederik Ruysch) were lacking. In her address to her readers, Merian notes:

[...] But in Holland I was astounded to see what lovely creatures were brought back from the East and West Indies, particularly when I had the honour of being able to see the precious collection of the Most Honourable Mr Nicolaas Witsen [...] as well as that of the Honourable Mr Jonas Witsen [...] Furthermore I also saw the collection of Mr Frederik Ruysch [...] In these collections I found these and countless other insects, but their origin and reproduction were lacking [...] This inspired me to undertake a long and costly journey [...] When I had returned to Holland and some amateurs had seen my painted pieces, they urged me to print and publish them, believing that this was

the first and most remarkable work ever to have been painted in America. The costs that had to be made in the production of this work deterred me at first, but I eventually resolved to do it [...] In making this work I have not been profit-seeking, and would be content if I just recover the expenses I have made. I have spared no expense in the production of this work, but I have had the plates cut by the most famous masters and used the best paper for that purpose, so that it would give pleasure and satisfaction to the art connoisseurs as well as to the amateurs of insects and plants, just as I will be pleased when I hear that I have reached my objective and at the same time will have provided pleasure [...][9]

To challenge openly the work of respected amateur naturalists and learned experts was rather bold. Merian did, however, anticipate and attempt to neutralise her critics by emphasising that she had been pressed into publishing her observations by the amateurs who had seen her watercolours and by appealing to the economic necessity of the publication. Furthermore, she insisted that what would please her was if her work gave pleasure to others, thereby restating the critical disavowal: this work was not about her. Merian's strategy, in other words, was to promote and boast of her achievement ('the first and most remarkable work ever to have been painted in America') by placing the words on the lips of others. In this, her approach was not dissimilar to that employed by other contemporary female authors.[10]

It is reasonable to conclude that Merian wanted her books to be popular and that she did wish to be recognised for her labour and for the quality of her observations and illustrations. She was well aware, however, that for a woman such as herself, divorced and engaging in what many would have considered the male pursuits of knowledge, travel and publication, there was no such thing as dignified and deserved fame – only notoriety.

EARLY RECEPTION: A WOMAN WHO PAINTED FLOWERS ADMIRABLY

Merian's earliest printed praise coincided with the publication of her first flower book, in 1675. It was her fellow resident of Nuremberg, Joachim von Sandrart, who included her in his reference work *Teutsche Academie der edlen Bau-, Bild- und Mahlerey-Künste*, a 'who's who' of those whom Von Sandrart considered to be the most significant German architects, sculptors and painters. Merian is part of the entry devoted to her husband: 'Johann Andreas Graff [. . .] married to Maria Sibylla Merian, a graceful painter of flowers', 'daughter of the copper engraver Matthäus Merian'. Merian's works, Von Sandrart notes 'are most perfect to be replicated with the needle'. She 'prepared interesting lessons for the benefit of those who demand to learn and follow her virtues'. Furthermore, in addition to comparing her virtues to the goddess Minerva, Von Sandrart writes that Merian performed 'regular, good housekeeping'.[11]

In many ways, the language Von Sandrart employs, perhaps not surprisingly, echoes that used by Merian herself in marketing her books on flowers. There was more, however, to Von Sandrart's use of language than simply (re)projecting her respectability and modesty. The reference to Merian's capable housekeeping, for example, suggests a concern with her gender and the domestic duties imposed upon or expected of those of her sex, something which resounds even more given that Von Sandrart's discussion of Merian is included under the entry dedicated to her husband.

In the 1679 edition of the *Teutsche Academie*, Von Sandrart promoted Merian to 'painter', and allotted her an entry under the name Maria Sibylla Graffin.[12] He notes that the artist was so well trained by her stepfather, Jacob Marrel, in the art of painting miniatures and flowers that she has attained perfection in this endeavour. This can be readily seen, he writes, in the Book of Flowers, in which she was 'excellently assisted by young [girls] through her teaching school' and which was 'to be praised'.[13]

This later entry by Von Sandrart is less overtly gendered. At first glance, his focus is on Merian's abilities as an artist and on her observations of nature. A close reading, however, reveals that socially constructed gender expectations continue to course through the text. Von Sandrart implies that Merian's artistic skills are owed to her stepfather, who trained her expertly, and perhaps even due to her lineage as Matthäus Merian's daughter. Von Sandrart's compliment regarding Merian's Book of Flowers could arguably be read as backhanded. Indeed, in highlighting the fact that Merian received the assistance of her pupils in assembling the book, Von Sandrart firmly anchors it as falling within the genre of household books, not unlike how-to books on cooking, the curing of childhood ailments or the farming of chickens. In other words, while Von Sandrart generously praises her work, he does so as a work by a woman, intended for women and children.

The use of gendered language is not unique to Von Sandrart. Part 1 of the Caterpillar Book, published in 1679, included a laudatory poem by Christoph Arnold, an eminent resident of Nuremberg. Because it is included in a volume that was published by Graff, her then husband, we can assume that Merian approved the poem. It appears before Merian's preface, thereby ensuring that this would be the first text readers perused. While Arnold's 'song of praise' extolls Merian's skills, what he appears to find most astonishing is that Merian – as a woman – should undertake and successfully complete her observations and descriptions of caterpillars:

It is remarkable that women, too, would venture / to treat the very matters / with serious intent / that scores of learned men have pondered without end.
[. . .]
What [well-known men of science] once did write, / we read with grateful pleasure; / But praise is due no

less / to a woman who aspires to do the same as they. [...]

for an ingenious woman has done all this herself, as if in idle hours.

[...]

we'll test by equal standards, / and show what can be done / by this industrious daughter of worthy Merian![14]

Arnold's *éloge* has points in common with Von Sandrart's commentary, in that he explicitly links Merian's skill to her parental lineage. In a line not quoted here, he goes on to note the ease with which Merian engraved the illustrations, writing that 'for her [this work] is but a trifle'. Combined with his comments regarding her fortunate parentage, Arnold arguably lessens Merian's accomplishment. On the other hand, by adding the names of well-known men of science, including Johannes Goedaert, mentioned in Chapter 2, Arnold elevates Merian's work to their standard. Nevertheless, this praise is diminished by Arnold's emphasis on Merian's gender, as it is by his note that her accomplishments were undertaken 'as if in idle hours', suggesting that the work was a way to occupy herself when her household, wifely and motherly duties had been satisfied. We cannot know how Merian felt about her motherly and wifely duties, or whether she included these observations by Arnold in an attempt to pre-empt critics, to maintain her reputation, or to highlight what was important to her. It is fair to assume, however, that Merian accepted the language used by Arnold and that it did not strike her as offensive or unusual.

Thus, although Von Sandrart and Arnold each recognise and celebrate Merian's skills as an artist and as an observer of nature, they insist on the significance of her gender, and on reassuring readers that her foremost duties – those related to her household – were not being neglected. Needless to say, no such assurances were required in the case of male artists.

A few years later, in 1687, the German intellectual Hermann Conring, in a chapter of his *In universam artem medicam singulasq* dedicated to 'metals, gems, water, earth, and individual writers', writes that a woman, the industrious Maria Sibylla Graff, the daughter of the celebrated Merian, has published a work on insects that is 'so elegant and pleasing to the eye as well as to the minds' of learned men (*opus tam elegans & gratum oculis aeque mentibusque elegantius doctorum*).[15] Like Von Sandrart and Arnold before him, Conring was duly impressed by Merian's talent. Also like them, however, it seemed inconceivable to judge and praise a woman on her merits alone; thus, she remained tethered to her husband, father and/or stepfather.

METAMORPHOSIS AND LATER: PRAISE, GENDERED LANGUAGE AND OMISSION

Metamorphosis is Merian's work that attracted, and continues to attract, most attention, in no small part because it is the product of a journey that most individuals could scarcely imagine taking during the long seventeenth century, let alone have a woman and her daughter undertake.[16] A frequently quoted anonymous seventeenth-century manuscript, which was once part of the papers related to the Amsterdam medical garden, reads: 'What experience does such a woman have after a short stay in a country such as Surinam [...] crawling about in forests and thickets [...] a fragile woman cannot do that, when a well-armed man would have a difficult enough time getting out of them [...].'[17] *Metamorphosis*, the same author noted, was simply a very expensive collection of images. Notwithstanding this dismissive opinion, which was likely never intended for public consumption, other commentators could scarcely contain their praise and enthusiasm of Merian in relation to *Metamorphosis*. Yet other individuals, perhaps a majority, opted for silence.

A Growing Love of Art and 'Quite Eccentric' Pursuits

In 1721, several years after the publication of *Metamorphosis* and after Merian's death, Arnold Houbraken devoted an extensive entry to her in the third volume of *De Groote schouburgh der Nederlantsche konstschilders en schilderessen* (The Great Theatre of Dutch Painters), which he accompanied with her portrait, an engraving based on the drawing made by Georg Gsell (fig.1).[18] At the outset, Houbraken notes that Merian's aptitude for the arts was evident from the age of eleven, when she 'tended more to the pencil than to domestic occupations'. But 'even with children and domestic worries', he continues, the 'love of art continued to grow in her'. About her work, he observes 'Those who have browsed and read the work speak of it with great praise' – thereby distancing himself from the praise on the substance of her books. He closes his entry on Merian with a poem, the last lines of which are as follows: 'What gave her the joy, what gave her the desire? / She found entertainment in art, and in contemplation / The Creator the cause of all things. / Her name lives, though death hath quenched her light.' Houbraken clearly admired Merian. One cannot escape the conclusion, however, that for him Merian was foremost a woman artist and naturalist. In his final analysis, Merian's art and observations of nature were for her entertainment and part of her devotion to God – not borne out of intellectual curiosity or from the desire to create and share knowledge.

By contrast, when discussing the work of the painter Herman Saftleven, for example, Houbraken limits himself to discussing the quality of his work, which he believed was at its highest in the painter's middle period.[19] When discussing the painter Johannes Bronkhorst, who belonged to the same artistic network as Merian and Saftleven, Houbraken notes that he had been apprenticed to a baker, which became his profession. However, his passion for art was so great that he learned how to paint, while continuing his work as a baker: 'He worked diligently in his spare time in art, and without any education got so far that he may be counted among the best artists in watercolor.'[20] Houbraken does not feel compelled to tell the reader whether Bronkhorst's baking suffered as a result of his artistic pursuits.

This intra-textual comparison between Merian, Saftleven and Bronkhorst is purposeful. Saftleven and Bronkhorst, like Merian, produced detailed, scientifically accurate illustrations of plants and insects, although only Merian published books containing her engravings. All three artists received commissions from the patron and (then) well-known amateur botanist Agnes Block to immortalise her rare and exotic plants, insects and birds; and all three earned the admiration of Houbraken. Yet, his approach to the memorialisation of the artists is strikingly different in the case of the two men when compared to his approach to Merian, notwithstanding the relatively similar circumstances of their respective artistic production.

In 1730, Johann Gabriel Doppelmayr, in his *Historische Nachricht von den Nürnbergischen Mathematicis und Künstlern*, describes Merian's pursuits of natural history as 'quite eccentric', but admiringly terms her findings in natural history 'completely new discoveries'.[21] Doppelmayr goes on to describe *Metamorphosis*, published in 1705, as 'a precious work with 60 copper plates in Regal-folio, with many beautiful observations included in Dutch and, with the generous assistance of the learned Casp. Commelini, in Latin at the same time'.[22] Doppelmayr was writing specifically to enhance the reputation of Nuremberg as a place where great artists and mathematicians flourished. Still, it is Caspar Commelin who is praised as learned: Merian had eccentric pursuits, completely new discoveries and precious copper plates, but Commelin was a physician with refined skills in Latin.

Metamorphosis *in Literary Circles*

At least two contemporary specialised literary magazines praised *Metamorphosis* soon after its publication. As was the case with artistic reference works, however, that praise was highly gendered. Willem Sewel, editor of the Dutch *De boekzaal der geleerde werreld* (The Library of the Learned World), could barely contain his astonishment that Merian – a woman – should have undertaken a trip to Suriname and produced *Metamorphosis*. The text is worth quoting in full:

> [...] It is here, Reader, that I ask you to stop with me for a little while, so you can be amazed at the great eagerness to investigate and the immeasurable diligence of this Lady; it is not new for men to make great efforts in the pursuit of the wonders and rarities of Nature; the scholarly world has seen many such undertakings. But that a woman, who is already quite old, should undertake a trip to the West Indies, and out of *liefhebberij* [amateur passion] decide to overlook the inconveniences of the heavy seas, the dangers of raging waves and roaring winds, only to investigate the reproduction of insects and to paint them closely after life, is something without precedent [...] No expense has been spared in carrying out this excellent work; the plates were engraved by the most famous masters, and printed on the best and heaviest paper, to please connoisseurs of art as well as those who love insects and plants [...][23]

Sewel goes on to provide a 'brief sketch of the precise and praiseworthy work of our renowned artist'. The anonymous author of a review of *Metamorphosis* in the Leipzig-based *Acta Eruditorum*, in 1707, was equally struck by Merian's gender:

> [...] But who would believe that a woman would be attracted [to lowly little animals] with such curiosity that she would collect insects with her own hands, paint them in vivid colors and engrave them in copper? Sparing no expense and unafraid of the danger threatened by a journey to America, a two-year stay in Surinam and the equally difficult return? Then again, she had already made an extraordinary name for herself before this, when she published the first part (1679) and then the most curious second part (1683) of *Observations on Insects*. But now with this work, which is definitely very beautiful, she deserves immortal fame among all the learned women who ever lived, because this book can undoubtedly compete with the efforts of the most famous craftsmen in this genre. Indeed among botanists as well she will henceforth be given a place of honor, because the foreign plants that she also depicts, as the insects' food and quasi incidentally, thus far were either completely unknown or had been less accurately described by others [...][24]

It seems beyond question that the author admired Merian's work. Indeed, the reference to the reception of Merian's publications amongst botanists and her characterisation as the *author* of the work (in a passage not cited here) are strikingly gender-neutral for the period. Nevertheless, it is amongst 'learned women' that Merian should receive immortal fame, and not simply amongst learned individuals. Furthermore, while the reviewer allows that *Metamorphosis* could 'undoubtedly compete' with the efforts of other craftsmen (not, it should be noted, 'artists' or 'learned men'), he would not go so far as to venture that Merian would win the competition.

Metamorphosis was the only publication by a woman to be reviewed in the 1705 *De boekzaal der geleerde werreld* and in the 1707 *Acta Eruditorum*, a fact from which we can infer the extraordinary nature of Merian's achievements, even if her gender seems to have garnered as much attention as her work. Merian was carefully kept aside, as an attraction of sorts but not as an equal to the many other self-taught male authors whose books were reviewed and recommended in these publications.

Omitted, Dismissed, Othered: The Male-Dominated World of Natural History

Although this book is concerned with Merian's artistic practice, it is important to review briefly the reception she received as a naturalist because it had a critical impact on the waning of her popularity in the post-Linnean world, the decline of which resulted in her artistic output being overlooked for a considerable period of time. As discussed below, reduced to its essence, Merian's reception as a naturalist was that of omission, dismissal or othering through the use of gendered language.

No commentator was as openly dismissive of Merian's work as the author who asked 'What experience does such a woman have[?]' Most commentators, to the contrary, praised Merian – in highly gendered terms, both explicitly and implicitly: women could be heroines and, in these cases, should be celebrated. But virtuous women were, essentially, women who behaved like virtuous men. Thus, while gendered expectations did not necessarily bar a woman from a given field, gender almost always affected the assessment of their activities outside of the domestic realm.[25]

Merian was careful to incorporate the practice of 'sociable citation', whereby she referred to individuals whose contributions to her work and/or to natural history she deemed important into *Metamorphosis*.[26] Her male counterparts, however, mostly failed to reciprocate, with three notable exceptions: the English apothecary James Petiver cited the Caterpillar Book numerous times in his *Musei Pevieriani* of 1695; the English botanist John Ray, in the epilogue to his *Historia insectorum* of 1710, referred his readers to Merian's 'elegantly engraved' insects in *Metamorphosis*; and Johann Christoph Volkamer referred to *Metamorphosis* and/or Merian multiple times in his *Nürnbergische Hesperides* (1708–14).[27] Even in these instances, however, Merian did not receive the effusive treatment reserved for the other 'learned'

and 'knowledgeable' male authors towards whom the authors felt deeply indebted.

The anonymous author of the note that opens this section said that Merian's caterpillar books were 'insignificant' and that *Metamorphosis* amounted to 'expensive prints'.[28] Given the location where the note was found, we can assume that the author was well known in the expert botanical circle surrounding the Amsterdam medical garden. It is difficult to imagine a more dismissive reception from a class of individuals that positioned itself at the top of the hierarchy of natural knowledge production, validation and dissemination.

By the middle of the seventeenth century, the young discipline had become increasingly institutionalised.[29] Experiments and discussions moved away from the domestic space and into the scientific academies and universities. A lack of formal education (women in Northern Europe could not enrol in university), the impossibility of becoming a member of scientific academies (at least in London, Paris, St Petersburg and Vienna), and general lack of Latin, the universal tongue of scientific inquiry, effectively pushed early modern women to the periphery of the creation and dissemination of natural knowledge.

Merian could not afford to publish *Metamorphosis* without first raising some funds, which she did by selling advance subscriptions (see Chapter 3). Part of Merian's success in England was undoubtedly attributable to James Petiver's membership of the Royal Society. Petiver was in a position to share early proofs and draft text from *Metamorphosis* with other members, which would have contributed to the demand for the work, and served to legitimise it.[30]

The use of language in the advertisement placed by Petiver in the *Philosophical Transactions*, reproduced in part in Chapter 3, however, confirms Merian's status as an outsider of the institution. In particular, Petiver refers to Merian as a 'Curious' person, which connotes her devotion to the promulgation of empirical knowledge. The term derives from the adjective, which denotes 'the mental disposition of being careful, assiduous, and inquisitive'.[31] The designation of Merian as a curious person was therefore not, in and of itself, gendered. Indeed, the masculine and plural forms of the adjective, *Curieux*, were used frequently during the same period, as an alternative to the noun *liefhebbers*, translated alternatively as *virtuoso*, amateur, lover of art.[32] Generally, referring to someone as a *curieux* meant that they were learned, albeit not professionals, in a given field.[33] The implied gendering (and attendant diminution) of Merian's achievement, however, becomes clear when one compares this advertisement with an account of the book *Paradisus Batavus* by Paul Hermann, the Director of the Leiden botanical garden, in the same publication a few years earlier:

> The learned and much celebrated Herbalist Dr. Paul Hermans, Author of this Work, whose Name alone is sufficient to recommend it to the ingenious Reader, designed therein to give us the History of such rare and non-descript Plants, as well European as Indian, as were cultivated either in publick Physick-Gardens, or those of private curious Persons, in and about Holland [. . .] All that I shall or need say of this Piece is, That the Descriptions are very accurate, and sufficient alone to lead us into a certain and unerring Knowledge of the Plants described [. . .][34]

The book produced by Hermann, although focused solely on plants, is similar to *Metamorphosis*, consisting of descriptions and illustrations. Both works offered information heretofore unknown regarding exotic specimens. Yet, Merian is described as a 'Curious Person', while Hermann is 'learned'. Hermann's name alone, the reader is told, is sufficient to recommend his book. In Merian's case, Petiver suggests that the public should encourage the author for a work so diligently and capably performed. Hermann offered 'certain and unerring Knowledge';

Merian offered rare insects admirably engraved and a work 'highly approved of' by unnamed persons.

Although Hermann occupied a high-profile position and was formally educated, the type of language used to promote his book was also used in cases of self-taught men operating outside of formal institutions. These include Antonie van Leeuwenhoek (1632–1723), known for his pioneering work in microscopy. Van Leeuwenhoek worked primarily in the textile industry and was largely self-taught; he did not write a book, nor did he write in Latin.[35] Yet, he became a Fellow of the Royal Society and his letters were frequently published in the *Philosophical Transactions*. Upon his death, he bequeathed his microscopes and cabinets of curiosities to the Royal Society, which acknowledged his contributions: 'Discoveries; they are so numerous as to make up a considerable Part of the *Philosophical Transactions* [. . .] And of such Consequence, as to have opened entirely new Scenes in some Parts of Natural Philosophy.'[36]

Discoveries, consequence, certain knowledge: none of these terms were applied to Merian or to her work by the formal institutions of natural history or by their members. In fact, her work as a naturalist only featured twice in the *Philosophical Transactions* during the eighteenth century, in addition to the advertisement placed by Petiver: once in reference to a certain type of cockroach that she had identified, and once more when a Fellow of the Society referred to Merian's description of a 'frog-fish' in order to buttress his identification of a slightly different specimen.[37] Neither Merian nor her work received a mention in the *Mémoires de l'Académie Royale des Sciences*, located in Paris. Merian remained an outsider, notwithstanding the diligence and devotion she brought to her subject, her commitment to empiricism and her careful observations. She was admired as a 'Curious Person' and as an artist, but was not considered a full participant in the creation and dissemination of natural knowledge, at least not insofar as her masculine professional contemporaries were concerned.

Merian's Afterlife

Within a few years of the publication of *Metamorphosis*, James Petiver published his own *South-Sea Herbal* (1715). On the first page there appeared a list of 'Books, Tracks &c. Published by the Author'. That list included 'Madam Merian's History of Surinam Insects, abbreviated and methodized, with some Remarks on them'. With this, Petiver telegraphed to his readers that he had improved Merian's *Metamorphosis*. By naming himself as publisher and including the title as part of a list of his own works, he presumed to give the work a veneer of legitimacy. In 1767, when James Epson published Petiver's entire body of work as *Jacobi Petiveri Opera*, he included a list of plates and tracks 'which completes all he ever wrote upon Natural History'. Number 112 on that list is Merian's *Surinam Insects*. Within a matter of decades, Merian's masterpiece had been assimilated into the body of work of one of the only men who had cited her earlier work and even promoted her in the *Philosophical Transactions*.

When she departed Amsterdam for St Petersburg after the death of her mother, Graff sold the remaining inventory of Merian's books, the plates for the Caterpillar Book and *Metamorphosis*, as well as the rights to both publications, to the publisher Joannes Oosterwyk. In 1718, Oosterwyk published a Latin version of the three parts of the Caterpillar Book, which he entitled *Erucarum ortus, alimentum et paradoxa metamorphosis*. The book opens on a frontispiece designed by the collector and botanical enthusiast Simon Schijnvoet, who was a member of Merian's network (fig.79). The design features four women dressed in an antique manner, two of whom are observing insects and two of whom personify Nature and Investigation, surrounded by *putti* variously pointing to illustrations and specimens of flowers and insects. The frontispiece is followed by a copy of the portrait made by Gsell, in which Merian is surrounded by her work and instruments (fig.1). By including these illustrations, the *Erucarum ortus* could therefore be understood as an homage to Merian and an effort to continue her legacy. However, unlike parts 1 and 11, which were published by Merian, and part 111, which was published by Graff, the *Erucarum ortus* separated the images from the text, relegating the former to the end of the book. By divorcing the images from their textual context, Oosterwyk fundamentally changed the nature of Merian's work, in which she intended the images to play a critical role.

Oosterwyk went on to publish two editions of *Metamorphosis* in 1719, one in Latin and one in Dutch. In these editions, he added 12 images, some of which do not appear to have been in Merian's hand and whose origins are unclear. As he had done in 1718 for the *Erucarum ortus*, these editions contain a new frontispiece honouring Merian. The frontispiece presents a woman, again dressed in an antique manner, seated at a table and holding flowers between her fingers (fig.80). There are six *putti* holding and pointing to boxes containing insects surrounding her. Various insects, leaves and flowers are strewn about the room. Clearly visible at the woman's feet is a copy of *Metamorphosis*, opened to show the illustration of the pomelo (fig.25) and an illustration with a tarantula (plate 18 in the book). A potted pineapple, immediately behind the open book, likely refers to the first two plates of *Metamorphosis*, which show the fruit from two different perspectives. The room features a wide window that opens onto a Surinamese landscape in which European men converse while enslaved persons and members of the indigenous population work.

The frontispiece, together with the ode to Merian that follows, conveys Oosterwyk's admiration for Merian and his understanding of the importance of her association to the success of the volume. The ode closes by addressing Merian, whose 'spirit and

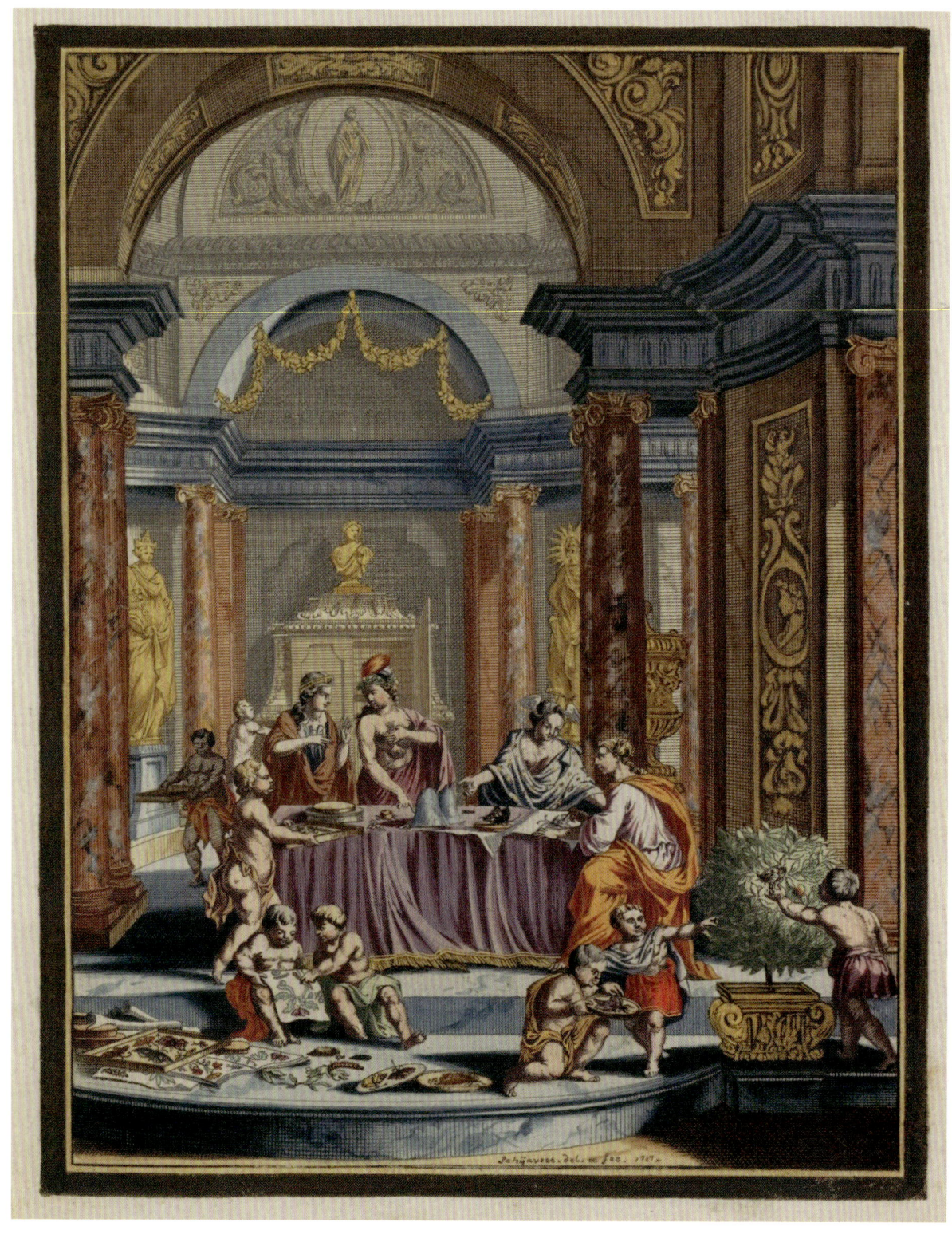

79 Simon Schijnvoet, 'Frontispiece', in Maria Sibylla Merian, *Erucarum ortus, alimentum et paradoxa metamorphosis*, Joannes Oosterwyk, Amsterdam, 1718, printed book, hand-coloured, Allard Pierson, Amsterdam

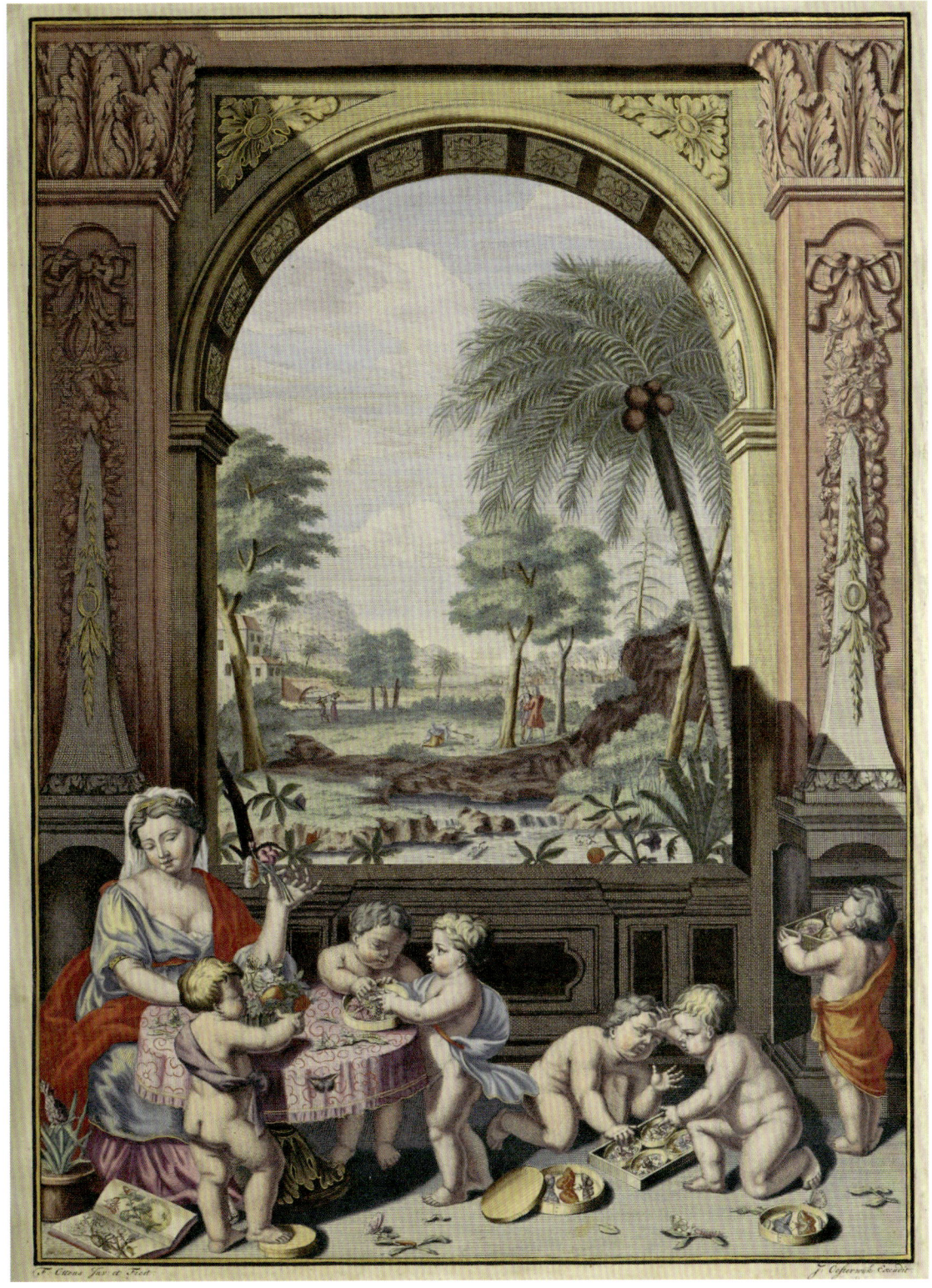

80 F. Ottens, 'Frontispiece', in *Maria Sibylla Meriaen Over de voortteeling en wonderbaerlyke veranderingen der Surinaemsche insecten*, Oosterwyk, Amsterdam, 1719, printed book, hand-coloured, Getty Research Institute, Los Angeles, CA

diligence, free from the gnawing of time, will put her name in everyone's mouth', now that Oosterwyk, 'out of compassion and gratitude for her daughter, has published this work, which will increase Merian's fame.'[38]

Later editions by publishers who bought the plates from Oosterwyk, however, contained no such laudation and, indeed, seem to have become further dissociated from Merian. In 1726, Pierre Gosse, a publisher in The Hague, produced an edition of *Metamorphosis* with French and Latin texts, which he entitled *Dissertatio de generatione et metamorphosibus insectorum surinamensium / Dissertation sur la generation et les insects de Surinam*. Another version in Dutch appeared in 1730 and, in 1771, the Parisian publisher Jacques Desnos issued a three-volume edition of *Metamorphosis* bound with the three parts of the Caterpillar Book in French, which he entitled *Histoire générale des insectes de Surinam et de toute l'Europe*. The formal title of the work explains that it has been 'revised, corrected and considerably expanded by M. Buch'oz'.

Some of the editions of *Metamorphosis* published after Merian's death were luxurious productions, carefully printed using Merian's original designs and then hand-coloured, as is the case with this illustration of a Rocu tree with caterpillars, moths and butterflies, which can only be dated as 1730 or 1771 (fig.81). In revising and altering her work, these publishers took away Merian's intellectual ownership and fundamentally and negatively altered her legacy. They communicated to their readers that the works that had been published by Merian herself were deficient. When readers and commentators consulted these posthumous editions, they were confronted with translations that did not always capture the nuances of Merian's original observations, with shortened descriptions and with images printed from worn plates or else not authored by Merian, and thus of lesser quality. Merian's work remained useful to some naturalists, however, and Carl Linnaeus, whose first edition of *Systema naturae*

appeared in 1735, relied upon it to name approximately 100 species of plants.[39]

As time went on, however, the posthumous editions of Merian's Caterpillar Book and *Metamorphosis* were more readily available than the originals, such that the public was deprived of her complete observations (particularly in the case of the Caterpillar Book) and of the beautiful images that were coloured by her workshop. As found by Kay Etheridge, a number of nineteenth-century writers were openly critical of Merian and of her work, based largely on their consideration of these posthumous editions.[40]

Connoisseurs and bibliophiles, however, continued to value the hand of Merian until at least the end of the eighteenth century. A study of eighteenth-century private libraries and auction catalogues in the Dutch Republic has found that hand-coloured editions of Merian's Book of Flowers, New Book of Flowers, Caterpillar Book and *Metamorphosis* were well represented in the book collections of wealthy owners.[41] The study also found that Merian's name was specifically mentioned on the title page or preface of 15 per cent of the auction catalogues where her books were amongst those sold. This is significant, considering that most auctions offered the works of dozens, if not hundreds, of authors. From this, we can infer that booksellers believed that Merian's name held a special power for potential purchasers long after her death.

Nevertheless, the proliferation of posthumous editions and their wide availability resulted in Merian's publications coming to be regarded as beautiful images without much scientific value. They were largely ignored by entomologists and historians of science until relatively recently, when the role of women in early modern science became an important topic of investigation. Merian did not fare better with art historians. From the foundation of art history as a scholarly discipline in Germany in the mid-nineteenth century through the first half of the twentieth century, Western art historians were not

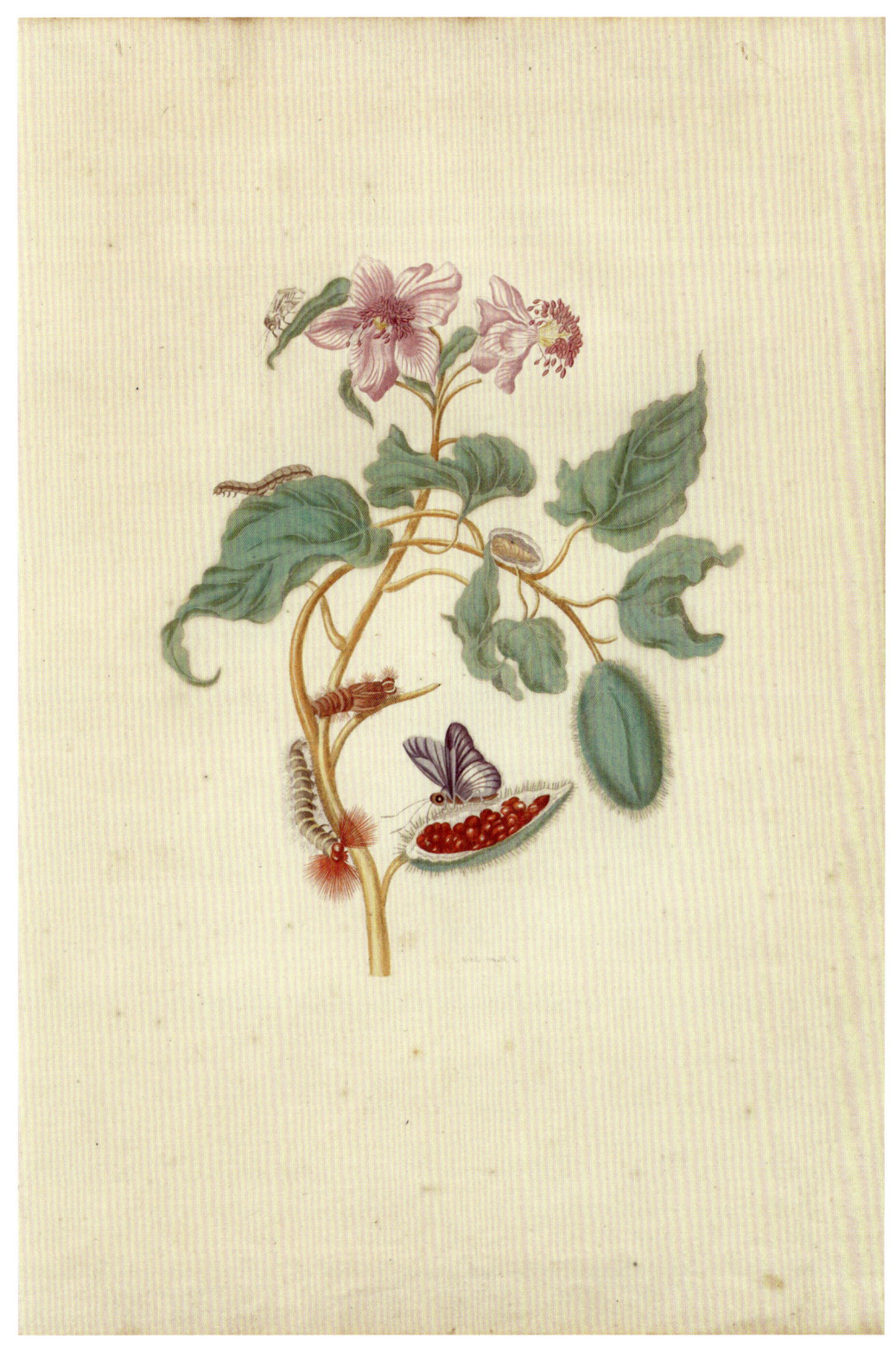

81 Maria Sybilla Merian, *The Rocu Tree with Caterpillars, Moths, and Butterflies*, 1730/71, watercolour, 52.7 × 34.8 cm (20 ¾ × 13 ¾ in), J. Paul Getty Museum, Los Angeles, CA

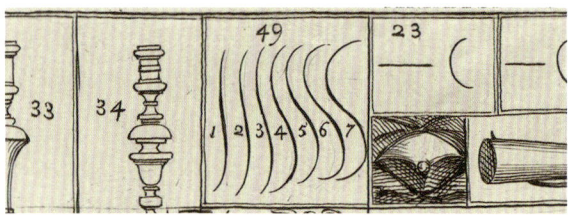

82 William Hogarth, 'The Line of Beauty', in *The Analysis of Beauty: Written with a View of Fixing the Fluctuating Ideas of Taste*, J. Reeves, London, 1753, figure 49, printed book, Metropolitan Museum of Art, New York, NY

interested in her books or her individual watercolours as valuable works of art. The illustration of nature, works in watercolour on paper or parchment, and scientific book illustrations did not fit into the canon of fine arts (architecture, sculpture and painting), and were therefore not the subject of scholarly study unless they were found in ancient or medieval manuscripts. It would take until 1967 for Merian's art to become the focus of public discourse again, when the art historian Elisabeth Rücker published a catalogue of Merian's art on the occasion of an exhibition at the Germanisches Nationalmuseum in Nuremberg.[42]

THE GREATEST COMPLIMENT

A common cliché holds that copying is the greatest compliment anyone can offer. In early modernity, the training of any visual artist, whether in Rembrandt's workshop or in art academies, included copying the work of the great artists who have come before, and emulating their teacher. Merian's illustrations served a similar purpose for a number of artists, naturalists including James Petiver, and artist-naturalists.

Merian's most direct successor was her elder daughter, Johanna Helena Herolt. As discussed in Chapter 4, Herolt's work is frequently so close to that

of her mother that it is difficult to make attributions. Other artists in the network that comprised Merian and Agnes Block, such as Alida Withoos, Maria Moninckx and Jan Moninckx, show her influence as well. This is particularly evident in the use of pronounced s-curves in the stems of plants, which exaggerate those found in nature. The s-curve, known to artists as 'the line of beauty' after William Hogarth's work (fig.82), was certainly not Merian's invention and had been used by artists earlier. It was she, however, who began using it in a pronounced way in illustrations of plants and flowers which, considering Leonhard Fuchs's directions for the correct illustration of nature (discussed in Chapter 2), was noteworthy. This is visible, for example, in her illustration of a flesh-coloured rose, included in part 1 of the Caterpillar Book (fig.83). The same marked s-curve is present in Alida Withoos's orange tiger lily (fig.84).

The spirit of Merian's art also emanates from the works of the Nuremberg artist Barbara Regina Dietzsch (1706–83). As the New Book of Flowers and part 1 of the Caterpillar Book were published and printed in Nuremberg, it is likely that Dietzsch may have had access to them. Indeed, a number of her illustrations have precedents in those early Merian works. This is the case, for example, with her depiction of a wallflower with an insect (fig.85). A similar wallflower is included in the second part of the New Book of Flowers (fig.86), as well as in part 1 of the Caterpillar Book (fig.87). It is undeniably the case that, to a certain extent, all illustrations of wallflowers will share similarities, as they depict the same flower. Dietzsch's image, however, shows more than a passing resemblance to those by Merian. The inclusion of an insect on the left-hand side, of unopened buds at the crest of the flower, and of a front-facing, open flower in the centre of the illustration, among other similarities, are all examples of the derivative use of Merian's printed illustrations.

Perhaps not surprisingly, given the collection of her works by the likes of James Petiver and Hans

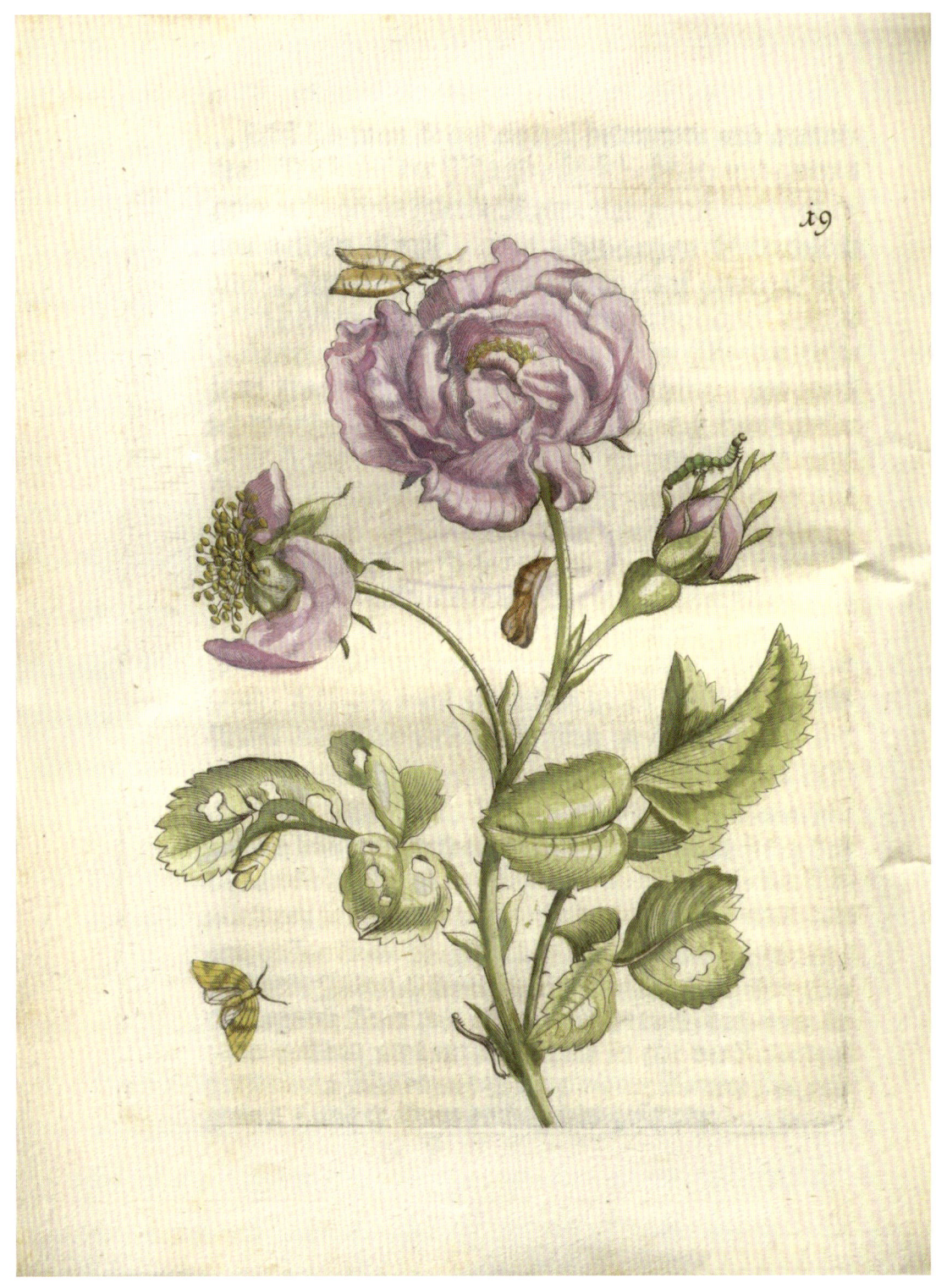

83 Maria Sibylla Merian, 'Flesh-Coloured Rose', in *Der Raupen wunderbare*, part 1, Johann Andreas Graff,
Nuremberg, 1679, plate 19, printed book, hand-coloured, Universitätsbibliothek Johann Christian Senckenberg,
Frankfurt am Main

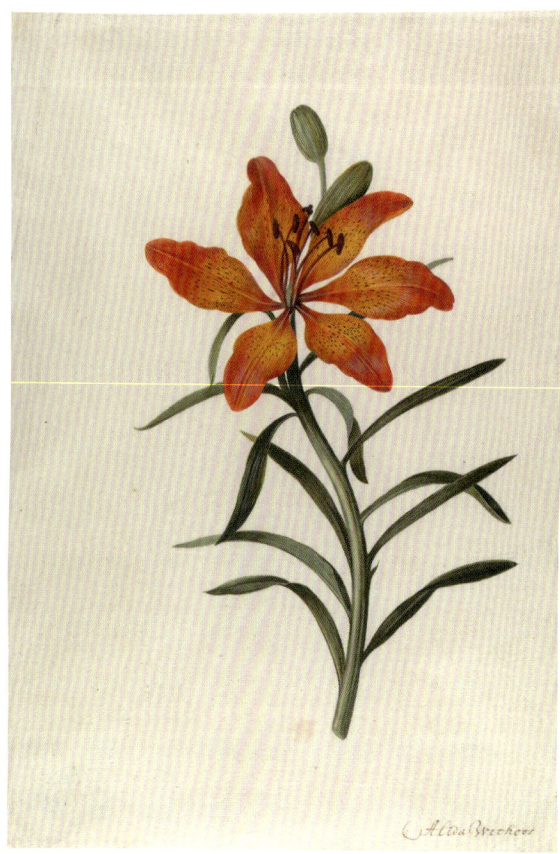
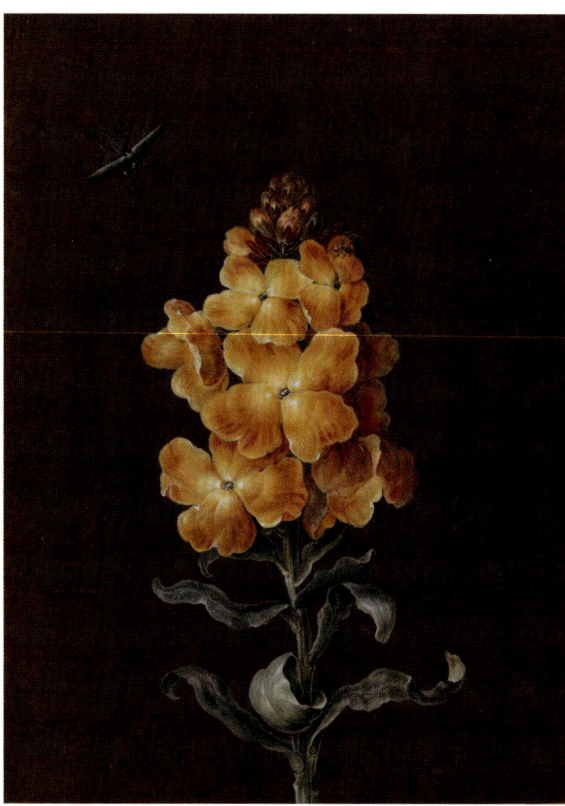

84 Alida Withoos, *Tiger Lily*, *c.*1680–1701, watercolour on paper, 37 × 24.3 cm (14 ⅝ × 9 ⅝ in), Amsterdam Museum, Amsterdam

85 Barbara Regina Dietzsch, *Yellow Wallflower with Insect*, undated, watercolour on parchment, 28.8 × 20.5 cm (11 ⅜ × 8 ⅛ in), Germanisches Nationalmuseum, Nuremberg

Sloane, Merian's influence is also clear in the works of the English naturalist Mark Catesby (1683–1749). We know that Sloane, who owned at least 251 watercolours by Merian, made his collection of albums with illustrations available for consultation to those who were interested, including Catesby.[43] Catesby was a self-taught artist; his two-volume *Natural History of Carolina, Florida, and the Bahama Islands* (1731–43) is extensively illustrated, although some of the illustrations were borrowed from George Ehret.

Catesby's illustrations are not nearly as artistically sophisticated as Merian's. In her footsteps, however, he depicted birds, amphibians, reptiles and insects with elements from their habitat and source of food. His illustration of a green lizard of Jamaica, from the second volume of the *Natural History*, for example, includes a branch of logwood on which are depicted leaves (front and back), and flowers in various stages of bloom (fig.88). Like the descriptions that accompany Merian's Caterpillar Book and *Metamorphosis*, his

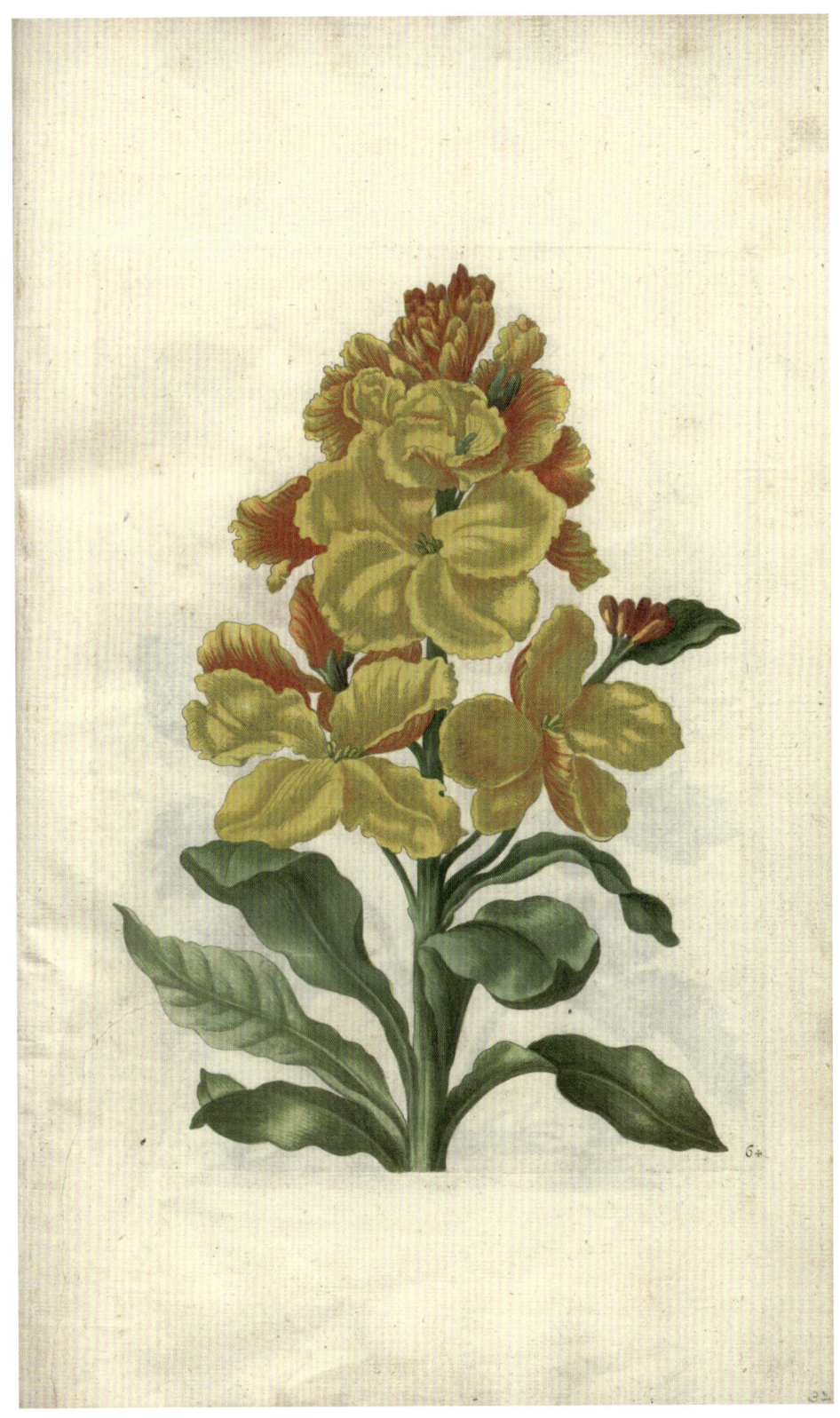

86 Maria Sibylla Merian, 'Wallflower', in *Neues Blumenbuch*, part 11, Johannes Andreas Graff,
Nuremberg, 1680 (originally published 1677), printed book, hand-coloured, Sächsische
Landesbibliothek – Staats- und Universitätsbibliothek (SLUB), Dresden

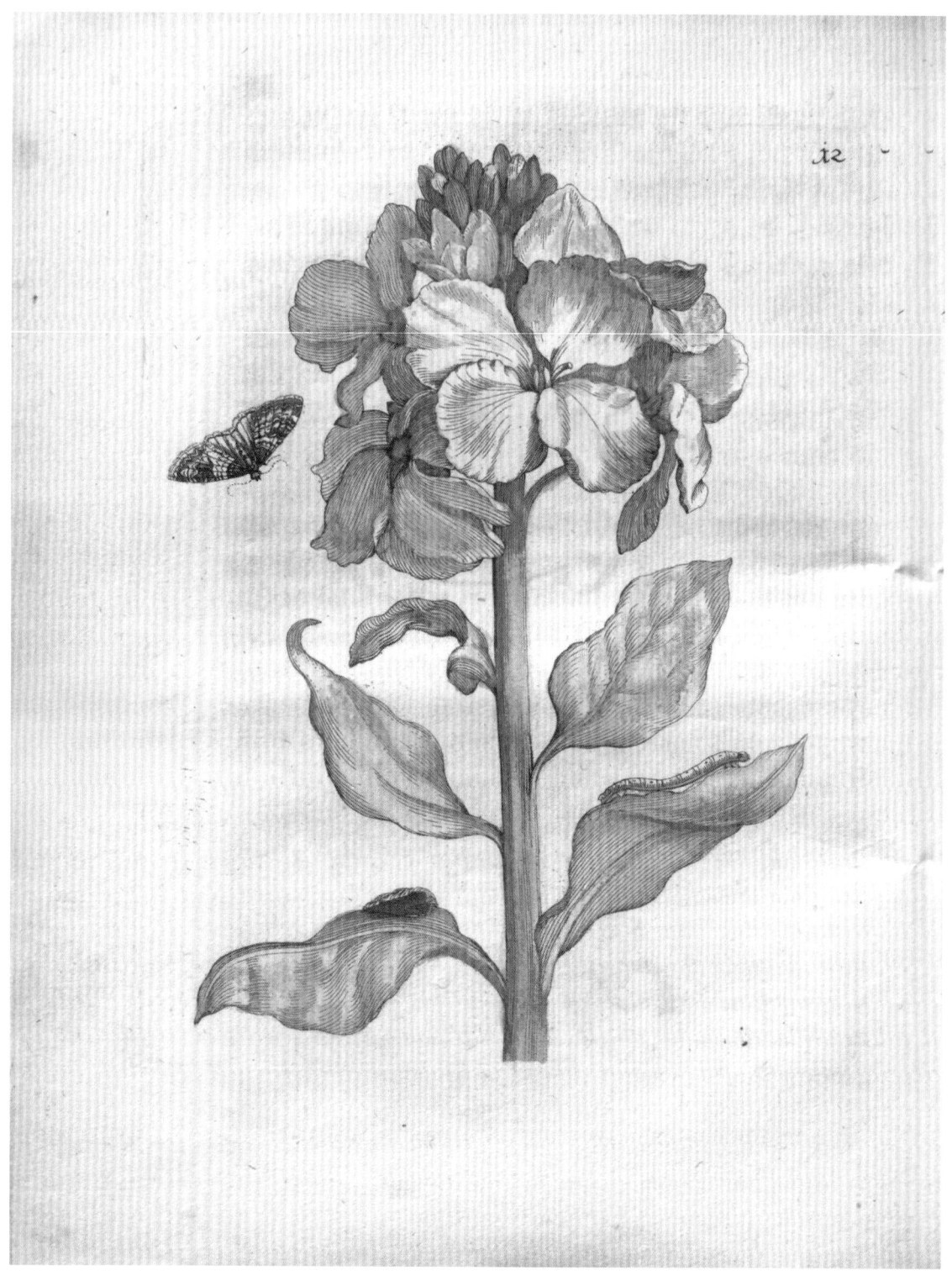

87 Maria Sibylla Merian, 'Wallflower with Insects', in *Der Raupen wunderbare*, part 1, Johann Andreas Graff,
   Nuremberg, 1679, plate 12, printed book, hand-coloured, Universitätsbibliothek Johann Christian Senckenberg,
   Frankfurt am Main

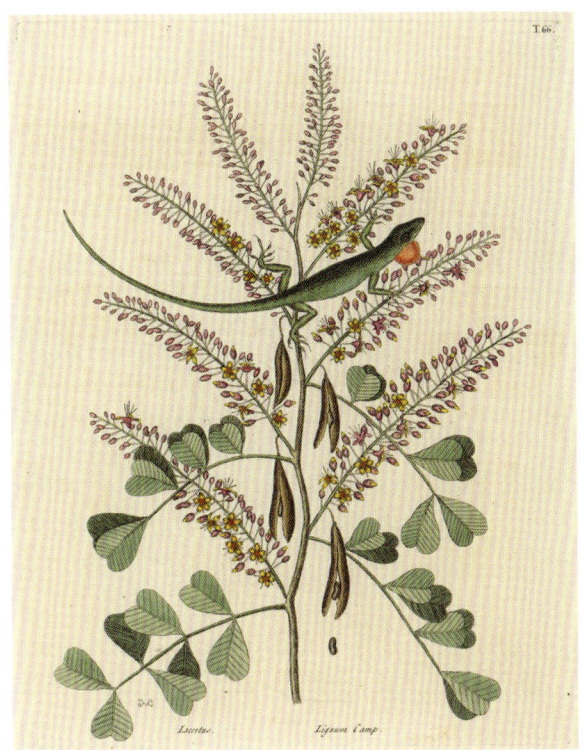
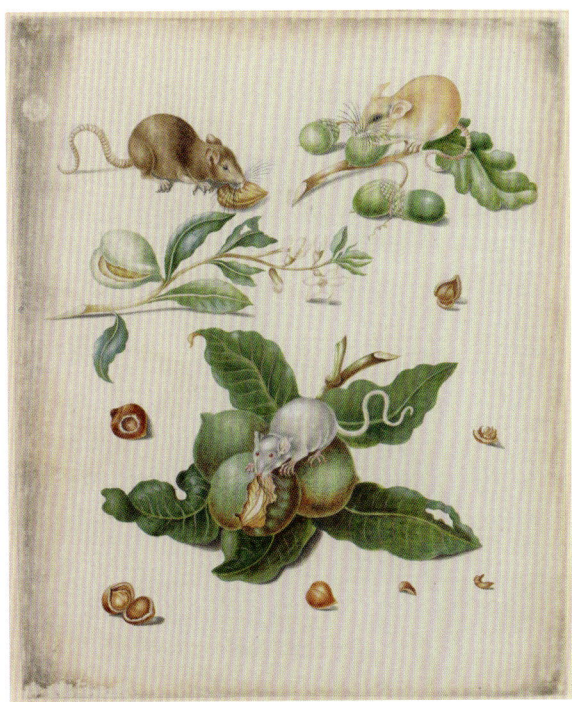

88 Mark Catesby, 'The Green Lizard of Jamaica', in *Natural History of Carolina, Florida, and the Bahama Islands*, vol.11, London, for the author, 1743, plate 66, printed book, hand-coloured, National Gallery, Washington, DC

89 Anonymous (currently attributed to Johanna Helena Herolt), *Three Mice with Hazelnut Branches*, eighteenth century, watercolour on parchment, 36.5 × 29.4 cm (14⅜ × 11⅝ in), Fondation Custodia, Paris

account of the lizard notes its colour (bright green with a red throat-flap), and the nature of his observation.

Withoos, Maria and Jan Moninckx, Dietzsch and Catesby were not the only ones whose work reflects the influence of and innovations by Merian. Her works marked a shift in the illustration of nature, for artists and naturalists alike, and her compositions and ecological, iconographic framework are pervasive in the art of natural history that came after her.

Perhaps the greatest compliment that can be paid to Merian, however, is to be found in the countless numbers of unnamed artists who have reproduced her works as exactly as possible in the decades and

centuries since her death. One such artist, probably working in the late eighteenth or early nineteenth century, reproduced a work that was painted both by Herolt (fig.60) and by Merian and Herolt together (fig.59): three mice with branches of hazelnuts (fig.89). The quality of the work is found wanting in certain areas, for example, in the handling of colour and shadows and in the faces of the mice, yet this copy of a favourite composition and subject matter of the workshop is a testament to Merian's lasting appeal.

Epilogue

We live at a time when understanding and reassessing the nature of the relationship between humans and the environment has reached an unprecedented level of urgency. Unimaginable until recently, plant life is now the subject not only of scientific inquiry, but also of the humanities. The appeal for collective environmental awareness, protection and sustainability echoes worldwide, as does the need to embrace and preserve whatever nature we can.

The pursuit of nature in Merian's time and place was of a different order, driven by curiosity, the thirst for knowledge and the promise of economic supremacy.[1] In the province of Holland, intensive land reclamation operations drove out the sea to create additional landmass, needed for a growing population. The Dutch Republic had achieved primacy in trade and was engaged in aggressive colonial expansion.[2] There was a palpable sense that one could possess nature – one dried blowfish, one coral branch, one pineapple at a time.[3]

While they may not be immediately obvious, there are several parallels between our world in crisis and the one inhabited by Merian and her daughters. Throughout the seventeenth century and beyond, corporations such as the Dutch East India Company, interested in expansion and the accumulation of natural resources, circumnavigated the globe, laying waste to waterways, forests and fields, picking, ploughing and plundering for the benefit of a wealthy merchant class in Amsterdam.[4] Not that life in the Republic was easy: international conflicts were a constant threat and, as a result of what is now known as the 'Little Ice Age', ruined crops and frozen canals made life challenging at best.[5]

Yet it is at that moment that the art of nature became more popular than ever before – just as it is once again today. Contemporary artists are reinvigorating landscape painting. Scholars are re-examining early *florilegia* and treatises of natural history to crack early modern recipes and remedies and learn about colour-making processes. Works like those of Merian and her daughters are now highly valuable at auction and are entering public collections. *Metamorphosis* and part 1 of the Caterpillar Book have been reproduced as facsimiles. Between September 2021 and December 2023, the works of Merian and her daughters have been shown in major exhibitions in Amsterdam, Baltimore, Hamburg, Los Angeles and Madrid.

These exhibitions and the ongoing scholarship provide us with new ways to understand and appreciate the art of Maria Sibylla Merian. They may also provide us with new ways to think about nature and, through art, our relationship with it. With Merian's exquisite watercolours as mediators, we may hope to regain our sense of curiosity and wonder at the incredible richness and diversity of plant and animal life, and to appreciate its ephemerality.

Notes

All of Merian's letters have been transcribed by the Maria Sibylla Merian Society, with a summary translation, at https://www.themariasibyllameriansociety.humanities.uva.nl.

INTRODUCTION

1   Lieke van Deinsen, 'Marketing Merian. The Visual Branding of the Late Female Naturalist', in Bert van de Roemer, Florence Pieters, Hans Mulder, Kay Etheridge and Marieke van Delft (eds), *Maria Sibylla Merian: Changing the Nature of Art and Science*, Lannoo, Tielt, 2022, pp 215–25, on pp 215–17.

2   Janice Neri, *The Insect and the Image: Visualizing Nature in Early Modern Europe, 1500–1700*, University of Minnesota Press, Minneapolis, MN, 2011, p.141. The expression 'undivided territory' comes from the essay of the same title by Erik Jorink and Bart Ramakers, 'Undivided Territory: "Art" and "Science" in the Early Modern Netherlands', in Eric Jorink and Bart Ramakers (eds), *Art and Science in the Early Modern Netherlands, Netherlands Yearbook for History of Art*, vol.61, W. Books, Zwolle, 2011, pp 6–32.

3   https://www.themariasibyllameriansociety.humanities.uva.nl/.

4   www.merianin.de.

5   Elisabeth Rücker, *Maria Sibylla Merian 1647–1717*, exh.cat., Germanisches Nationalmuseum, Nuremberg, 1967.

6   Ann Sutherland Harris and Linda Nochlin, *Women Artists, 1550–1950*, exh.cat., Random House and Los Angeles County Museum of Art, Los Angeles, CA, 1976, p.366.

7   Katlijne van der Stighelen, Mirjam Westen, Koninklijk Museum voor Schone Kunsten and Museum voor Moderne Kunst Arnhem, *A chacun sa grâce*, Flammarion, Ludion, 1999, pp 186–7.

8   Sam Segal, 'Maria Sibylla Merian as a Flower Painter', in Kurt Wettengl (ed.), *Maria Sibylla Merian 1657–1717: Artist and Naturalist*, Gerd Hatje, Ostfildern-Ruit, 1998, pp 68–87, on p.86.

9   Carin Grabowski, *Maria Sibylla Merian Zwischen Malerei und Naturforschung*, Reimer, Berlin, 2017.

10 For example, Catherine Powell-Warren, *Gender and Self-Fashioning at the Intersection of Art and Science: Agnes Block, Botany, and Networks in the Dutch Seventeenth Century*, Amsterdam University Press, Amsterdam, 2023; Babette Bohn, *Women Artists, Their Patrons, and Their Publics in Early Modern Bologna*, Pennsylvania State University Press, University Park, PA, 2021; Adelina Modesti, *Women's Patronage and Gendered Cultural Networks in Early Modern Europe: Vittoria della Rovere, Grand Duchess of Tuscany*, Routledge, London, 2020.

11 Andrea Pearson, 'Gender, Sexuality, and the Future of Agency Studies in Northern Art, 1400–1600', *Journal of Historians of Netherlandish Art*, vol.15, no.2, Summer 2023, pp 1–41, on p.18.

I THE ARC OF A PERIPATETIC CAREER

1. Christening of Maria Sibylla Merianin, Taufbücher (Christening Records), Frankfurt 10 (1642–7), fol.292ᵛ. Reproduced at www.merianin.de/home/archivalien.

2. Natalie Zemon Davis, *Women on the Margins: Three Seventeenth-Century Lives*, Harvard University Press, Cambridge, MA, 1997, p.142.

3. Kurt Wettengl, 'Between Frankfurt and Surinam', in Kurt Wettengl (ed.), *Maria Sibylla Merian 1657–1717: Artist and Naturalist*, Gerd Hatje, Ostfildern-Ruit, 1998, pp 12–35, on p.15.

4. Elizabeth S. Cohen and Margaret Reeves (eds), *The Youth of Early Modern Women*, Amsterdam University Press, Amsterdam, 2018.

5. Thea Vignau-Wilberg, *Joris and Jacob Hoefnagel: Art and Science around 1600*, Hatje Cantz, Berlin, 2017; Carin Grabowski, *Maria Sibylla Merian Zwischen Malerei und Naturforschung*, Reimer, Berlin, 2017, pp 29–32.

6. Arnold Houbraken, *De Groote schouburgh der Nederlantsche konstschilders en schilderessen*, Widow of the author, Amsterdam, 1721, vol.III, p.220.

7. Wettengl, 'Between Frankfurt and Surinam', p.17.

8. Clare Crowston, 'Women, Gender, and Guilds in Early Modern Europe: An Overview of Recent Research', *International Review of Social History*, vol.53, 2008, pp 19–44; Anna Bellavitis, *Women's Work and Rights in Early Modern Urban Europe*, Palgrave Macmillan/Springer Nature, Cham, 2018, pp 43–56.

9. A term I borrow from Ariadne Schmidt, 'The Profits of Unpaid Work. "Assisting Labour" of Women in the Early Modern Urban Dutch Economy', *The History of the Family*, vol.19, no.3, 2014, pp 301–22.

10. Sam Segal, 'Maria Sibylla Merian as a Flower Painter', in Wettengl (ed.), *Maria Sibylla Merian*, pp 68–87, on p.69; Grabowski, *Maria Sibylla Merian*, pp 33–5.

11. Heidrun Ludwig, 'Nürnberger Blumenmalerinnen un 1700: zwischen Dilettantismus und Professionalität', *Kritische Berichte*, vol.4, 1996, pp 21–9; Hans Bösch, *Die Nürnberger Maler, ihre Lehrlinge, Probestücke, Vorgeher u.s.w. von 1596–1659*, no publisher, Nuremberg, 1899.

12. Stadtarchiv Nürnberg, Handwerksarchiv / Maler (reichsstädtische Zeit), ref.no.E 5/43.

13. Jeffrey Chipps Smith, *Nuremberg, a Renaissance City, 1500–1618*, exh.cat., University of Texas Press, Austin, TX,1983, pp 3–16.

14. Manfred H. Grieb, *Nürnberger Künstlerlexikon Bildende Künstler Kunsthandwerker Gelehrte Sammler Kulturschaffende Und Mäzene Vom 12. Bis Zur Mitte Des 20. Jahrhunderts*, vol.1, A–G, Saur, Munich, 2007, pp 499–500; Margot Lölhöffel, 'Johann Andreas Graff. Forgotten Artist and Partner of Maria Sibylla Merian for Twenty Years', in Bert van de Roemer, Florence Pieters, Hans Mulder, Kay Etheridge and Marieke van Delft (eds), *Maria Sibylla Merian: Changing the Nature of Art and Science*, Lannoo, Tielt, 2022, pp 52–62, on pp 52–5.

15. Smith, *Nuremberg, a Renaissance City*, Introduction; Hans Bien, *Bird's Eye View of Nuremberg*, c.1630, original paper on canvas, pen and ink drawing, coloured, scale about 1:2900, 48 × 66.6 cm (18 ⅞ × 26 ¼ in), Nuremberg City Archives, A4, plan collection 517/4.

16. Lölhöffel, 'Johann Andreas Graff', p.58.

17. Frima Fox Hofrichter, 'An Intimate Look at Baroque Women Artists: Birth, Babies, and Biography', in Rosalynn Voaden and Diane Wolfthal (eds), *Framing the Family: Narrative and Representations in the Medieval and Early Modern Periods*, Arizona Center for Medieval and Renaissance Studies, Tempe, AZ, 2005, pp 139–58.

18. Letters from Merian to Clara Regina Imhoff: Nuremberg, 25 July 1682; Nuremberg, 24 March 1683; Frankfurt am Main, 8 December 1684; Frankfurt am Main, 8 May 1685; Frankfurt am Main, 3 June 1685; Amsterdam, 27 August 1697.

19. Margot Lölhöffel, 'Erster Teil. Maria Sibylla Merianin und Johann Andreas Graff. Gemeinsames und Trennendes', *Nürnberger Altstadtberichte*, vol.40, 2015, pp 37–76.

20. Maria Sibylla Merian, ed. Wolf-Dietrich Beer, *Schmetterlinge, Käfer und andere Insekten: Leningrader Studienbuch*, 2 vols, Edition Leipzig, Leipzig, 1976, vol.1, p.221.

21. Kim Todd, *Chrysalis: Maria Sibylla Merian and the Secrets of Metamorphosis*, Harcourt, New York, 2007, pp 67, 73.

22. Tomomi Kinukawa, 'Natural History as Entrepreneurship: Maria Sibylla Merian's

Correspondence with J.G. Volkamer II and James Petiver', *Archives of Natural History*, vol.38, no.2, 2011, pp 313–27.

23   Merian to Johann Georg Volkamer, Amsterdam, 8 October 1702. Translation my own.

24   Merian to Johann Georg Volkamer, Amsterdam, 16 April 1705.

25   Lölhöffel, 'Johann Andreas Graff', p.55.

26   Trevor Saxby, *The Quest for the New Jerusalem, Jean de Labadie and the Labadists, 1610–1744*, Nijhoff, Dordrecht, 1987.

27   Todd, *Chrysalis*, p.93.

28   Johann Gabriel Doppelmayr, *Historische Nachricht von den Nürnbergischen Mathematicis und Künstlern* [...], 1730. Transcribed and translated by Renate Ell, Frau Ludwig, Katharina Schmidt-Loske and Brigitte Wirth and reproduced by the Maria Sibylla Merian Society, at https://www.themariasibyllameriansociety.humanities.uva.nl.

29   Johann Andreas Graff, *Ground Plan of the Famous Estate in Wieuwarden*, c.1686, coloured pen and brush drawing, 33.7 × 42 cm (13 ¼ × 16 ½ in), Staatsarchiv Nürnberg, Handschriftliche Karten, inv.no.212, 1686; Elisabeth Rücker, *Maria Sibylla Merian 1647–1717. Ihr Wirken in Deutschland und Holland*, Nachbarn 24, Kgl. Niederländischen Botschaft, Bonn, 1980, p.15.

30   Grieb, *Nürnberger Künstlerlexikon*, pp 499–500.

31   Lorraine Daston and Katharine Park, *Wonders and the Order of Nature: 1150–1750*, Zone Books, New York, 2001, p.215; see also Claudia Swan, *Rarities of These Lands: Art, Trade, and Diplomacy in the Dutch Republic*, Princeton University Press, Princeton, NJ, 2021, pp xii and 17; and Marisa Anne Bass, Anne Goldgar, Hanneke Grootenboer and Claudia Swan (eds), *Conchophilia: Shells, Art, and Curiosity in Early Modern Europe*, Princeton University Press, Princeton, NJ, 2021.

32   Claudia Swan, 'Dutch Diplomacy and Trade in *Rariteyten*: Episodes in the History of Material Culture of the Dutch Republic', in Zoltán Biedermann, Anne Gerritsen and Giorgio Riello (eds), *Global Gifts: The Material Culture of Diplomacy in Early Modern Eurasia*, Cambridge University Press, Cambridge, 2018, pp 171–97, on p.196.

33   *Amsterdamsche Courant*, 21 November 1684, no.47.

34   Martha C. Howell, 'Michaelina Wautier and Working Women in Early-Modern Europe', in Katlijne van der Stighelen, Gerlinde Gruber, Martha C. Howell, Jahel Sanzsalazar, Francesca Del Torre Scheuch, Ben van Beneden and Martine van Elk, *Michaelina Wautier, 1604–1689: Glorifying a Forgotten Talent*, exh.cat., Rubenshuis, Antwerp, and BAI, Kontich, 2018, pp 100–119, on p.102.

35   Davis, *Women on the Margins*, p.166.

36   Martha Moffitt Peacock, *Joanna Koerten*, Lund Humphries, London, forthcoming.

37   Translation by Florence Pieters and Bert van de Roemer, in their chapter 'In Search of Friendship. Maria Sibylla Merian's Traces in Friendship Albums (*alba amicorum*)', in Van de Roemer et al. (eds), *Maria Sibylla Merian*, pp 74–86, on p.86.

38   Procuration by Maria Sibylla Merian in favour of Jacob Hendrik Herolt and Michiel van Musscher, 23 April 1699, notary Samuel Wijmer, Stadsarchief Amsterdam, Notarial archives 5075, inv.4830, doc.49, pp 186–7.

39   Eveline Sint Nicolaas, Valika Smeulders, Maria Holtrop, Stephanie Archangel, Lisa Lambrechts, Karwan Fatah-Black and Martine Gosselink, *Slavery: The Story of João, Wally, Oopjen, Paulus, Van Bengalen, Surapati, Sapali, Tula, Dirk, Lohkay*, Rijksmuseum and Atlas Contact, Amsterdam, 2021, pp 86–8.

40   Marieke van Delft, 'Maria Sibylla Merian and the People of Suriname', in Van de Roemer et al. (eds), *Maria Sibylla Merian*, pp 118–30, on p.123.

41   ibid., pp 120–27.

42   Merian to Johann Georg Volkamer, Amsterdam, 8 October 1702. Translation my own.

43   ibid.

44   'Timeline', in Van de Roemer et al. (eds), *Maria Sibylla Merian*, pp 8–12.

45   Todd, *Chrysalis*, p.223.

2 THE ART OF NATURE IN PRINT:
MERIAN'S EARLY BOOKS

1   Kay Etheridge, *The Flowering of Ecology: Maria Sibylla Merian's Caterpillar Book*, Brill, Leiden, 2021, p.130.

2   ibid., pp 134–6.

3   Andrew Griebeler, 'Production and Design of Early

Illustrated Herbals', *Word & Image*, vol.38, no.2, 2022, pp 104–22, on p.104; Wilfrid Blunt and William T. Stearn, *The Art of Botanical Illustration*, revised edn, ACC Art Books, Woodbridge, 2021, pp 31–42.

4   Griebeler, 'Production and Design of Early Illustrated Herbals', pp 104–14.

5   Stephen A. Harris, *The Beauty of the Flower: The Art and Science of Botanical Illustration*, Reaktion, London, 2023, p.71.

6   Jaya Remond, 'Drawing in the Tropics. Maria Sibylla Merian's and Charles Plumier's Pictures of Caribbean Nature', in Bert van de Roemer, Florence Pieters, Hans Mulder, Kay Etheridge and Marieke van Delft (eds), *Maria Sibylla Merian: Changing the Nature of Art and Science*, Lannoo, Tielt, 2022, pp 184–94, on p.184.

7   Sachiko Kusukawa, *Picturing the Book of Nature: Image, Text, and Argument in Sixteenth-Century Human Anatomy and Medical Botany*, University of Chicago Press, Chicago, IL, 2012, p.3; see also Sarah Neville, *Early Modern Herbals and the Book Trade: English Stationers and the Commodification of Botany*, Cambridge University Press, Cambridge, 2022, pp 53–122; and Claudia Swan, 'Illustrated Natural History', in Susan Dackerman, Harvard Art Museums and Mary and Leigh Block Museum of Art, *Prints and the Pursuit of Knowledge in Early Modern Europe*, exh.cat., Harvard Art Museums, Distributed by Yale University Press, Cambridge, MA, 2011, pp 186–99.

8   Sachiko Kusukawa, 'The Use of Pictures in the Formation of Learned Knowledge: The Cases of Leonhard Fuchs and Andreas Vesalius', in Sachiko Kusukawa and Ian Maclean (eds), *Transmitting Knowledge: Words, Images, and Instruments in Early Modern Europe*, Oxford University Press, Oxford, 2006, pp 73–96, on p.77.

9   Meghan C. Doherty, *Engraving Accuracy in Early Modern England: Visual Communication and the Royal Society*, Amsterdam University Press, Amsterdam, 2022, p.29; Lorraine Daston, 'Epistemic Images', in Alida Payne (ed.), *Vision and Its Instruments: Art, Science, and Technology in Early Modern Europe*, Pennsylvania State University Press, University Park, PA, 2015, pp 13–35, on p.17.

10   Doherty, *Engraving Accuracy*, pp 13–14.

11   Catherine Powell-Warren, *Gender and Self-Fashioning at the Intersection of Art and Science: Agnes Block, Botany, and Networks in the Dutch Seventeenth Century*, Amsterdam University Press, Amsterdam, 2023, pp 216–17.

12   Claudia Swan, '*Ad vivum, Naer het leven*, From the Life: Defining a Mode of Representation', *Word & Image*, vol.11, no.4, October–December 1995, pp 353–72, on p.364.

13   Pamela H. Smith, 'Art, Science, and Visual Culture in Early Modern Europe', *Isis*, vol.97, no.1, March 2006, pp 83–100, on p.91.

14   Jaya Remond, 'The Pictorial Idioms of Nature: Image Making as Phytographic Translation in Early Modern Northern Europe', in Katja Krause, Maria Auxent and Dror Weil (eds), *Premodern Experience of the Natural World in Translation*, Routledge, New York, 2023, pp 273–96.

15   Brian Ogilvie, *The Science of Describing: Natural History in Renaissance Europe*, University of Chicago Press, Chicago, IL, 2008, pp 12–13; Swan, '*Ad vivum*', p.354; Robert Felfe, '*Naer het leven*: Between Image-Generating Techniques and Aesthetic Mediation', in Thomas Balfe, Joanna Woodall and Claus Zittel (eds), *Ad vivum? Visual Materials and the Vocabulary of Life-Likeness in Europe before 1800*, Brill, Leiden, 2019, pp 44–88, on pp 44–9.

16   Florike Egmond, *Eye for Detail: Images of Plants and Animals in Art and Science 1500–1630*, Reaktion Books, London, 2017, pp 94–5; Swan, '*Ad vivum*', p.363; Thomas Balfe and Joanna Woodall, 'Introduction: From Living Presence to Lively Likeness – The Lives of *ad vivum*', in Balfe et al. (eds), *Ad vivum?*, pp 1–43, on p.9.

17   Kusukawa, 'The Use of Pictures', p.79.

18   Blunt and Stearn, *The Art of Botanical Illustration*, pp 63–72; Pamela H. Smith, 'The Use of Artisanal Knowledge and the Representation of Nature in Sixteenth-Century Germany', in Therese O'Malley and Amy R.W. Meyers (eds), *The Art of Natural History: Illustrated Treatises and Botanical Paintings, 1400–1850*, Yale University Press, New Haven, CT, 2008, pp 15–32.

19   Museum Plantin-Moretus, Antwerp: https://museumplantinmoretus.be/nl/pagina/500-jaar-dodoens.

20 Egmond, *Eye for Detail*, p.99. For an in-depth discussion of the evolution of plant imagery over time, see Harris, *The Beauty of the Flower*, pp 49–79.

21 Harris, *The Beauty of the Flower*, pp 29–31.

22 Jessie Wei-Hsuan Chen, 'A Woodblock's Career: Transferring Visual Botanical Knowledge in the Early Modern Low Countries', *Nuncius*, vol.35, no.1, 2020, pp 20–63.

23 The blocks are now preserved at the Museum Plantin-Moretus in Antwerp, a UNESCO World Heritage site.

24 Anna Marie Roos, *Martin Lister and His Remarkable Daughters: The Art of Science in the Seventeenth Century*, Bodleian Library, University of Oxford, Oxford, 2019.

25 Harris, *The Beauty of the Flower*, pp 32–4.

26 Janice Neri, 'Fantastic Observations: Images of Insects in Early Modern Europe', PhD diss., University of California, Irvine, CA, 2003, pp 135–8.

27 Kusukawa, *Picturing the Book of Nature*, pp 4–6.

3 CREATIVITY AND INNOVATION IN METAMORPHOSIS

1 Translation Patrick Lennon, in Marieke van Delft and Hans Mulder (eds), *Maria Sibylla Merian. Metamorphosis 1705*, Lannoo, Tielt, 2016, p.177.

2 In this book, figures referring to Merian's *Metamorphosis insectorum Surinamensium* (1705) have frequently been sourced from the 1719 edition of her work published by Joannes Oosterwyk, *Maria Sybilla Meriaen Over de voortteeling en wonderbaerlyke veranderingen der Surinaemsche insecten*, simply owing to the higher quality of the images available. Images from the 1719 edition have been used in lieu of images from the 1705 edition only where identical.

3 Translation Patrick Lennon, in Van Delft and Mulder (eds), *Metamorphosis*, p.177.

4 Text accompanying plate 6, translation Patrick Lennon, in ibid., p.177.

5 Text accompanying plate 55, translation Patrick Lennon, in ibid., p.186.

6 *Amsterdamse Courant* (Donderdaegse), no.19, 12 February 1699. Translation my own.

7 *Oprechte Haerlemsche Courant*, 30 October 1698. Translation my own.

8 Merian to Johann Georg Volkamer, Amsterdam, 8 October 1702. Translation my own.

9 Catherine Powell-Warren, *Gender and Self-Fashioning at the Intersection of Art and Science: Agnes Block, Botany, and Networks in the Dutch Seventeenth Century*, Amsterdam University Press, Amsterdam, 2023, pp 235–6.

10 Merian to James Petiver, Amsterdam, 4 June 1703. Translation my own.

11 The Royal Society, *Philosophical Transactions*, vol.23, no.285, 30 June 1703.

12 Elizabeth Tebeaux, 'Women and Technical Writing, 1475–1700: Technology, Literacy, and Development of a Genre', in Lynette Hunter and Sarah Hutton (eds), *Women, Science and Medicine 1500–1700: Mothers and Sisters of the Royal Society*, Sutton, Stroud, 1997, pp 29–62.

13 Merian to James Petiver, Amsterdam, 14 April 1704. Translation my own.

14 *Oprechte Haerlemsche Courant*, 15 November 1703. Translation my own.

15 *Amsterdamse Courant* (Donderdaegse), no.50, 24 April 1704. Translation my own.

16 Merian to Christian Schlegel, Amsterdam, 2 October 1711. Translation Bert van de Roemer.

17 Hans Mulder and Marieke van Delft, 'The Production of *Metamorphosis insectorum Surinamensium 1705*', in Van Delft and Mulder (eds), *Metamorphosis*, pp 40–50, on pp 43–4; Kate Heard, *Maria Merian's Butterflies*, Royal Collection Trust, London, 2016, p.33.

18 Merian to Christian Schlegel, Amsterdam, 2 October 1711. Translation Bert van de Roemer.

19 Mulder and Van Delft, 'The Production of *Metamorphosis*', p.43.

20 Van Delft and Mulder (eds), *Metamorphosis*, pp 187–9.

21 Translation Patrick Lennon, in Van Delft and Mulder (eds), *Metamorphosis*, p.177.

22 Text accompanying plate 27, translation Patrick Lennon, in ibid., p.182.

23 Text accompanying plate 57, translation Patrick Lennon, in ibid., p.184.

24 For example, see Tomomi Kinukawa, 'Science and

Whiteness as Property in the Dutch Atlantic World: Maria Sibylla Merian's *Metamorphosis Insectorum Surinamensium* (1705)', *Journal of Women's History*, vol.24, no.3, 2012, pp 91–116; and Marieke van Delft, 'Maria Sibylla Merian and the People of Suriname', in Bert van de Roemer, Florence Pieters, Hans Mulder, Kay Etheridge and Marieke van Delft (eds), *Maria Sibylla Merian: Changing the Nature of Art and Science*, Lannoo, Tielt, 2022, pp 118–30.

4 A FAMILY WORKSHOP: MARKETING MATRIARCHY

1   Marriage Registration, 28 June 1692, Amsterdam Notarial Archives. Stadsarchief Amsterdam, Ondertrouwboek (Marriage Register), archive 5001, inv.697, p.366.

2   *Amsterdamsche Courant*, 5 August 1692, p.2. Translation my own.

3   Abigail Newman and Lieneke Nijkamp (eds), *Many Antwerp Hands: Collaborations in Netherlandish Art*, Harvey Miller Publishers, Turnhout, 2021; see also Anne T. Woollett, 'Two Celebrated Painters: The Collaborative Ventures of Rubens and Brueghel, ca.1598–1625', in Anne T. Woollett and Ariane van Suchtelen (eds), *Rubens & Brueghel: A Working Friendship*, exh.cat., The J. Paul Getty Museum, Los Angeles, CA, Mauritshuis, The Hague, and Waanders Publishers, Zwolle, 2006, pp 1–41, on p.3.

4   For an explanation of the historical context in which the term 'master' is used in this book, refer to Chapter 1, p.17.

5   I.H. van Eeghen, trans. Jasper Hillegers, 'The Amsterdam Guild of Saint Luke in the 17th Century', *Journal of Historians of Netherlandish Art*, vol.4, no.2, Summer 2012.

6   J.G. van Dillen, *Bronnen tot de geschiedenis van het bedrijfsleven en het gildewezen van Amsterdam 1510–1672*, Huygens Instituut, at https://resources.huygens.knaw.nl/retroboeken/ gildewezen/#page=940&accessor=toc&source=3 (accessed 1 July 2023).

7   ibid., entry no.460.

8   Based on a review of Van Dillen, *Bronnen*.

9   Frima Fox Hofrichter, *Judith Leyster 1609–1660*, exh.cat., National Gallery of Art, Washington, DC, 2009; Marianne Berardi, 'Science into Art: Rachel Ruysch's Early Development as a Still-Life Painter', PhD diss., University of Pittsburg, PA, 1998; see also Elizabeth A. Honig, 'The Art of Being "Artistic": Dutch Women's Creative Practices in the 17th Century', *Woman's Art Journal*, vol.22, no.2, Autumn–Winter 2001–2, pp 31–9.

10   Merian to Johann Georg Volkamer, Amsterdam, 16 April 1705. Translation my own.

11   Ella Reitsma and Sandrine Ulenberg, *Maria Sibylla Merian & Daughters: Women of Art and Science*, exh.cat., Rembrandt House Museum, Amsterdam, 2008, p.114.

12   Merian to Clara Regina Imhoff, Frankfurt am Main, 25 July 1682. Translation my own.

13   Alicia C. Montoya and Reindert Jagersma, 'Marketing Maria Sibylla Merian, 1720–1800: Book Auctions, Gender, and Reading Culture in the Dutch Republic', *Book History*, vol.21, 2018, pp 56–88.

14   For technical information regarding the process of pasting insect wings onto canvasses, see the blog of the Hamilton Kerr Institute, which has conducted ground-breaking research on Otto Marseus van Schrieck and his practice: https://blogs.fitzmuseum. cam.ac.uk/hki/2020/04/30/paint-and-butterflies- conserving-and-researching-a-painting-by-otto- marseus-van-schrieck/.

15   See discussion regarding the meaning and significance of 'from life' in Chapter 2, pp 29–30.

16   'Register zu Een Bloem Boek, geschildert door Johanna Helena Herolt in Amsterdam 1698', Herzog Anton Ulrich Museum, Braunschweig, Z 6524 recto.

17   Celeste Brusati, 'Stilled Lives: Self-Portraiture and Self-Reflection in Seventeenth-Century Netherlandish Still-Life Painting', *Simiolus: Netherlands Quarterly for the History of Art*, vol.20, no.2/3, 1990–91, pp 168–82; see also Martha Moffitt Peacock, 'Mirrors of Skill and Renown: Women and Self-Fashioning in Early Modern Dutch Art', *Mediaevistik*, vol.28, no.1, 2015, pp 325–52; and Alejandro Vergara-Sharp, *Clara Peeters*, Lund Humphries, London, 2025.

18   Reitsma and Ulenberg, *Merian & Daughters*, pp 158–67.

19   Working identification.

20 Sophie Reinders, *De mug en de kaars. Vriendenboekjes van adellijke vrouwen, 1575–1640*, Vantilt, Nijmegen, 2017, p.9; Mara Wade, 'Women's Networks of Knowledge: The Emblem Book as *Stammbuch*', *Daphnis*, vol.45, 2017, pp 492–509.

21 Reitsma and Ulenberg, *Merian & Daughters*, p.121.

22 ibid., p.105.

23 Joachim von Sandrart, *Der Teutschen Academie Zweyter und letzter Haupt-Theil/ von Der Edlen Bau- Bild- und Mahlerey-Künste,* part III, Endter, Nuremberg, 1679, p.85.

24 Reitsma and Ulenberg, *Merian & Daughters*, p.112.

25 Sam Segal, 'Maria Sibylla Merian as a Flower Painter', in Kurt Wettengl (ed.), *Maria Sibylla Merian 1657–1717: Artist and Naturalist*, Gerd Hatje, Ostfildern-Ruit, 1998, pp 68–87, on p.82.

26 Joris Hoefnagel and Jacob Hoefnagel, *Diana and Actaeon*, 1597, Musée du Louvre, Paris, inv./cat.nr. REC 85.

27 Thea Vignau-Wilberg, *Joris and Jacob Hoefnagel: Art and Science around 1600*, Hatje Cantz, Berlin, 2017, p.40.

28 Natalie Zemon Davis, *Women on the Margins: Three Seventeenth-Century Lives*, Harvard University Press, Cambridge, MA, 1997, p.199.

29 Kay Etheridge, *The Flowering of Ecology: Maria Sibylla Merian's Caterpillar Book*, Brill, Leiden, 2021, p.109.

30 Contract between Dorothea Maria Merian, Wed. Pieter Henrici, and Johannes Oosterwyk, 28 September 1717, notary Pieter Schabaelje, Stadsarchief Amsterdam, inv.6107; see also Lieke van Deinsen, 'Marketing Merian. The Visual Branding of the Late Female Naturalist', in Bert van de Roemer, Florence Pieters, Hans Mulder, Kay Etheridge and Marieke van Delft (eds), *Maria Sibylla Merian: Changing the Nature of Art and Science*, Lannoo, Tielt, 2022, pp 215–25, p.215.

31 Etheridge, *The Flowering of Ecology*, p.117.

32 Theresa Kemp, Beth Link and Catherine Powell, 'Accounting for Early Modern Women in the Arts: Reconsidering Women's Agency, Networks, and Relationships', in Merry Wiesner-Hanks (ed.), *Challenging Women's Agency and Activism in Early Modernity*, Amsterdam University Press, Amsterdam, 2021, pp 283–308, esp. pp 302–3; Gerda Lerner, *The Creation of Feminist Consciousness: From the Middle Ages to Eighteen-Seventy*, Oxford University Press, New York, 1993.

33 Reitsma and Ulenberg, *Merian & Daughters*, p.237.

5 FLOWERS, ART AND COLLECTORS

1 Michael North, *Art and Commerce in the Dutch Golden Age*, Yale University Press, New Haven, CT, 1999, p.109.

2 Mary D. Garrard, *Brunelleschi's Egg: Nature, Art, and Gender in Renaissance Italy*, University of California Press, Berkeley, CA, 2010, pp 9–30; Alisha Rankin, 'Medicine for the Uncommon Woman. Experience, Experiment and Exchange in Early Modern Germany', PhD diss., Harvard University, Cambridge, MA, 2005; Lynette Hunter and Sarah Hutton (eds), *Women, Science and Medicine 1500–1700: Mothers and Sisters of the Royal Society*, Sutton, Stroud, 1997; Anne Mieke Backer, *Er stond een vrouw in de tuin. Over de rol van vrouwen in het Nederlandse landschap*, De Hef, Rotterdam, 2016.

3 Norman Bryson, *Looking at the Overlooked: Four Essays on Still Life Painting*, Reaktion Books, London, 2004, pp 136–77; see also Paris A. Spies-Gans, *A Revolution on Canvas: The Rise of Women Artists in London and Paris, 1760–1830*, Paul Mellon Centre for Studies in British Art, London, 2022; and Virginia Treanor, 'Women and the Art of Science', in Andaleeb Banta, Alexa Greist and Theresa Kutasz Christensen (eds), *Making her Mark: A History of Women Artists in Europe, 1400–1800*, exh.cat., Goose Lane Editions, Fredericton, 2023, pp 106–21, on p.107.

4 Catherine Powell-Warren, 'A Strange Attraction. Women Artists and Patrons and the Creatures that No One Can Love', in Jan de Hond, Eric Jorink and Hans Mulder (eds), *Crawly Creatures: Little Animals in Art and Science*, exh.cat., Rijksmuseum, Amsterdam, 2022, pp 105–114, on p.110; Lucia Tongiorgi Tomasi, '"*La femminil pazienza*": Women Painters and Natural History in the Seventeenth and Early Eighteenth Centuries', in Therese O'Malley and Amy R.W. Meyers (eds), *The Art of Natural History: Illustrated Treatises and Botanical Paintings, 1400–1850*, Yale University Press, New Haven, CT, 2008, pp 158–85, on p.160; Alison Kettering,

'Watercolour and Women: Between Mirror and Comb', *Women's Art Journal*, vol.42, no.1, Spring/Summer 2021, pp 27–35, on pp 27–8.

5   Willem Goeree, *Verligterie-kunde, of regt gebruik der water-verwen*, Goeree, Middelburg, 1670, addendum; Kettering, 'Watercolor and Women', p.28.

6   Stefania Branchetti, 'Petronella de la Court. Egen haard is goud waard', in Judith Noorman (ed.), *Gouden vrouwen van de 17de eeuw. Van kunstenaars tot verzamelaars*, W. Books, Zwolle, 2020, pp 36–9.

7   Michelle Moseley-Christian, 'Seventeenth-Century *Pronk Poppenhuisen*: Domestic Space and the Ritual Function of Dutch Dollhouses for Women', *Home Cultures*, vol.7, no.3, 2010, pp 341–63.

8   Catherine Powell-Warren, *Gender and Self-Fashioning at the Intersection of Art and Science: Agnes Block, Botany, and Networks in the Dutch Seventeenth Century*, Amsterdam University Press, Amsterdam, 2023.

9   Inventory of Valerius Röver, 1730, University of Amsterdam, Special Collections, MS II A 18.

10 Getty Provenance Index, Sale Catalog Br-A254, Lot 0309: '2 a foreign Plant, and a Corant-bush, on Vellum, by S. Merian', drawing on vellum. Auction house: Cooper. Sale: 1–8 February 1725. This lot 8 February, together with 'Water Colours and Miniatures'.

11 Zacharias Conrad Von Uffenbach, *Herrn Zacharias Conrad von Uffenbach Merkwürdige Reisen durch Niedersachsen, Holland und Engelland*, part 11, Johann Freiderich Gaum, Ulm, 1753, p.583.

12 Zacharias Conrad von Uffenbach, *Herrn Zacharias Conrad von Uffenbach Merkwürdige Reisen durch Niedersachsen, Holland und Engelland*, part 111, Gaum, Ulm und Memmingen, 1754, p.250. Translations my own.

13 ibid., part 111, pp 352–4.

14 Maria Sibylla Merian, ed. Wolf-Dietrich Beer, *Schmetterlinge, Käfer und andere Insekten: Leningrader Studienbuch*, 2 vols, Edition Leipzig, Leipzig, 1976, vol.1, p.43.

15 Kim Todd, *Chrysalis: Maria Sibylla Merian and the Secrets of Metamorphosis*, Harcourt, New York, 2007, p.223.

16 Merian, ed. Beer, *Schetterlinge, Käfer und andere Insekten*, pp 46–7.

6 RECEPTION AND LEGACY

1   Willem Sewel, *De boekzaal der geleerde werreld*, vol.1, Francois Halma, Amsterdam, 1705, p.91, quoted in full below. Translation my own.

2   This chapter relies upon and reproduces in part my essay '"What Experience Does Such a Woman Have?" Maria Sibylla Merian (1647–1717) and the Gendered Language of her Reception in Natural History at the Dawn of the Dutch Eighteenth-Century', *Women's Writing*, special issue: 'Textual Misogynies', ed. Carme Font Paz, forthcoming.

3   Elizabeth Tebeaux, 'Women and Technical Writing, 1475–1700: Technology, Literacy, and Development of a Genre', in Lynette Hunter and Sarah Hutton (eds), *Women, Science and Medicine 1500–1700: Mothers and Sisters of the Royal Society*, Sutton, Stroud, 1997, pp 29–62.

4   George Cuvier, *Cuvier's History of the Natural Sciences: Nineteen Lessons from the Sixteenth and Seventeenth Centuries*, new edn, Publications Scientifiques du Muséum, Paris, 2015.

5   Natalie Zemon Davis, *Women on the Margins: Three Seventeenth-Century Lives*, Harvard University Press, Cambridge, MA, 1997, p.155.

6   Martine van Elk, *Early Modern Women's Writing: Domesticity, Privacy, and the Public Sphere in England and the Dutch Republic*, Palgrave Macmillan/Springer Nature, Cham, 2017.

7   Carme Font Paz and Nina Geerdink (eds), *Economic Imperatives for Women's Writing in Early Modern Europe*, pp 124–46, Brill, Boston, MA, 2018, p.1.

8   Maria Sibylla Merian, *Der Raupen wunderbare Verwandelung und sonderbare Blumennahrung*, part 1, Johann Andreas Graff, Nuremberg, 1679, preface; Kay Etheridge, *The Flowering of Ecology: Maria Sibylla Merian's Caterpillar Book*, Brill, Leiden, 2021, p.143.

9   Translation Patrick Lennon, in Marieke van Delft and Hans Mulder (eds), *Maria Sibylla Merian. Metamorphosis 1705*, Lannoo, Tielt, 2016, p.177.

10 Nina Geerdink, 'Economic Advancement and Reputation Strategies: Seventeenth-Century Dutch Women Writing for Profit', *Renaissance Studies*, vol.34, no.3, 2019, pp 350–73; Nina Geerdink, 'Possibilities of Patronage: The Dutch Poet Elisabeth

Hoofman and Her German Patrons', in Paz and Geerdink (eds), *Economic Imperatives*, pp 124–46.

11 Joachim von Sandrart, *Teutsche Academie der edlen Bau-, Bild- und Mahlerey-Künste*, part III, Miltenberger, Nuremberg, 1675, p.339.

12 Joachim von Sandrart, *Der Teutschen Academie Zweyter und letzter Haupt-Theil/ von Der Edlen Bau- Bild- und Mahlerey-Künste*, part III, Endter, Nuremberg, 1679, p.85.

13 ibid.

14 Etheridge, *The Flowering of Ecology*, p.134.

15 Hermann Conring, *Introductio in universam artem medicam singulasq*, Ernest. Gottlieb. Crugium, Halle and Leipzig, 1726, p.294. The 1687 version of the text has been transcribed by the Maria Sibylla Merian Society.

16 This section draws from Catherine Powell-Warren, *Gender and Self-Fashioning at the Intersection of Art and Science: Agnes Block, Botany, and Networks in the Dutch Seventeenth Century*, Amsterdam University Press, Amsterdam, 2023, pp 113–20; and from Powell-Warren, '"What Experience Does Such a Woman Have?"'.

17 Manuscript note reproduced and transcribed in Hans Mulder, *De Ontdekking van de Natuur*, Terra, Amsterdam, 2021, pp 136–40; see also Ella Reitsma and Sandrine Ulenberg, *Maria Sibylla Merian & Daughters: Women of Art and Science*, exh.cat., Rembrandt House Museum, Amsterdam, 2008, p.242.

18 Arnold Houbraken, *De Groote schouburgh der Nederlantsche konstschilders en schilderessen*, Widow of the author, Amsterdam, 1721, vol.III, pp 220–24. Translations my own.

19 ibid., vol.I, pp 340–42.

20 ibid., vol.III, p.242.

21 Johann Gabriel Doppelmayr, *Historische Nachricht von den Nürnbergischen Mathematicis und Künstlern* [. . .], 1730, pp 268–9. Translations my own.

22 ibid.

23 Sewel, *De boekzaal der geleerde werreld*, vol.I, pp 91–9. Translation my own.

24 Anonymous, *Acta Eruditorum, publicata Lipsiae, Calendis Novembris, Anno m dcc vii* (November 1707), pp 481–2. Translation from the Latin Dr Roek (C.L.) Vermeulen.

25 Frederika H. Jacobs, *Defining the Renaissance Virtuosa: Women Artists and the Language of Art History and Criticism*, Cambridge University Press, Cambridge, 1997, pp 9–10, 40–41.

26 Leah Knight, 'Horticultural Networking and Sociable Citation', in Helen A. Curry, Nicholas Jardine, James A. Secord and Emma C. Spary (eds), *Worlds of Natural History*, Cambridge University Press, Cambridge, 2018, pp 61–77, on p.61.

27 John Ray, *Historia insectorum opus posthumum jussu Regiae Societatis Londinensis editum*, Impensis A. and J. Churchill, London, 1710, p.398; Etheridge, *The Flowering of Ecology*, pp 28–9.

28 Reitsma and Ulenberg, *Merian & Daughters*, p.242.

29 Brian Ogilvie, *The Science of Describing: Natural History in Renaissance Europe*, University of Chicago Press, Chicago, IL, 2008; Londa Schiebinger, *The Mind Has No Sex? Women in the Origins of Modern Science*, Harvard University Press, Cambridge, MA, 1996.

30 Tomomi Kinukawa, 'Natural History as Entrepreneurship: Maria Sibylla Merian's Correspondence with J.G. Volkamer II and James Petiver', *Archives of Natural History*, vol.38, no.2, 2011, pp 313–27, on pp 318–21.

31 Lukas Rieppel, 'Museums and Botanical Gardens', in Bernard V. Lightman (ed.), *A Companion to the History of Science*, Wiley-Blackwell, Chichester, 2016, pp 238–51.

32 Claudia Swan, '*Liefhebberij*: A Market Sensibility', in Inger Leemans and Anne Goldgar (eds), *Early Modern Knowledge Societies as Affective Economies*, Routledge, New York, 2021, pp 141–64, on p.142.

33 ibid.

34 The Royal Society, *Philosophical Transactions*, vol.21, no.249, 28 February 1699, pp 63–7, on pp 63–4.

35 Iain C. Sutcliffe (ed.), 'Still Going Strong: Leeuwenhoek at Eighty', Special Issue: Antonie van Leeuwenhoek, *Journal of Microbiology*, vol.106, 2014; see also Antonie van Leeuwenhoek and Leeuwenhoek-Commissie, *Alle de brieven van Antoni van Leeuwenhoek. The Collected Letters of Antoni van Leeuwenhoek*, part XIV, 1701–4, Swets & Zeitlinger, Lisse, 1996; and Antonie van Leeuwenhoek and Leeuwenhoek-Commissie, *Alle de brieven van Antoni*

van Leeuwenhoek. *The Collected Letters of Antoni van Leeuwenhoek*, part xv, 1704–7, Swets & Zeitlinger, Lisse, 1999.

36 The Royal Society, *Philosophical Transactions*, vol.32, no.38, 31 December 1723, pp 446–53, on p.449.

37 The Royal Society, *Philosophical Transactions*, vol.41, no.457, 31 August 1740, pp 441–8, on p.443; The Royal Society, *Philosophical Transactions*, vol.51, 31 December 1759, pp 653–7, on p.653.

38 Brouerius van Niedek, 'Op de verhandeling der Surinaemsche Insecten van wyle Juffr. Maria Sibylla Meriaen', in Merian, *Maria Sibylla Meriaen Over de voortteeling and wonderbaerlyke veranderingen der Surinaemsche insecten*, Joannes Oosterwyk, Amsterdam, 1719, n.p.

39 Kay Etheridge, 'The Biology of *Metamorphosis insectorum Surinamensium*', in Van Delft and Mulder (eds), *Metamorphosis*, pp 29–39, on p.39.

40 Etheridge, *The Flowering of Ecology*, pp 125–6.

41 Alicia C. Montoya and Reindert Jagersma, 'Marketing Maria Sibylla Merian, 1720–1800: Book Auctions, Gender, and Reading Culture in the Dutch Republic', *Book History*, vol.21, 2018, pp 56–88.

42 Elisabeth Rücker, *Maria Sibylla Merian 1647–1717*, exh.cat., Germanisches Nationalmuseum, Nuremberg, 1967.

43 Henrietta McBurney, 'The Influence of Maria Sibylla Merian's Work on the Art and Science of Mark Catesby', in Bert van de Roemer, Florence Pieters, Hans Mulder, Kay Etheridge and Marieke van Delft (eds), *Maria Sibylla Merian: Changing the Nature of Art and Science*, Lannoo, Tielt, 2022, pp 195–205, on p.196.

EPILOGUE

1 Claudia Swan, *Rarities of These Lands: Art, Trade, and Diplomacy in the Dutch Republic*, Princeton University Press, Princeton, NJ, 2021.

2 Jonathan Israel, *The Dutch Republic: Its Rise, Greatness, and Fall: 1477–1806*, Clarendon Press, Oxford, 2007.

3 Paula Findlen, *Possessing Nature: Museums, Collecting, and Scientific Culture in Early Modern Italy*, University of California Press, Berkeley, CA, 1994.

4 Londa Schiebinger and Claudia Swan (eds), *Colonial Botany: Science, Commerce, and Politics in the Early Modern World*, University of Pennsylvania Press, Philadelphia, PA, 2005; Dániel Margócsy, *Commercial Visions: Science, Trade, and Visual Culture in the Dutch Golden Age*, University of Chicago Press, Chicago, IL, 2014.

5 Dagomar Degroot, *The Frigid Golden Age: Climate Change, the Little Ice Age and the Dutch Republic 1560–1720*, Cambridge University Press, Cambridge, 2019.

Bibliography

Note: Notarial records and letters are sorted by date, whereas books and articles are sorted alphabetically.

SA = Gemeente Amsterdam Stadsarchief

NOTARIAL DOCUMENTS

Christening of Maria Sibylla Merianin, 4 April 1647, Taufbücher (Christening Records), Frankfurt 10 (1642–7), fol.292^v, at www.merianin.de/home/archivalien.

Johanna Helena Graff and Hendrick Herolt, Marriage Registration, 28 June 1692, SA, Ondertrouwboek (Marriage Register), archive 5001, inv.697, p.366, at https://archief.amsterdam/inventarissen/scans/5001/2.2.38/start/180/limit/10/highlight/7.

Procuration by Maria Sibylla Merian in favour of Jacob Hendrik Herolt and Michiel van Musscher, 23 April 1699, notary Samuel Wijmer, SA, Notarial archives 5075, inv.4830, doc.49, pp 186–7, at https://archief.amsterdam/inventarissen/scans/5075/196.1.21/start/140/limit/10/highlight/1.

Contract between Dorothea Maria Merian, Wed. Pieter Henrici, and Johannes Oosterwyk, 28 September 1717, notary Pieter Schabaelje, SA, inv.6107, at https://archief.amsterdam/inventarissen/scans/5075/241.1.151/start/260/limit/10/highlight/7.

OTHER ARCHIVAL DOCUMENTS

Bien, Hans, *Bird's Eye View of Nuremberg*, c.1630, original paper on canvas, pen and ink drawing, coloured, scale about 1:2900, 48 × 66.6 cm (18 7/8 × 26 ¼ in), Nuremberg City Archives, A4, plan collection 517/4.

Graff, Johann Andreas, *Ground Plan of the Famous Estate in Wieuwarden*, c.1686, coloured pen and brush drawing, 33.7 × 42 cm (13 ¼ × 16 ½ in), Staatsarchiv Nürnberg, Handschriftliche Karten, inv.no.212, 1686.

Röver, Valerius. Inventory, 1730, University of Amsterdam, Special Collections, MS II A 18.

LETTERS OF MARIA SIBYLLA MERIAN

Transcriptions available at https://www.themariasibyllamieriansociety.humanities.uva.nl/sources/letters/

Maria Sibylla Merian to Clara Regina Imhoff, Nuremberg, 25 July 1682. Germanisches Nationalmuseum, Nürnberg, HA, Familie Imhoff, Teil II, Fasz.50.

—, Nuremberg, 24 March 1683. Stadtbibliothek Nürnberg, Autogr.164.

—, Frankfurt am Main, 8 December 1684. Stadtbibliothek Nürnberg, Autogr.172.

—, Frankfurt am Main, 8 May 1685. Germanisches Nationalmuseum, Nürnberg, HA, Familie Imhoff, Teil II, Fasz.50.

—, Frankfurt am Main, 3 June 1685. Stadtbibliothek Nürnberg, Autogr.166.

—, Amsterdam, 27 August 1697. Stadtbibliothek Nürnberg, Autogr.167.

Maria Sibylla Merian to Johann Georg Volkamer, Amsterdam, 8 October 1702. Universitätsbibliothek Erlangen-Nürnberg, Erlangen, Briefsammlung Trew.

Maria Sibylla Merian to James Petiver, Amsterdam, 4 June 1703. The British Library, London, Department of Manuscripts, Sloane 4063, fol.201^f.

—, Amsterdam, 14 April 1704. The British Library, London, Department of Manuscripts, Sloane 4064, fol.5.

Maria Sibylla Merian to Johann Georg Volkamer, Amsterdam, 16 April 1705. Universitatsbibliothek Erlangen, Trew-Bibliothek, Brief-Sammlung MS 1834, Merian No.4.

Maria Sibylla Merian to Christian Schlegel, Amsterdam, 2 October 1711. Fondation Custodia, Paris, Collection Frits Lugt, inv.7578.

NEWSPAPERS, BULLETINS AND PERIODICALS

Amsterdamsche Courant, 21 November 1684, no.47, not digitised.

—, 5 August 1692, at https://resolver.kb.nl/resolve?urn=MMSAA06:165523098:mpeg21:p00002.

Amsterdamse Courant (Donderdaegse), no.19, 12 February 1699, at https://resolver.kb.nl/resolve?urn=MMSAA06:166469019:mpeg21:p00002.

—, no.50, 24 April 1704, at https://www.delpher.nl/nl/kranten/view?coll=ddd&identifier=ddd:010707971:mpeg21:p002.

Anonymous, *Acta Eruditorum, publicata Lipsiae, Calendis Novembris, Anno m dcc vii* (November 1707), pp 481–2.

Oprechte Haerlemsche Courant, 30 October 1698, at https://www.delpher.nl/nl/kranten/view?coll=ddd&identifier=ddd:011227094:mpeg21:p002.

—, 15 November 1703, at https://resolver.kb.nl/resolve?urn=ddd:011221053:mpeg21:p004.

Sewel, Willem, *De boekzaal der geleerde werreld*, vol.1, Francois Halma, Amsterdam, 1705.

The Royal Society, *Philosophical Transactions*, vol.21, no.249, 28 February 1699, pp 63–7, at https://doi.org/10.1098/rstl.1699.0012.

—, vol.23, no.285, 30 June 1703, at https://doi.org/10.1098/rstl.1702.0069.

—, vol.32, no.38, 31 December 1723, pp 446–53, at https://doi.org/10.1098/rstl.1722.0090.

—, vol.41, no.457, 31 August 1740, pp 441–8, at https://doi.org/10.1098/rstl.1739.0074.

—, vol.51, 31 December 1759, pp 653–7, at https://doi.org/10.1098/rstl.1759.0062.

BOOKS BY MARIA SIBYLLA MERIAN

Gräffin, Maria Sibylla, *Florum fasciculus prima*, Johannes Andreas Graff, Nuremberg, 1675.

—, *Florum fasciculus, Alter Zweyter Blumen-Theil*, Johannes Andreas Graff, Nuremberg, 1677.

—, *Der Raupen wunderbare Verwandelung und sonderbare Blumennahrung*, part 1, Johann Andreas Graff, Nuremberg, 1679.

—, *Florum fasciculus tertius, Dritter Blumen Theil*, Johannes Andreas Graff, Nuremberg, 1680.

—, *Neues Blumenbuch*, Johannes Andreas Graff, Nuremberg, 1680.

—, *Der Raupen wunderbare Verwandelung und sonderbare Blumennahrung*, part 11, David Funken, Frankfurt am Main, 1683.

Merian, Maria Sibylla, *Metamorphosis insectorum Surinamensium*, by the author, Amsterdam, 1705.

—, *Der rupsen begin, voedzel en wonderbaare verandering*, part 1, for and sold by the author, sold by G. Valck, Amsterdam, 1712.

—, *Der rupsen begin, voedzel en wonderbaare verandering*, part 11, for and sold by the author, sold by G. Valck, Amsterdam, 1712.

POSTHUMOUS BOOKS PUBLISHED UNDER MARIA SIBYLLA MERIAN'S NAME

Merian, Maria Sibylla, *Derde en laatste deel der Rupsen begin, voedzel, en wonderbaare verandering* [...] *In print gebracht en in't licht gegeven door haar jongste dochter Dorothea Maria Henricie*, for and sold by the author, Amsterdam, 1717.

—, *Erucarum ortus, alimentum et paradoxa metamorphosis*, Joannes Oosterwyk, Amsterdam, 1718.

—, *Dissertatio de generatione et metamorphosibus insectorum*

Surinamensium, Joannes Oosterwyk, Amsterdam, 1719.

—, *Maria Sibylla Meriaen Over de voortteeling en wonderbaerlyke veranderingen der Surinaemsche insecten*, Joannes Oosterwyk, Amsterdam, 1719.

—, *Dissertatio de generatione et metamorphosibus insectorum surinamensium / Dissertation sur la generation et les insects de Surinam*, Pierre Gosse, The Hague, 1726.

—, *De Europische insecten*, Jean Frederic Bernard, Amsterdam, 1730.

—, *Histoire des insectes de L'Europe*, Jean Frederic Bernard, Amsterdam, 1730.

—, *Over de voortteeling en wonderbaerlyke veranderingen der Surinaemsche Insecten*, Jean Frederic Bernard, Amsterdam, 1730.

—, *Histoire générale des insectes de Surinam et de toute l'Europe* [. . .]. *Troisième édition, revue, corrigée & considérablement augmentée par M. Buch'oz. A laquelle on a joint une troisième partie qui traite des plus belles fleurs, telles que des plantes bulbeuses, liliacées, caryophillées*, Tome premier[–troisième], L.C. Desnos, Paris, 1771.

Merian, Maria Sibylla, ed. Wolf-Dietrich Beer, *Schmetterlinge, Käfer und andere Insekten: Leningrader Studienbuch*, 2 vols, Edition Leipzig, Leipzig, 1976.

OTHER PRIMARY SOURCES

Conring, Hermann, *Introductio in universam artem medicam singulasq*, Ernest. Gottlieb. Crugium, Halle and Leipzig, 1726.

Cuvier, George, *Cuvier's History of the Natural Sciences: Nineteen Lessons from the Sixteenth and Seventeenth Centuries*, new edn, Publications Scientifiques du Muséum, Paris, 2015, at https://doi.org/10.4000/books.mnhn.2761.

Doppelmayr, Johann Gabriel, *Historische Nachricht von den Nürnbergischen Mathematicis und Künstlern* [. . .], 1730, Germanisches Nationalmuseum, Nürnberg, ref. no.Hs 108571.

Goeree, Willem, *Verligterie-kunde, of regt gebruik der water-verwen*, Goeree, Middelburg, 1670.

Houbraken, Arnold, *De Groote schouburgh der Nederlantsche konstschilders en schilderessen*, Widow of the author, Amsterdam, 1721.

Petiver, James. *Musei Petiveriani: centuria prima, rariora naturae: continens, viz., animalia, fossilia, plantas*, Smith & Walford, London, 1695.

Ray, John, *Historia insectorum opus posthumum jussu Regiae Societatis Londinensis editum*, Impensis A. and J. Churchill, London, 1710.

Van Leeuwenhoek, Antonie, and Leeuwenhoek-Commissie, *Alle de brieven van Antoni van Leeuwenhoek. The Collected Letters of Antoni van Leeuwenhoek*, part XIV, 1701–4, Swets & Zeitlinger, Lisse, 1996.

—, *Alle de brieven van Antoni van Leeuwenhoek. The Collected Letters of Antoni van Leeuwenhoek*, part XV, 1704–7, Swets & Zeitlinger, Lisse, 1999.

Von Sandrart, Joachim, *Teutsche Academie der edlen Bau-, Bild- und Mahlerey-Künste*, Miltenberger, Nuremberg, 1675, at http://ta.sandrart.net.

—, *Der Teutschen Academie Zweyter und letzter Haupt-Theil/ von Der Edlen Bau- Bild- und Mahlerey-Künste*, Endter, Nuremberg, 1679.

Von Uffenbach, Zacharias Conrad, *Herrn Zacharias Conrad von Uffenbach Merkwürdige Reisen durch Niedersachsen, Holland und Engelland*, part II, Johann Freiderich Gaum, Ulm, 1753.

—, *Herrn Zacharias Conrad von Uffenbach Merkwürdige Reisen durch Niedersachsen, Holland und Engelland*, part III, Gaum, Ulm und Memmingen, 1754.

SECONDARY SOURCES

Anker, Peder, *Imperial Ecology: Environmental Order in the British Empire, 1895–1945*, Harvard University Press, Cambridge, MA, 2001.

Backer, Anne Mieke, *Er stond een vrouw in de tuin. Over de rol van vrouwen in het Nederlandse landschap*, De Hef, Rotterdam, 2016.

Balfe, Thomas, and Joanna Woodall, 'Introduction: From Living Presence to Lively Likeness – The Lives of *ad vivum*', in Balfe et al. (eds), *Ad vivum?*, pp 1–43.

Balfe, Thomas, Joanna Woodall and Claus Zittel (eds), *Ad vivum? Visual Materials and the Vocabulary of Life-Likeness in Europe before 1800*, Brill, Leiden, 2019.

Banta, Andaleeb, Alexa Greist and Theresa Kutasz Christensen (eds), *Making her Mark: A History of Women Artists in Europe, 1400–1800*, exh.cat., Goose Lane Editions, Fredericton, 2023.

Bass, Marisa Anne, 'Florilegium: The Origins of the Flower Still Life in the Early Modern Netherlands', in Claudia Swan (ed.), *Tributes to David Freedberg: Image and Insight*, Brepols, Turnhout, 2019, pp 11–26.

Bass, Marisa Anne, Anne Goldgar, Hanneke Grootenboer and Claudia Swan (eds), *Conchophilia: Shells, Art, and Curiosity in Early Modern Europe*, Princeton University Press, Princeton, NJ, 2021.

Bellavitis, Anna, *Women's Work and Rights in Early Modern Urban Europe*, Palgrave Macmillan/Springer Nature, Cham, 2018.

Berardi, Marianne, 'Science into Art: Rachel Ruysch's Early Development as a Still-Life Painter', PhD diss., University of Pittsburg, PA, 1998.

Beuys, Barbara, *Maria Sibylla Merian: Künstlerin, Forscherin, Geschäftsfrau*, Insel, Berlin, 2017.

Blunt, Wilfrid, and William T. Stearn, *The Art of Botanical Illustration*, revised edn, ACC Art Books, Woodbridge, 2021.

Bohn, Babette, *Women Artists, Their Patrons, and Their Publics in Early Modern Bologna*, Pennsylvania State University Press, University Park, PA, 2021.

Bösch, Hans, *Die Nürnberger Maler, ihre Lehrlinge, Probestücke, Vorgeher u.s.w. von 1596–1659*, no publisher, Nuremberg, 1899.

Branchetti, Stefania, 'Petronella de la Court. Egen haard is goud waard', in Noorman (ed.), *Gouden vrouwen*, pp 36–9.

Braun, Juliane, 'Bioprospecting Breadfruit: Imperial Botany, Transoceanic Relations, and the Politics of Translation', *Early American Literature*, vol.54, no.3, September 2019, pp 643–71. DOI: 10.1353/eal.2019.0062.

Brosens, Koenraad, Leen Kelchtermans and Katlijne van der Stighelen (eds), *Family Ties: Art Production and Kinship Patterns in the Early Modern Low Countries*, Brepols, Turnhout, 2012.

Brusati, Celeste, 'Stilled Lives: Self-Portraiture and Self-Reflection in Seventeenth-Century Netherlandish Still-Life Painting', *Simiolus: Netherlands Quarterly for the History of Art*, vol.20, no.2/3, 1990–91, pp 168–82.

Bryson, Norman, *Looking at the Overlooked: Four Essays on Still Life Painting*, Reaktion Books, London, 2004.

Chen, Jessie Wei-Hsuan, 'A Woodblock's Career: Transferring Visual Botanical Knowledge in the Early Modern Low Countries', *Nuncius*, vol.35, no.1, 2020, pp 20–63, at https://doi.org/10.1163/18253911-03501002.

Cohen, Elizabeth S., and Margaret Reeves (eds), *The Youth of Early Modern Women*, Amsterdam University Press, Amsterdam, 2018.

Cook, Harold J., *Matters of Exchange: Commerce, Medicine, and Science in the Dutch Golden Age*, Yale University Press, New Haven, CT, 2007.

Crowston, Clare, 'Women, Gender, and Guilds in Early Modern Europe: An Overview of Recent Research', *International Review of Social History*, vol.53, 2008, pp 19–44.

Daston, Lorraine, 'Epistemic Images', in Alida Payne (ed.), *Vision and Its Instruments: Art, Science, and Technology in Early Modern Europe*, Pennsylvania State University Press, University Park, PA, 2015, pp 13–35.

Daston, Lorraine, and Katharine Park, *Wonders and the Order of Nature: 1150–1750*, Zone Books, New York, 2001.

Davis, Natalie Zemon, *Women on the Margins: Three Seventeenth-Century Lives*, Harvard University Press, Cambridge, MA, 1997.

Degroot, Dagomar, *The Frigid Golden Age: Climate Change, the Little Ice Age and the Dutch Republic 1560–1720*, Cambridge University Press, Cambridge, 2019.

Doherty, Meghan C. *Engraving Accuracy in Early Modern England: Visual Communication and the Royal Society*, Amsterdam University Press, Amsterdam, 2022.

Egmond, Florike, 'The Making of the *Libri Picturati* A16–30', in Jan de Koning (ed.), *Drawn After Nature: The Complete Botanical Watercolours of the 16th-Century Libri Picturati*, KNNV Publishing, Zeist, 2008, pp 12–21.

—, *Eye for Detail: Images of Plants and Animals in Art and Science 1500–1630*, Reaktion Books, London, 2017.

Etheridge, Kay, 'The Biology of *Metamorphosis insectorum Surinamensium*', in Van Delft and Mulder (eds), *Metamorphosis*, pp 29–39.

—, 'The History and Influence of Maria Sibylla Merian's Bird-Eating Tarantula: Circulating Images and the Production of Natural Knowledge', in P. Manning and D. Rood (eds), *Global Scientific Practice in the Age of Revolutions, 1750–1850*, University of Pittsburgh Press, Pittsburgh, PA, 2016, pp 54–70.

—, *The Flowering of Ecology: Maria Sibylla Merian's Caterpillar Book*, Brill, Leiden, 2021.

Felfe, Robert, '*Naer het leven*: Between Image-Generating Techniques and Aesthetic Mediation', in Balfe et al. (eds), *Ad vivum?*, pp 44–88.

Findlen, Paula, *Possessing Nature: Museums, Collecting, and Scientific Culture in Early Modern Italy*, University of California Press, Berkeley, CA, 1994.

—, *Empires of Knowledge: Scientific Networks in the Early Modern World*, Routledge, Taylor & Francis Group, London, 2017.

Friedewald, Boris, *A Butterfly Journey: Maria Sibylla Merian, Artist and Scientist*, Prestel, Munich, 2015.

Garrard, Mary D., *Brunelleschi's Egg: Nature, Art, and Gender in Renaissance Italy*, University of California Press, Berkeley, CA, 2010.

Geerdink, Nina, 'Possibilities of Patronage: The Dutch Poet Elisabeth Hoofman and Her German Patrons', in Paz and Geerdink (eds), *Economic Imperatives*, pp 124–46.

—, 'Economic Advancement and Reputation Strategies: Seventeenth-Century Dutch Women Writing for Profit', *Renaissance Studies*, vol.34, no.3, 2019, pp 350–73.

Grabowski, Carin, *Maria Sibylla Merian Zwischen Malerei und Naturforschung*, Reimer, Berlin, 2017.

Grieb, Manfred H., *Nürnberger Künstlerlexikon Bildende Künstler Kunsthandwerker Gelehrte Sammler Kulturschaffende Und Mäzene Vom 12. Bis Zur Mitte Des 20. Jahrhunderts*, vol.1, A–G, Saur, Munich, 2007.

Griebeler, Andrew, 'Production and Design of Early Illustrated Herbals', *Word & Image*, vol.38, no.2, 2022, pp 104–22. DOI: 10.1080/02666286.2021.1951518.

Harris, Ann Sutherland, and Linda Nochlin, *Women Artists, 1550–1950*, exh.cat., Random House and Los Angeles County Museum of Art, Los Angeles, CA, 1976.

Harris, Stephen A., *The Beauty of the Flower: The Art and Science of Botanical Illustration*, Reaktion, London, 2023.

Heard, Kate, *Maria Merian's Butterflies*, Royal Collection Trust, London, 2016.

Hofrichter, Frima Fox, 'An Intimate Look at Baroque Women Artists: Birth, Babies, and Biography', in Rosalynn Voaden and Diane Wolfthal (eds), *Framing the Family: Narrative and Representations in the Medieval and Early Modern Periods*, Arizona Center for Medieval and Renaissance Studies, Tempe, AZ, 2005, pp 139–58.

—, *Judith Leyster 1609–1660*, exh.cat., National Gallery of Art, Washington, DC, 2009.

Honig, Elizabeth A., 'The Art of Being "Artistic": Dutch Women's Creative Practices in the 17th Century', *Woman's Art Journal*, vol.22, no.2, Autumn–Winter 2001–2, pp 31–9.

Howell, Martha C., 'Michaelina Wautier and Working Women in Early-Modern Europe', in Katlijne van der Stighelen, Gerlinde Gruber, Martha C. Howell, Jahel Sanzsalazar, Francesca Del Torre Scheuch, Ben van Beneden and Martine van Elk, *Michaelina Wautier, 1604–1689: Glorifying a Forgotten Talent*, exh.cat., Rubenshuis, Antwerp, and BAI, Kontich, 2018, pp 100–119.

Hunter, Lynette, and Sarah Hutton (eds), *Women, Science and Medicine 1500-1700: Mothers and Sisters of the Royal Society* Sutton, Stroud, 1997.

Israel, Jonathan, *The Dutch Republic: Its Rise, Greatness, and Fall: 1477–1806*, Clarendon Press, Oxford, 2007.

Jacobs, Frederika H., *Defining the Renaissance Virtuosa: Women Artists and the Language of Art History and Criticism*, Cambridge University Press, Cambridge, 1997.

Jorink, Erik, and Bart Ramakers, 'Undivided Territory: "Art" and "Science" in the Early Modern Netherlands', in Eric Jorink and Bart Ramakers (eds), *Art and Science in the Early Modern Netherlands, Netherlands Yearbook for History of Art*, vol.61, W. Books, Zwolle, 2011, pp 6–32.

Kemp, Theresa, Beth Link and Catherine Powell, 'Accounting for Early Modern Women in the Arts: Reconsidering Women's Agency, Networks, and Relationships', in Merry Wiesner-Hanks (ed.), *Challenging Women's Agency and Activism in Early Modernity*, Amsterdam University Press, Amsterdam, 2021, pp 283–308.

Kettering, Alison, 'Watercolour and Women: Between Mirror and Comb', *Women's Art Journal*, vol.42, no.1, Spring/Summer 2021, pp 27–35.

Kinukawa, Tomomi, 'Natural History as Entrepreneurship: Maria Sibylla Merian's Correspondence with J.G. Volkamer II and James Petiver', *Archives of Natural History*, vol.38, no.2, 2011, pp 313–27.

—, 'Science and Whiteness as Property in the Dutch Atlantic World: Maria Sibylla Merian's *Metamorphosis Insectorum Surinamensium* (1705)', *Journal of Women's History*, vol.24, no.3, 2012, pp 91–116.

Knight, Leah, 'Horticultural Networking and Sociable Citation', in Helen A. Curry, Nicholas Jardine, James A. Secord and Emma C. Spary (eds), *Worlds of Natural History*, Cambridge University Press, Cambridge, 2018, pp 61–77.

Kusukawa, Sachiko, 'The Uses of Pictures in the Formation of Learned Knowledge: The Cases of Leonhard Fuchs and Andreas Vesalius', in Sachiko Kusukawa and Ian Maclean (eds), *Transmitting Knowledge: Words, Images, and Instruments in Early Modern Europe*, Oxford University Press, Oxford, 2006, pp 73–96.

—, *Picturing the Book of Nature: Image, Text, and Argument in Sixteenth-Century Human Anatomy and Medical Botany*, University of Chicago Press, Chicago, IL, 2012.

Leis, Arlene, and Kacie L. Wills (eds), *Women and the Art and Science of Collecting*, Routledge, London, 2018.

Lerner, Gerda, *The Creation of Feminist Consciousness: From the Middle Ages to Eighteen-Seventy*, Oxford University Press, New York, 1993.

Lölhöffel, Margot, 'Erster Teil. Maria Sibylla Merianin und Johann Andreas Graff. Gemeinsames und Trennendes', *Nürnberger Altstadtberichte*, vol.40, 2015, pp 37–76.

—, 'Johann Andreas Graff. Forgotten Artist and Partner of Maria Sibylla Merian for Twenty Years', in Van de Roemer et al. (eds), *Maria Sibylla Merian*, pp 52–62.

Ludwig, Heidrun, 'Nürnberger Blumenmalerinnen un 1700: zwischen Dilettantismus und Professionalität', *Kritische Berichte*, vol.4, 1996, pp 21–9.

Margócsy, Dániel, *Commercial Visions: Science, Trade, and Visual Culture in the Dutch Golden Age*, University of Chicago Press, Chicago, IL, 2014.

McBurney, Henrietta, 'The Influence of Maria Sibylla Merian's Work on the Art and Science of Mark Catesby', in Van de Roemer et al. (eds), *Maria Sibylla Merian*, pp 195–205.

Modesti, Adelina, *Women's Patronage and Gendered Cultural Networks in Early Modern Europe: Vittoria della Rovere, Grand Duchess of Tuscany*, Routledge, London, 2020.

Montoya, Alicia C., and Reindert Jagersma, 'Marketing Maria Sibylla Merian, 1720–1800: Book Auctions, Gender, and Reading Culture in the Dutch Republic', *Book History*, vol.21, 2018, pp 56–88.

Moseley-Christian, Michelle, 'Seventeenth-Century *Pronk Poppenhuisen*: Domestic Space and the Ritual Function of Dutch Dollhouses for Women', *Home Cultures*, vol.7, no.3, 2010, pp 341–63.

Mulder, Hans, *De Ontdekking van de Natuur*, Terra, Amsterdam, 2021.

Mulder, Hans, and Marieke van Delft, 'The Production of *Metamorphosis insectorum Surinamensium* 1705', in Van Delft and Mulder (eds), *Metamorphosis*, pp 40–50.

Neri, Janice, 'Fantastic Observations: Images of Insects in Early Modern Europe', PhD diss., University of California, Irvine, CA, 2003.

—, *The Insect and the Image: Visualizing Nature in Early Modern Europe, 1500–1700*, University of Minnesota Press, Minneapolis, MN, 2011.

Neville, Sarah, *Early Modern Herbals and the Book Trade: English Stationers and the Commodification of Botany*, Cambridge University Press, Cambridge, 2022.

Newman, Abigail, and Lieneke Nijkamp (eds), *Many Antwerp Hands: Collaborations in Netherlandish Art*, Harvey Miller Publishers, Turnhout, 2021.

Noorman, Judith (ed.), *Gouden vrouwen van de 17de eeuw. Van kunstenaars tot verzamelaars*, W. Books, Zwolle, 2020.

North, Michael, *Art and Commerce in the Dutch Golden Age*, Yale University Press, New Haven, CT, 1999.

Ogilvie, Brian, *The Science of Describing: Natural History in Renaissance Europe*, University of Chicago Press, Chicago, IL, 2008.

Ogilvie, Sheilagh C., *A Bitter Living: Women, Markets, and Social Capital in Early Modern Germany*, Oxford University Press, Oxford, 2003.

O'Malley, Therese, and Amy R.W. Meyers (eds), *The Art of Natural History: Illustrated Treatises and Botanical Paintings, 1400–1850*, Yale University Press, New Haven, CT, 2008.

Ozment, Steven E., *When Fathers Ruled: Family Life in Reformation Europe*, Harvard University Press, Cambridge, MA, 1983.

Paravisini-Gebert, Lizabeth, 'Maria Sibylla Merian: The Dawn of Field Ecology in the Forests of Suriname, 1699–1701', *Review: Literature and Arts of the Americas*, vol.45, no.1, 2012, pp 10–20.

Paz, Carme Font, and Nina Geerdink (eds), *Economic Imperatives for Women's Writing in Early Modern Europe*, Brill, Boston, MA, 2018.

Peacock, Martha Moffitt, 'Mirrors of Skill and Renown: Women and Self-Fashioning in Early Modern Dutch Art', *Mediaevistik*, vol.28, no.1, 2015, pp 325–52.

—, *Joanna Koerten*, Lund Humphries, London, forthcoming.

Pearson, Andrea, 'Gender, Sexuality, and the Future of Agency Studies in Northern Art, 1400–1600', *Journal of Historians of Netherlandish Art*, vol.15, no.2, Summer 2023, pp 1–41. DOI: 10.5092/jhna.15.2.3.

Pedersen, Eva de la Fuente, and Hanne Kolind Poulsen (eds), *Flowers and World Views*, exh.cat., Narayana Press, Odder, 2013.

Pieters, Florence, and Bert van de Roemer, in their chapter 'In Search of Friendship. Maria Sibylla Merian's Traces in Friendship Albums (*alba amicorum*)', in Van de Roemer et al. (eds), *Maria Sibylla Merian*, pp 74–86.

Powell, Catherine, 'Locating Early Modern Women in the Public Sphere of Botany: Agnes Block (1629–1704) and Networks in Print', *Early Modern Low Countries*, vol.4, no.2, December 2020, pp 234–58. DOI: 10.18352/emlc.147.

Powell-Warren, Catherine, 'A Strange Attraction. Women Artists and Patrons and the Creatures that No One Can Love', in Jan de Hond, Eric Jorink and Hans Mulder (eds), *Crawly Creatures: Little Animals in Art and Science*, exh.cat., Rijksmuseum, Amsterdam, 2022, pp 105–114.

—, *Gender and Self-Fashioning at the Intersection of Art and Science: Agnes Block, Botany, and Networks in the Dutch Seventeenth Century*, Amsterdam University Press, Amsterdam, 2023.

—, 'Scientific Illustration', in Banta et al. (eds), *Making her Mark*, pp 225–33.

—, '"What Experience Does Such a Woman Have?"

Maria Sibylla Merian (1647–1717) and the Gendered Language of her Reception in Natural History at the Dawn of the Dutch Eighteenth-Century', *Women's Writing*, special issue: 'Textual Misogynies', ed. Carme Font Paz, forthcoming.

Rankin, Alisha, 'Medicine for the Uncommon Woman. Experience, Experiment and Exchange in Early Modern Germany', PhD diss., Harvard University, Cambridge, MA, 2005.

Reinders, Sophie, *De mug en de kaars. Vriendenboekjes van adellijke vrouwen, 1575–1640*, Vantilt, Nijmegen, 2017.

Reitsma, Ella, and Sandrine Ulenberg, *Maria Sibylla Merian & Daughters: Women of Art and Science*, exh.cat., Rembrandt House Museum, Amsterdam, 2008.

Remond, Jaya, 'Drawing in the Tropics. Maria Sibylla Merian's and Charles Plumier's Pictures of Caribbean Nature', in Van de Roemer et al. (eds), *Maria Sibylla Merian*, pp 184–94.

—, 'The Pictorial Idioms of Nature: Image Making as Phytographic Translation in Early Modern Northern Europe', in Katja Krause, Maria Auxent and Dror Weil (eds), *Premodern Experience of the Natural World in Translation*, Routledge, New York, 2023, pp 273–96.

Rieppel, Lukas, 'Museums and Botanical Gardens', in Bernard V. Lightman (ed.), *A Companion to the History of Science*, Wiley-Blackwell, Chichester, 2016, pp 238–51.

Roos, Anna Marie, *Martin Lister and His Remarkable Daughters: The Art of Science in the Seventeenth Century*, Bodleian Library, University of Oxford, Oxford, 2019.

Rücker, Elisabeth, *Maria Sibylla Merian 1647–1717*, exh. cat., Germanisches Nationalmuseum, Nuremberg, 1967.

—, *Maria Sibylla Merian 1647–1717. Ihr Wirken in Deutschland und Holland*, Nachbarn 24, Kgl. Niederländischen Botschaft, Bonn, 1980.

Saxby, Trevor, *The Quest for the New Jerusalem, Jean de Labadie and the Labadists, 1610–1744*, Nijhoff, Dordrecht, 1987.

Schiebinger, Londa, *The Mind Has No Sex? Women in the Origins of Modern Science*, Harvard University Press, Cambridge, MA, 1996.

Schiebinger, Londa, and Claudia Swan (eds), *Colonial Botany: Science, Commerce, and Politics in the Early*

Modern World, University of Pennsylvania Press, Philadelphia, PA, 2005.

Schmidt, Ariadne, 'The Profits of Unpaid Work. "Assisting Labour" of Women in the Early Modern Urban Dutch Economy', *The History of the Family*, vol.19, no.3, 2014, pp 301–22.

Scrase, David, *Flower Drawings*, Cambridge University Press, Cambridge, 1997.

Segal, Sam, 'Maria Sibylla Merian as a Flower Painter', in Wettengl (ed.), *Maria Sibylla Merian*, pp 68–87.

Segal, Sam, and Klara Alen, *Dutch and Flemish Flower Pieces: Paintings, Drawings and Prints up to the Nineteenth Century*, 2 vols, Brill, Leiden, 2020.

Sint Nicolaas, Eveline, Valika Smeulders, Maria Holtrop, Stephanie Archangel, Lisa Lambrechts, Karwan Fatah-Black and Martine Gosselink, *Slavery: The Story of João, Wally, Oopjen, Paulus, Van Bengalen, Surapati, Sapali, Tula, Dirk, Lohkay*, Rijksmuseum and Atlas Contact, Amsterdam, 2021.

Smith, Jeffrey Chipps, *Nuremberg, a Renaissance City, 1500–1618*, exh.cat., University of Texas Press, Austin, TX, 1983.

Smith, Pamela H., 'Art, Science, and Visual Culture in Early Modern Europe', *Isis*, vol.97, no.1, March 2006, pp 83–100.

—, 'The Use of Artisanal Knowledge and the Representation of Nature in Sixteenth-Century Germany', in O'Malley and Meyers (eds), *The Art of Natural History*, pp 15–32.

Spies-Gans, Paris A., *A Revolution on Canvas: The Rise of Women Artists in London and Paris, 1760–1830*, Paul Mellon Centre for Studies in British Art, London, 2022.

Swan, Claudia, '*Ad vivum*, *Naer het leven*, From the Life: Defining a Mode of Representation', *Word & Image*, vol.11, no.4, October–December 1995, pp 353–72.

—, 'Illustrated Natural History', in Susan Dackerman, Harvard Art Museums and Mary and Leigh Block Museum of Art, *Prints and the Pursuit of Knowledge in Early Modern Europe*, exh.cat., Harvard Art Museums, Distributed by Yale University Press, Cambridge, MA, 2011, pp 186–99.

—, 'Dutch Diplomacy and Trade in *Rariteyten*: Episodes in the History of Material Culture of the Dutch Republic', in Zoltán Biedermann, Anne Gerritsen and Giorgio Riello (eds), *Global Gifts: The Material Culture of Diplomacy in Early Modern Eurasia*, Cambridge University Press, Cambridge, 2018, pp 171–97.

—, '*Liefhebberij*: A Market Sensibility', in Inger Leemans and Anne Goldgar (eds), *Early Modern Knowledge Societies as Affective Economies*, Routledge, New York, 2021, pp 141–64.

—, *Rarities of These Lands: Art, Trade, and Diplomacy in the Dutch Republic*, Princeton University Press, Princeton, NJ, 2021.

Sutcliffe, Iain C. (ed.), 'Still Going Strong: Leeuwenhoek at Eighty', Special Issue: Antonie van Leeuwenhoek, *Journal of Microbiology*, vol.106, 2014.

Tebeaux, Elizabeth, 'Women and Technical Writing, 1475–1700: Technology, Literacy, and Development of a Genre', in Hunter and Hutton (eds), *Women, Science and Medicine*, pp 29–62.

Todd, Kim, *Chrysalis: Maria Sibylla Merian and the Secrets of Metamorphosis*, Harcourt, New York, 2007.

Tomasi, Lucia Tongiorgi, '"*La femminil pazienza*": Women Painters and Natural History in the Seventeenth and Early Eighteenth Centuries', in O'Malley and Meyers (eds), *The Art of Natural History*, pp 158–85.

Treanor, Virginia, 'Women and the Art of Science', in Banta et al. (eds), *Making her Mark*, pp 106–21.

Van de Roemer, Bert, Florence Pieters, Hans Mulder, Kay Etheridge and Marieke van Delft (eds), *Maria Sibylla Merian: Changing the Nature of Art and Science*, Lannoo, Tielt, 2022.

Van Deinsen, Lieke, 'Marketing Merian. The Visual Branding of the Late Female Naturalist', in Van de Roemer et al. (eds), *Maria Sibylla Merian*, pp 215–25.

Van Delft, Marieke, 'Maria Sibylla Merian and the People of Suriname', in Van de Roemer et al. (eds), *Maria Sibylla Merian*, pp 118–30.

Van Delft, Marieke, and Hans Mulder (eds), *Maria Sibylla Merian. Metamorphosis 1705*, Lannoo, Tielt, 2016.

Van der Stighelen, Katlijne, 'Amateur Artists: Amateur Art as a Social Skill and a Female Preserve', in Delia Gaze (ed.), *Dictionary of Women Artists*, vol.1, Fitzroy Dearborn Publishers, London, 1997, pp 66–80.

Van der Stighelen, Katlijne, Mirjam Westen, Koninklijk Museum voor Schone Kunsten and Museum voor Moderne Kunst Arnhem, *A chacun sa grâce*, Flammarion, Ludion, 1999.

Van Dillen, J.G., *Bronnen tot de geschiedenis van het bedrijfsleven en het gildewezen van Amsterdam 1510–1672*, Huygens Instituut, at https://resources.huygens.knaw.nl/retroboeken/gildewezen/#page=940&accessor=toc&source=3 (accessed 1 July 2023).

Van Eeghen, I.H., trans. Jasper Hillegers, 'The Amsterdam Guild of Saint Luke in the 17th Century', *Journal of Historians of Netherlandish Art*, vol.4, no.2, Summer 2012. DOI: 10.5092/jhna.2012.4.2.4.

Van Elk, Martine, *Early Modern Women's Writing: Domesticity, Privacy, and the Public Sphere in England and the Dutch Republic*, Palgrave Macmillan/Springer Nature, Cham, 2017.

Van Suchtelen, Ariane (ed.), trans. Diane Webb, *In Full Bloom*, exh.cat., Mauritshuis, The Hague, and Waanders Publishers, Zwolle, 2022.

Vergara-Sharp, Alejandro, *Clara Peeters*, Lund Humphries, London, 2025.

Vignau-Wilberg, Thea, *Joris and Jacob Hoefnagel: Art and Science around 1600*, Hatje Cantz, Berlin, 2017.

Wade, Mara, 'Women's Networks of Knowledge: The Emblem Book as *Stammbuch*', *Daphnis*, vol.45, 2017, pp 492–509.

Wettengl, Kurt, 'Between Frankfurt and Surinam', in Wettengl (ed.), *Maria Sibylla Merian*, pp 12–35.

— (ed.), *Maria Sibylla Merian 1657–1717: Artist and Naturalist*, Gerd Hatje, Ostfildern-Ruit, 1998.

Wiesner-Hanks, Merry, 'Gender Theory and the Study of Early-Modern Europe', in Megan Cassidy-Welch and Peter Sherlock (eds), *Practices of Gender in Late Medieval and Early Modern Europe*, Brepols, Turnhout, 2008, pp 7–24.

— (ed.), *Women and Gender in the Early Modern World: Critical Concepts in Women's History*, 4 vols, Routledge, Abingdon, 2016.

Woollett, Anne T., 'Two Celebrated Painters: The Collaborative Ventures of Rubens and Brueghel, ca.1598–1625', in Anne T. Woollett and Ariane van Suchtelen (eds), *Rubens & Brueghel: A Working Friendship*, exh.cat., The J. Paul Getty Museum, Los Angeles, CA, Mauritshuis, The Hague, and Waanders Publishers, Zwolle, 2006, pp 1–41.

Image Credits

The publisher would like to thank the copyright holders for granting permission to reproduce the images illustrated. Every attempt has been made to trace accurate ownership of copyrighted images in this book. Any errors or omissions will be corrected in subsequent editions provided notification is sent to the publisher. The copyright for reproduction of photos is listed below.

Index

Note: italic page numbers indicate figures; Maria Sibylla Merian has been abbreviated to MSM in headings and subheadings.